ecpr
monographs

Series Editor: Alan Ware
University of Oxford

citizenship:
the history of an idea

Paul Magnette

translated by Katya Long

ecpr PRESS

© Paul Magnette

First published in French by Bruylant in 2001

First published by the ECPR Press in 2005

The ECPR Press is a department of the European Consortium for Political
Research (ECPR), an independent, scholarly association, which supports and
encourages the training, research and cross-national cooperation of political sci-
entists in institutions throughout Europe and beyond. The ECPR's Central
Services are located at the University of Essex, Wivenhoe Park,
Colchester, CO4 3SQ, UK

Typeset in Times 10pt by the ECPR Press
Printed and bound in the UK by the University of Essex Print Centre

British Library Cataloguing in Publication Data
A catalogue record for this book is available from the British Library

ISBN 0-9547966-5-9

ecpr monographs

The ECPR Monographs series is published by the ECPR Press, the publishing imprint of the European Consortium for Political Research (ECPR).

As an independent, scholarly, institution, one of the ECPR's objectives is to facilitate research in political science among European universities. To that end, the ECPR has developed a strong publishing portfolio since the 1970s.

The policy to extend that portfolio by launching its own publishing imprint was discussed by the Executive Committee of the ECPR in 2002, and the decision to proceed was taken in early 2003.

It was decided that the first two series to be published under the imprint should be complementary. The ECPR Classics series facilitates scholarly access to significant works from earlier eras of political science by re-publishing books that have been out of print. The ECPR believes this will enable contemporary students and researchers to develop their own work more effectively.

The ECPR Monographs series publishes major new research in all sub-disciplines of political science including revised versions of manuscripts that were originally submitted as PhD theses, as well as manuscripts from established members of the profession.

Alan Ware
Editor, ECPR Classics and ECPR Monographs
Worcester College, Oxford University, UK

Other titles in this series:

Paying for Democracy: Political Finance and State Funding for Parties, Kevin Casas-Zamora
Representing Women? Female Legislators in West European Parliaments, Mercedes Mateo Diaz

Titles in the ECPR Classics series:

System and Process in International Politics, Morton A. Kaplan
Political Elites, Geraint Parry
Parties and Party Systems: A Framework for Analysis, Giovanni Sartori

acknowledgements

This book was first published in French in 2001. It would never have seen the light of the day without the invaluable intellectual support of Professor John Dunn, who also wrote a very generous foreword. The book would never have been published in English without the encouragement of another very distinguished historian of political thought, Professor Richard Bellamy. Working with these two brilliant minds has been one of the greatest intellectual experiences of my short academic career.

Translating the manuscript proved a much harder task than I imagined, and I am very grateful to Katya Long for her rigour and resolution, and to Deborah Savage for her very careful and demanding work of edition - while also feeling somewhat guilty for all the pain I gave them.

This has also been my first experience in the world of Anglo-Saxon academic publishing, and the excellent impression this left me owes a lot to the patience, professionalism and kindness of the first Publications Manager of the ECPR Press, Rebecca Knappett.

| foreword

Citizenship is the main axis of modern political legitimacy. It is as citizens that we authorize the powers of the states which rule us; and it is through our citizenship alone that we can coherently explain how and why we have special obligations to obey them more than any other states in which we happen to find ourselves, or why we should belong to our own societies more deeply and decisively than we do to any other assemblage of human beings amongst whom we happen at the time to be. Citizenship is the privileged site of the modern link between protection and obedience, and the crucial combat zone within which we interpret the political health or pathology of our own country, or those of others'. It epitomizes the relation between political right and political duty within the modern world. But for all its evident centrality to modern politics, it would be quite wrong to assume that citizenship itself is well understood.

What does it mean to be a citizen? Who should be citizens of where? Where and why did the term citizen (or compelling translations of it within other languages) first appear in the political speech of human communities? How has it travelled between them since that initial appearance; and what does its appearance and disappearance, its massive diffusion and its lengthy absences, really mean? Is citizenship a single clear conception with a specifiable and readily intelligible history? Is it a miscellany of very different conceptions jostling against one another, or serenely ignoring each other, and dispersed out across time and space in a way which makes no overall political or historical sense? Is it the principal organizing component of one or more especially powerful and dynamic theories of what politics is and what it means? Or is it simply a bemusing lexical shadow of more opaque and insistent struggles for power, the outcome of which is always determined by quite other forces, and which, insofar as they are intelligible at all, must always in the end be understood in quite other terms? How does it stand in relation to the Great (and endless) Game between men and women, which goes back as far as the recoverable history of human consciousness, and will presumably continue until that consciousness comes to an end? Is it the brand of an ancient and curiously integrated culture and practice of exclusion and subjugation? Or is it the most apt current title for a full, if overwhelmingly belated, opportunity for equality of justice?

What does citizenship really consist in? Is it an inherently urban phenomenon, of direct self-expression and free participatory self-government, truly at home only long ago and on the scale of a substantial Mediterranean neighbourhood, but now stretched, with purposeful metaphorical effrontery, to cover the often vast, always intensely governed, and heavily bureaucratic states of the twenty first century, or even to the irritable political incoherence of a globalized capitalist economy? Or is it better seen as an open and potentially limitless process of political construction, extending accountability and authorization fluently out, in due course to the globe as a whole, or even well beyond it? Is it possible to be citizens at all within polities which are still ghosts of pre-modern empires: the Commonwealth of Independent States, the United Kingdom, Japan, dare one say it, the People's Republic of China? Could our descendants one day find themselves citizens, not merely of an overcrowded globe, but of the universe as a whole?

Political theorists, political scientists and historians of political ideas have no agreed method for handling such questions, let alone any shared and generally convincing set of answers to them. Paul Magnette is too modest to insist on the jejune and confused quality of most recent attempts to analyse citizenship; and his book, very wisely, does not pretend to answer all of the weighty and intractable questions which it raises. But he has an excellent grasp of the complex and challenging relations between the history of political terms, the history of political conceptions, the history of political practices, and the more refined (and sometimes more pretentious) history of our cumulative attempts to understand our political experiences and predicaments. His book offers an economical and illuminating guide through many of the elements which have gone into the intellectual and ideological history of modern citizenship. In doing so, he clearly surpasses any other recent analysis in any language known to me. But the merits of his book reach well beyond this and do much to expose the impoverished and doctrinaire character of anglophone or German discussions of the politics and social significance of citizenship over the last two decades.

As the European Union stumbles determinedly onwards, the issue of just what citizenship is and means is likely to become ever more insistent; and the need to understand far more clearly than we now do both our own political conceptions, and the great strategic options which they can focus and open up for us, will grow steadily more urgent. This is a book to read closely and reflect on with the utmost care. It is our story; and to make a wiser future we must learn to understand it a great deal better. In that exacting and pressing task Paul Magnette's lucid and patient book offers nothing but help.

John Dunn
King's College, Cambridge

| contents

                                                                    page

Introduction   1

Chapter one: The Invention of Citizenship   7

Chapter two: The Eclipse and Renaissance of the Concept of Citizenship   31

Chapter three: Modern Citizenship: Between Rights and State   62

Chapter four: From Theory to Politics: Citizenship and Modern Revolutions   103

Chapter five : Citizenship and Modern Society   140

Chapter six: Citizenship and Diversity   167

Conclusion: The Alternatives of Citizenship   182

Index   195

introduction

Long ignored by political scientists, confined to the sphere of law,[1] citizenship is now one of the keywords of the science of politics, having impacted on every aspect of the discipline. No doubt we owe this taste for the concept to Thomas H. Marshall. The British sociologist, interested at the end of the Second World War in the effect of democracy on social inequalities, seized on the term for analytical ends: 'The limit of my ambition', he wrote, 'has been to regroup familiar facts in a pattern which may make them appear ... in a new light'.[2] In studying 'industrial citizenship' or the 'social dimension', Marshall joined the vast current of research dedicated to relationships between the market and the state. He meant to show that the 'social issue' – placed at the time at the summit of the political agenda in Europe – was not a breaking-off but an extension of the political movement of modernity. The concept of citizenship had this heuristic advantage: it permitted the schematisation of the history of western political modernity as the succession of three phases – protection by the state, participation in democratic life and control of the market – and emphasised that these three components of citizenship were complementary. Without losing sight of his analytic pretension, let us note that Marshall did deliberately normative work: for this 'ethical socialist', it was a question of giving the 'social issue' a nobility and importance equal to those given in preceding centuries to the issues of rights to protection and of democratic participation.

What might have been merely a small conference soon forgotten became a scientific event. Firstly because the study of the Welfare State and its impact on the condition of the citizen imposed itself as one of the major themes of European political science, to such an extent that the expression 'social citizenship', a bit exotic in Marshall's time, became almost banal thereafter. But also, and above all, because other fields of political science followed Marshall's approach: in political theory, in the study of nationalism and migrations, in the analysis of democratic life, the heuristic virtues of the concept of citizenship were discovered during the middle of the 1960s.

Political theorists took an interest in the origins and the transformations of this concept, which had remained until then relatively marginal. Dedicating their efforts to the understanding of the basic grammar of politics, to the analysis of the

ways in which the concepts through which we think politics are formed and transformed, they could not help but be struck by the semantic vogue which suddenly
surrounded the word citizenship. In the spirit of questioning of received authority
that characterised the western world at that time, it became common to talk of
industrial citizenship, of citizenship in school or in the neighbourhood, or even in
the Church. In the era of the triumphant individual, political theory could no
longer be content with the terms of state, sovereignty, liberty, obedience, subjection. To reflect on the recomposition of political ties, it needed a concept that cap-
tured both the autonomy of the individual and his insertion in a community.[3]

There, also, the analysis of the origins of the concept slipped imperceptibly
towards normative elaboration. During the 1980s and 1990s, the clearer and clearer opposition between 'liberals' and 'republicans' or 'communitarians' was formalised around conceptions of the citizen. Laying out rapid and often superficial
genealogies, political theorists claimed to identify in the history of western political thought 'two different traditions of what it means to be a citizen'. 'According
to the first, the citizen is the primary political actor; law-making and administration are everyday business. According to the second, law-making and administration are someone else's business; the citizen's business is private'.[4] According to
this interpretation, which radicalises the distinction between the liberty of the
moderns and that of the ancients which Benjamin Constant made at the beginning
of the nineteenth century, a constant thread would link Aristotle, Machiavelli,
Rousseau and their disciples, and would oppose them to the family issued from
Bodin, Hobbes and Montesquieu. Deliberately exaggerated, this conceptualisation
of two confrontational conceptions of citizenship hides poorly, or not at all, its
polemical intentions.

In their turn, researchers who dedicate themselves to the functioning of
democracy have also seized on citizenship. Since democracy was becoming more
liberal, more individualistic, more detached from its old theological-political base,
the condition of the citizen needed to be rethought. It was necessary to take up
again, at new cost and in a renovated language, the reflection begun by
Tocqueville and John Stuart Mill on the construction, maintenance and development of the civic ties that are the warp and weft of contemporary democracies.[5] To
examine the construction of the civic sense and the acquisition by the citizen of
civic literacy and civic loyalty; to study the manner in which citizens understand
politics and develop a feeling of confidence in and solidarity with their fellow citizens; to understand why adhesion to the community is sometimes weakened and
sometimes reinforced. While neither Tocqueville nor Mill used the word citizenship, from the beginning of the seventies all this was schematised under the concept of citizenship. From then on the term no longer designated simply a set of
rights and duties, a legal status, it also covered the representations, roles and identities that are formed around the exercise of these rights.[6] This extension of meaning permitted examination of how the gender issue has, for centuries, been
obscured, and the impact of its recent discovery on the redefinition of democracy.

Some years later, researchers studying transformations of national identity in their turn used the notion of citizenship to heuristic ends. After all, among the ancients this term had been the instrument of a social closure serving to distinguish the members of the city from foreigners, and it was with the same finality that it was rediscovered in the sixteenth century in the Europe of reviving cities, and then in the seventeenth during the age of the nation-state formation. In a world where movements of population are intensifying, where the sovereignty of states is said to be eroding, where 'communities' are rediscovering the ethnic foundations that nations in construction had attempted to dissimulate, where legal discrimination between nationals and foreigners is fading, it seems indispensable to rethink the meaning of political communities. All those who are working today to expose the ethnic foundations of national citizenships and the oppression they imply, all those who are measuring the awakening of intra- and extra-national identities and are questioning the possibility of detaching democracy from an ethnic foundation see in 'multicultural citizenship' a useful analytical and discursive tool.

The success that this concept has met with over the last years is such that it could nearly be said to have become the cardinal point of political science. The four great fields of political science that Karl Mannheim and Stein Rokkan[7] identified – the study of the state and its normative and coercive foundations; research on the nation and exclusion; work on the development of democracy; and work on the public control of the market – have appropriated the concept and placed it at the centre of their analyses. All reason in terms of citizenship, as much as a tool of analysis as of normative elaboration.

The discipline of international relations has not been left out either. For as long as it was conceived to be an area of interaction between discrete states, the concept of citizenship was not used in the field of international relations. But since international relations has discovered the porosity of the state and ascertained the emergence of the individual as an actor in international politics, citizenship has found its place. There is more and more interrogation today on the emergence of multinational or global citizenship – no longer merely as an abstract cosmopolitan idea but as a fact – and the ever-stronger institutionalisation of ceaselessly more numerous international organisations leads naturally to speculation on the possibility of construction beyond the state of the statutes, representations and social roles comparable to those of citizenship formed in the mould of the state.

The acknowledgement of this general taste that political science has acquired is the point of origin of this book.[8] If the concept of citizenship occupies such a central strategic position, the time may have come to take up again the investigation of its origins. The history of its formation, of its eclipses, of its rediscoveries and its transformations may help us to understand the manipulations it is the object of today. It can help us above all to be aware of two dangers which lurk when a concept attracts all the attention. The first is that of semantic dilution. By stretching the meaning of a word, introducing into it all our contemporary preoccupations, we risk causing it to lose its heuristic virtue. After the manner of other grand concepts of contemporary political science, citizenship today suffers from a certain 'analytical debility' that is the 'simple product of the struggle to impose intellectual order through too few ideas upon too vast and heterogeneous a range of experience'.[9] One may wonder, for instance, what sense there is to speak of 'monastic citizenship' as an eminent medievalist does,[10] or if one does not yield to the most flagrant misconstruction when one speaks of 'fascist citizenship'.[11] What significance does a concept preserve when it covers both one thing and its opposite? What, again, in these conditions, is its analytical strength?

The other danger is that of the confusion that accompanies normative elaboration. It is certainly known that political theory has always been conceived as a form of political activity, and that according to the expression of Quentin Skinner 'the pen is a mighty sword'.[12] But there comes a moment when, by dint of mixing interpretation and combat, of playing on 'the art of writing', one obscures more than one sheds light. Nothing forbids a scholar from playing at politics, wrote Max Weber at the beginning of the last century, as long as he respects the rhetorical rules proper to each of these two roles and he indicates when he slips from one to the other. Contemporary political theory has abandoned this prudence. To it nothing comes amiss; it no longer conceives of interpretation as other than political combat. Hence, if 'There is no notion more central in politics than citizenship', none is 'more variable in history, or contested in theory'.[13] Each scholar searches in the texts for the foundations of his own thesis. (Of course, all the great authors of western political thought have done the same, from Machiavelli to Marx. But they did it without concealing their polemical intentions.) The instrumentalisation of the history of political thought does harm to its comprehension. Anyone who has skimmed through the texts of Benjamin Constant, Tocqueville or John Stuart Mill knows how artificial the opposition of so-called liberal and republican conceptions of citizenship is, how much that alleged distinction prevents us from seeing that it is precisely in the permanent tension between these two dimensions of the concept that the resiliency of its evolution resides.

The history of the concept of citizenship, followed step by step, in its great moments of elaboration as well as in its eclipses and its wanderings, is certainly less gratifyingly spectacular than flashy syntheses. It discovers, at best, conceptual continuities and constantly bumps up against the eventualities of history. From all time, in all eras, men have sought to find the meaning of living in a community and to protect themselves from injustice. Their discourses on citizenship bear the marks of time: political science is political in that it reflects the worries of societies; it is science in that it depends on the progress of knowledge. It is at this double horizon that reflection on the meaning of community, the rule of law and autonomy takes place and perceptions change. And it is always between these two boundaries that we navigate today.

NOTES

1 This word that we use to describe the condition of the citizen was for a long time a technical term, used only for the narrow meaning of nationality, still used today by lawyers. It appeared in the English language in the fourteenth century to designate the status of the inhabitant of a city, with a much more geographical than political connotation. It was only in 1792 that it was first used to mean a member of a state. A few decades later appeared the derivatives *citizenry* (1819), which means the civic body, and *citizenhood* (1871), synonymous with what we call today citizenship. It is only in the second half of the twentieth century, and more so since the 1970s, that the word has been in common use and that it has taken on a clearly political meaning. The same evolution is found in the other European languages. The derivative 'citizenship' only appeared in the French language in 1783, and only took on a 'patriotic meaning' during the few years that followed the revolution of 1789. For a long time the word citizen meant the inhabitant of a city, had no political meaning and only became synonymous with a member of a state at the beginning of the seventeenth century. In Italian, the derivative *cittadinanza* appears as early as the fourteenth century but only means the title of member of the city and competes with the words *civilità* and *città* which have the same meaning – all of these terms also mean all of the citizens, and the *città* also means the city in an urban sense. The word is basically technical and does not bear the republican ethos that was being reinstated by the 'civic humanists' at the time; they expressed the ideas of independence, autonomy and patriotism that were at the heart of their discourse through the concept of *libertà*. Once more, it was only around the time of the French revolution that the word takes on the meaning of belonging to a sovereign state. Spanish borrowed the words and their meaning from Italian, the *ciudad* meaning as early as the fourteenth century and the *ciudadania* in the sixteenth century meaning both city and nationality. In Germany, until the end of the nineteenth century, the *Bürger* meant the national or the subject and its patriotic meaning is only present in the works of the republican philosophers. *Cf.* P. Costa, 'La Cittadinanza: un Tentativo di Ricostruzione Archeologica', in D. Zolo (ed.), *La Cittadinanza, Appartenenza, Identità*, (Diritti, Bari: Laterza, 1994), pp. 47–92.

2 T.H. Marshall, *Citizenship and Social Class, and Other Essays* (Cambridge, Cambridge University Press, 1950), p. 27.

3 *Cf.* R. Dahrendorf, 'Citizenship: the social dynamics of an idea', *Social Research* 1974, 41/4, pp. 673–701.

4 M. Walzer, 'Citizenship', in T. Ball, J. Farr and R. L. Hanson (eds), *Political Innovation and Conceptual Change* (Cambridge, Cambridge University Press, 1989), p. 216. This interpretation is generally the work of 'republicans' or 'communitarians', who tend to distance themselves from the liberal view. It became very common in the 1990s. See, notably, in Canada, C. Taylor, 'The Liberal-Communitarian debate', in N. Rosenbaum (ed.), *Liberalism and Moral Life* (Cambridge MA, Harvard University Press, 1989), pp. 175–189; in Germany, J. Habermas, 'Citizenship and national identity: reflections on the future of Europe', *Praxis International*, 1991, 12/1, pp. 1–19; in Italy, S. Veca, *Cittadinanza, Riflessioni Filosofiche sull'idea di Emancipazione* (Milan, Feltrinelli, 1990); and in France, D. Schnapper, *La Communauté des Citoyens* (Paris, Gallimard, 1994).

5 One of the first works on the political sociology of democratic citizenhip is the book by D.

Thompson, *Democratic Citizenship, Social Science and Democratic Theory in the Twentieth Century* (Cambridge, Cambridge University Press, 1970). For a more communitarian view, see also M. Janowitz, 'Observations on the sociology of citizenship: obligations and rights', *Social Forces*; 1980, 59/1 pp. 1–24; and for the Marxist perspective see J.M. Barbalet, *Citizenship, Rights, Struggle and Class Inequality* (Milton Keynes, Open University Press, 1988).

6 *Cf.* Jean Leca, 'Questions sur la citoyenneté', *Projet* 1983, 171–172, pp. 113–25.

7 K. Mannheim, *Essays on Sociology and Social Psychology* (London, Routledge, 1950) and P. Flora, Stein Kuhnle and D. Urwin (eds.), *State Formation, Nation-Building and Mass Politics in Europe: The Theory of Stein Rokkan*, (Oxford, Oxford University Press, 1999).

8 Following the works on conceptual genealogy by R. Koselleck, W. Conze and O. Brunner (eds), *Geschichtliche Grundbegriffe: historisches Lexikon zur politisch-sozialen Sprache in Deutschland* (Stuttgart, Klett-Cotta, 1972–1997) and more specifically on citizenship, P. Costa, *Civitas. Storia della cittadinanza in Europa*, 4 vols., (Laterza, Roma-Bari, 1999–2001) and R. Bellamy and D. Castiglione (eds), *Lineages of Citizenship* (Basingstoke, Palgrave, 2004).

9 J. Dunn, 'Revolution', in T. Ball *et al.*, *Political Innovation*, p. 333.

10 P. Reisenberg, *Citizenship in the Western Tradition, From Plato to Rousseau* (Chapel Hill NC, North Carolina University Press, 1992).

11 See, for example, B. S. Turner's comparative analysis of political regimes in B. S. Turner, 'Outline of a theory of citizenship', in C. Mouffe (ed.), *Dimensions of Radical Democracy* (London, Verso, 1992), pp. 33–62.

12 *Cf.* J. Tully (ed.), *Meaning and Context, Quentin Skinner and his Critics* (Cambridge, Polity Press, 1988).

13 J. Shklar, *American Citizenship, The Quest for Inclusion* (Cambridge MA, Harvard University Press, 1991), p. 1.

chapter one | the invention of citizenship

Men have always come together in communities and tried to find collective means of solving the problems before them. In this sense, politics and citizenship are inherent to every form of human community. Nevertheless, historians agree on the fact that politics as we use the term today, that is, as distinct from other sorts of collective action, was invented by the Greeks. More precisely, as Moses Finley puts it, politics is 'an invention made separately by the Greeks and the Etruscans'. Having 'invented politics', the Greeks were compelled to 'innovate continuously',[1] to create new and unprecedented institutions as political problems arose. Moreover, their philosophers produced the theory of these institutions and thus gave politics its cardinal concepts.

At first, citizenship in the time of the ancients appears in the texts to be an institution meant to *draw the outline of the political community*, by defining who belongs to and who is excluded from the civic body. This is what, nowadays, we call nationality. From Athens to Rome, the terms of political inclusion varied: in the former case they were ethnically expressed while they translated a legal-political civilisation in the latter. But the reasoning remains the same and defines the political entity as the whole of its citizens – rather than as a territory or a 'sovereignty' – by opposing it to what is external or foreign.

In the sense that the city was a society defined by its laws and rules, citizenship also described the *modes of legal relations that established themselves between members*. To be a citizen meant, foremost, to enjoy civil rights, to be governed in one's married relations, affiliations, property and inheritance by a set of laws particular to the members of a particular political community and to submit to their jurisdiction; while non-citizens fell under the authority of other rules or of simple power struggles. Citizenship defined all aspects of citizens' lives. The ancients made no distinction between what would come to be called public and private spheres. The Roman 'civil law' was the law of fellow-citizenship, codifying every form of relationship between citizens, 'economic' or political, domestic or public, secular or religious, civil or military.

Participation in the practice of public power seems, nevertheless, if one reads between the lines, to be the heart of this status. As a proof of this, the rights of citizenship that were granted to foreigners only rarely included 'political rights', and were limited to the *civitas sine suffragio* ('citizenship without a vote') as the Roman law had it. To be a citizen was to be a member of a community defined by its autonomy, which gave itself its own laws. There was no city, no republic, in the full meaning of the word, if the people were not the source and the measure of authority: a sign of this is the fact that the same word (*politeia* in Greek and *civitas* in Latin) means both the city, the civic body and citizenship. For the ancients, a community is not conceptually separable from its members, nor is it from its political regime.

The ancients did not know 'representation', used by the moderns as the main tool to tame the people by designating some of its members, presumed to be wiser than the rest, to govern in the name of all.[2] This mechanism was unknown in Athens, where judges and magistrates were designated by lot, which is the most egalitarian process since it supposes that all citizens are equally worthy of being chosen. Besides, the short-term mandates were meant to guarantee a rotation of the leading posts so that all citizens would occupy them at some point. And the antique cities always guaranteed a direct power of decision for citizens: laws were not the work of representatives but the will of the people itself, which, in principle, decided on them in its assemblies. To be a citizen, in the first ages of politics, was not to choose leaders but, as Cicero said, was to have no master and to be one's own master.

This axiom was so strong in the political culture of the ancient world that citizens continued to back it even when, in fact, their institutions directly or indirectly kept them out of public office. Social life, mirroring the nature that it was part of, was seen as a harmony of differences. A just society, answering to a natural purpose, was one that set up balanced hierarchical relations between men. In the same way, the 'good' regime was one that grouped social forces in a way that cancelled out their tensions and so contributed to harmony. Democratic Athens, short-lived and in practice more oligarchic than its panegyrics imply, was an exception in the ancient world in considering all its citizens to be equal, interchangeable, in turn governed and governing. Generally speaking, equality was less absolute. Indeed, Athens was organised in such a way that its power, in principle exercised by all citizens, was exercised in fact by 'the best' among them. In Rome, if the *potestas* belonged to the people, the magistrates were the ones who had *imperium*, while the Senate – made up of the highest magistrates, most of them from the big patrician families – had the *auctoritas*. The difference between the *arche* and the *politeuma* in Athens, and between *potestas*, *auctoritas* and *imperium* in Rome, all terms which are subsumed within the inclusive category of 'sovereignty' in modern times, translates the mixed character of ancient regimes, in which social forces are balanced in such a way that the people were guided, like a herd by its shepherd, by its best components, its *pars valentior*, as in the pastoral metaphor which Christianity would make so powerful.

The concept of citizenship was, in ancient times, a cardinal tool of the legitimisation of authority: it allowed the exclusion of many individuals considered to be of inferior worth, and forged a sense of ethnic or political community between the 'included'. It made possible the assertion of equal rights between citizens, a legal and political identity that commanded their obedience while establishing between them a hierarchy that reproduced, in social and political life, differences that were thought to be natural.

POLIS, POLITES AND POLITEIA: THE SHAPING OF THE CONCEPT OF CITIZENSHIP IN ATHENS

The history of the words by which the antique notion of citizenship was crystallised shows well the political use of language. The Greek term that we translate today as 'citizenship', the one that means being a citizen, is the word *politeia*, derived abstractly from *polites* (citizen), the latter itself derived from *polis* (city). Etymology teaches us that the words *polis* and *polites* were formed when the denomination by 'groups determined by common habitat' succeeded the 'ancient social divisions based on genealogy'.[3] When, in other terms, the social group took over from the family as the community of reference. On the other hand, the derivative *politeia* appears much later, in the middle of the fifth century BC, when the city had long been established and its belonging members clearly defined. Moreover, it appears in various semantic contexts in which it sometimes means the citizen's status but also sometimes refers more globally to the city, of which it names the 'constitution', the 'regime', the 'civic body'. The term's polysemy shows that the concept it names was not clearly isolated from related notions.

Herodotus' Neologism

In Book IX of his *Histories*,[4] Herodotus introduces, probably for the first time,[5] the derivative *politeia*. Despite the anecdotal quality of this first occurrence, it is worthwhile to give it some attention because it fixes two crucial dimensions of this concept that still characterise it today. In paragraphs 33–35 Herodotus broaches the way in which Tisamenus (IX, 33) acquired Spartan citizenship. While he was consulting the oracle in Delphi in order to know whether he would have children, Tisamenus learned from the Pythia 'that he would conquer in greater struggles, five times over'. This was certainly not the answer he was expecting but, obeying the oracles and having understood that he would win the Olympic Games, he unsuccessfully started to practise. On the other hand, the Lacedaemonians had understood that the oracle was predicting military triumphs for him, and thus offered him the co-direction of their battles for a salary. Tisamenus 'however, when he saw that they set great store by his friendship, forthwith raised his price, and told them if they would *receive him among their citizens, and give him equal rights with the rest*, he was willing to do as they desired, but on no other terms would they ever gain his consent' [my emphasis]. Having overcome the Spartans' reluctance he then went on to ask that 'they must likewise make his brother Hagias a *Spartan*, with the same rights as himself" [my emphasis]. Herodotus goes on to show that Tisamenus was following the example of Melampous, who had demanded from the Argians, in exchange for his services, one-third of royal power for himself and another third for his brother, 'at least if kingship may be compared with citizenship' concluded Herodotus. Having won, Tisamenus and his brother became 'the only men whom the Spartans ever admitted to citizenship' (IX, 33–35).

From a semantic point of view, this short passage is full of teachings. Firstly we notice that Herodotus is conscious of the fact that he is introducing a new term and he defines it with great care. On the one hand he uses the word *politeia* as a synonym of 'citizen of Sparta', thus underlining the equivalence between 'citizenship' and 'nationality'. But on the other hand he parallels Tisamenus's demand with that of Melampous: royalty and citizenship. This confrontation is cleverly staged: nationality and royalty are paired here in harmony as two components of citizenship and *politeia* comes at the end of the sentence as a keynote. By this Herodotus seeks to underline the power of action held within citizenship; his character says nothing else when he demands to be admitted as a 'full-fledged' citizen. Subsequent history would confirm the dual meaning of this first use: belonging and participation, belonging to a community that is defined by its capacity for action.

If the word *politeia* was created around 460 BC, it was only between 430 and the end of the fifth century that it became a common usage. It is found in the *Athenien politeia* of Pseudo-Xonophon, in the funeral oration that Thucydides wrote for Pericles and in several inscriptions. However it does not penetrate poetic vocabulary, which allows us to suppose that it was from the start the prerogative of political prose.[6]

The Invention of Citizenship (594–450 BC)

Why, in the middle of the fifth century, it seemed necessary to invent a word while there already were several conceptual dichotomies used to underline the links of belonging and exclusion, still needs to be explained. The Achean-Mycenian civilisation already opposed the *doulos* (slave) to the *eleupos* (free man), defining the latter by his belonging to the community.[7] In Athens, well before the laws of Solon, *epitimos* and *atimos* were opposed, only the first being protected by the public authority.[8] In order to understand why a new term was deemed necessary, we need to turn to etymology and seek in political history a new reasoning that calls for its own language.

Modern and ancient history acknowledge Solon as one of the founders of Greek civic institutions. Archon in 594/593 BC, sensed the dangers of social divisions within Athens, the civil war and tyranny that were brewing. He decided to put an end to this by laws (*thesmoi*) to ease the divisions of Athenian society; marking its difference from what was exterior to it was an unintended side effect.

The main threats to Athenian harmony were conflicts about land: too many men, under various statuses, were working on too little land. Solon tackled these tensions by acknowledging to all the ownership of the land they were working on in the fields of Attica, abolishing current debts and prohibiting enslavement for debt. In order to prevent this equilibrium from crumbling under external pressure, he also took measures that limited immigration into Athenian territory. These were the heralds of an 'Athenian identity', defined by individual ownership of land and by its opposite: the situation of slaves and foreigners.

Among the Athenians, Solon weakened private influence and the monopoly of aristocrats; a growing part of the lives of individuals were no longer entirely submitted to the constraints of other individuals but, rather, were under the care of the public (versus private) authority. Attica's population was divided into categories based on the wealth they produced and not on hereditary nobility, each of them having their own honours and duties in their assemblies – the *ekklesia* and the Council of the Four Hundred – and popular courts. Matters that formerly were private began to be codified, such as matrimony, the education of orphans, offerings and religious celebrations, weights, measures and currencies. Simultaneously, Athenians could have their conflicts settled by public 'courts of justice' made up of juries of Athenians, and had the right of appeal against the courts' decisions. Their participation in meetings and votes of the assemblies was increased, maybe even to the point of electing the magistrates. Solon thus contributed to the establishment of mechanisms used to solve social conflicts, which presaged what we now call a 'public sphere'. He hadn't levelled out social differences at either the 'economic' level (since land property respected traditional hierarchy) or at the political level (since the high judiciaries were allotted to the 'elite'). In this still aristocratic perception, the cosmos was understood as a harmony, established by law by balancing differences without eradicating them. The art of moderation, of proportion, contributed to the importation into the social world of the differences seen in nature.

Some modern historians hailed the birth of the citizen in these reforms 'because at last the society had become, as Solon proclaimed in his poetry, *hèmeterè polis*, "our polis". He established...politeia, which now certainly meant citizenship'.[9] But this word only appeared a century and a half later. Solon still only spoke of Athenians and not of citizens, or in legal terms of *epitimoi*.[10] Admittedly the foundations of a political conception of the community had been laid, but the lack of appropriate vocabulary leads us to doubt whether the concept of citizenship had already been formed in the sixth century.

This is undoubtedly explained by the fact that Athenian society was still rather precarious at the dawn of the sixth century. It was prey to factional divisions, struggles between the people of the coasts, the plains and the hills, stirred up by those aristocrats who, like Peisistratos in the middle of the century, relied on them to set up their tyranny. The famous tyrant was never capable of totally erasing the Solonian institutions: Peisistratos himself appeared before the Areopagos (the hill on which the court of justice for capital crimes was held), to answer for the hideous crime of homicide. It can even be thought that his tyranny prepared the way for classical citizenship: the weight and magnitude of the power he wielded against aristocratic factions helped to reduce their rivalry and undoubtedly contributed, along with internal migrations, to the homogenisation of the population of Attica and Athens.

And by one of those strange cycle effects that so fascinated the ancients, tyranny helped the progressive emergence of a republican regime. At first degenerating into internal struggles between aristocratic families, the rule of aristocrats then gave way to a regime of terror marked by arbitrariness: the *diapsiphismos* – civic inquisition – set up to prosecute the defenders of tyranny (510/509 BC), was used by factions against one another and threatened all Athenians with the loss of civic rights, exile or even death. In this violent and frightful context, Kleisthenes understood that he could only reinforce his own faction by bringing it the support of those who weren't part of the governing families. Aware that the striking collective fear Athenians were experiencing was connected with status, because the fate of men depended on it, he successfully established reforms that took away from aristocratic families the control of Athenians' identity and reinforced their participation in political decisions. Throughout the whole of Attica, Athenians were assigned to one of the thirty newly created *trittyes* (groupings of *demes*), in accordance to their belonging to the city, the coast or the country's midland. The trittyes themselves were brought together, by lot, in tribes, in such a way that each tribe has elements of each of the three regions. Thus, these tribes, who were to be the base of political activities and military divisions, joined together groups of individuals who came from different regions and were taken away from the influence of local families. Fifty members of each tribe were drawn by lot to make up the Council of Five Hundred, which prepared the work of the Assembly (*ekklesia*). This Assembly, in which all could be present, voted on war and peace and fines and death penalties, and elected military leaders. This set of reforms was aimed at destroying traditional social relations, mixing populations and imposing formal rules.

Classical cosmogony was turned around by these reforms. The aristocratic conception of geometrical equality, a harmony based on the comprehensiveness of differences, was replaced by the democratic conception of arithmetic equality: all are equal and linked by relations of equivalency, identity and reversibility. A single status institutionalises this simple equality: all citizens can be seen or see themselves as identical and interchangeable. The *polis* is no longer a harmony of different notes but a circular unity between points equidistant from the centre. Jean-Pierre Vernant gave a remarkable definition of this new representation:

The Polis appears as a homogeneous universe, without hierarchy, without floors, without differentiation. The *arche* is no longer concentrated in a unique figure at the top of the social organization. It is evenly distributed throughout the entire field of public life, in that common space in which the city finds its core, its *mesogeois*. In accordance with a settled cycle, sovereignty goes from one group to the other, from one individual to another, in such a way that to order and to obey, rather than opposing each other as two Absolutes, become two inseparable terms of a unique reversible rapport. Under the *isonomia* law, the social world takes on the form of a circular and centred cosmos, within which every citizen, because he is equal to all others, will cover the whole of the circuit, successively and regularly holding and relinquishing every symmetrical position that makes up the civic space.[11]

The fact that an equal status was in principle awarded to every Athenian on a strictly formal basis and that he was endowed with real powers of political and legal participation undoubtedly explains why modern historians date the birth of a 'fully developed citizenship'[12] to the end of the sixth century BC. But before this unnamed citizenship was associated with social representations, before it was understood by its holders and its concept formed, a further half-century was to elapse. During this period, Athens asserted its power on the external scene: the victories of Marathon (490 BC) and Salamis (480) won by armies of citizens against the permanent troops of the king of Persia, and the leading role of Athens in the Delian League from 478, helped give the Athenians strong self-confidence, to the point where they started to believe themselves to be stronger than the Persians and than all the other Greek people, and even to conceive themselves as an 'ethnic' group.

During the same period, Athens experienced a striking demographic and economic growth. Its population probably doubled between 480 and 430, the growth being particularly strong amongst metics and slaves.[13] Many Athenians emigrated and set up colonies of citizen-soldiers (*klerouchies*). The city's leading role, besides stimulating the naval industry, supplied Athens with proceeds from the mines, port taxes and other levies. The Athenians' feelings of self-confidence and pride that stemmed from these tangible successes 'were not confined to Athenian leaders of a limited group, but in the men of Marathon and the sailors of Salamis and their sons – that is in the Athenian people at large – there was a growing political consciousness and sense of power'.[14]

It is around 450 that the word *demokratia* appears, when participation in Athenian institutions broadened. At that point, citizens probably made up only one-tenth of the total population of Athens, but these privileged members of society, listed in their *demes* (townships), members of *trittyes* and tribes, were statutory equals, be they peasants, craftsmen, merchants or landowners. All could be drawn by lot as members of the council or of juries, all could take part in assemblies and vote in them. It is true that only one-fifth of these citizens truly attended these deliberations and these were older, richer and more urban than the average. Without a doubt, geographical distance and professional employment, without being insurmountable obstacles, were not conducive to participation. Legal equality made the best of a *de facto* inequality. As an implicit counterpart, the rich underwrote the costs of the civil and military functioning of the city. Their lavish spending during liturgies helped legitimise their domination: 'Their boasting…helped to justify the *demos'* entrustment of political leadership to them as a class'.[15] This 'functional specialisation' within a civic body renowned to be equal was even translated in the language. At the end of the fifth century, it was common practice to call citizens who didn't take an active part in the affairs of the city or that were thought to be more concerned by their private business (*ta idia*, 'unto his own things') *idiôtai* or 'ignorant men', while the *politeuomenoi* ('professional' politicians) *de facto* represented the whole of the civic body: magistrates, strategists and speakers, they weighed heavily in the decision-making mechanism in the city, within assemblies and tribunals, conveying the voices of their 'partisans'.[16] The whole of the people accepted this form of leadership, and those who suffered as a result of it did not consider themselves to be second-class citizens.

The definition of 'others', of 'non-citizens' who are carefully put aside, testifies to the value the holders conferred to the status of citizenship. In fact, at the same time, appeared the statuses of foreigners (*xenos*) and of metics (*metoïkos*), with limited rights and prohibitions. Metics had to comply with some citizen's duties, such as taxation or military service, while they were deprived of citizen's fundamental rights: the right to own land and to take an active part in assemblies and legal proceedings. It was also around the mid-century that the conditions of access to citizenship were made more rigorous. Kleisthenes' reforms had allowed as citizens those who were sons of a male citizen and were registered in a *deme*. The *demes* having perhaps been lax, the laws of Pericles (451/450) require a double-citizen descent. Whatever were the catalysing events of these measures, still largely debated by contemporary historiography, they testify to the fact that citizens were aware of the value of their status and the privileges that it entailed.

It is only after a long legal, political, social and cultural evolution that the word citizenship appears. When Solon asserted public power and acknowledged 'citizens' of Attica a certain amount of 'rights', free men were still only defined by opposition to slaves. When, a century later, Kleisthenes codified an administrative status for Athenians and gave them the power of legal and political participation, 'citizenship' was not yet known. The growing power of Athens in Greece, its military glory and economic growth finally made Athenians feel like 'citizens', proud of their privileges even though only a minority could enjoy them. And it was only then, when consciousness met fact, that it became necessary to use an abstraction to name this jealously guarded condition.

The different uses of the term *politeia* in Greece during the fifth and fourth centuries BC are a testimony to its double meaning: in its strict sense it is a precise, technical political term, most often used in official formulations bestowing citizenship, in place of the 'ethnic' qualification (Athenian, Spartan and so on); in fact, a formula of nationality. On the other hand, the political conflicts around this status bear witness to the fact that it only meant something to those who held it because of what it entailed: a group of privileges that organised the political and judicial participation of citizens in the *polis*.

Jacqueline Bordes has found four different contexts in which the word *politeia* in its 'individual' meaning is most often used. Significantly, they have in common the fact that they are all 'negative', that is to say that they refer to citizenship not in its 'normality' but in its exceptions. The word first appeared when the Athenian started granting citizenship to foreigners; they only handed it out parsimoniously and let it be known that this was an important privilege. A law banned the granting of citizenship to anyone who had not been of great use to the city; the right of citizenship for a foreigner only became legally binding after it had been confirmed by a secret ballot of at least six thousand Athenians.[17] In fact, the conditions for granting the citizenship right to a single foreigner were as strict as those for a vote for war or for collecting new taxes. Various partial 'rights' could be granted to non-citizens, such as *epigamia* or ownership rights, but citizenship was seen as 'the maximum a *polis* can offer to a foreigner'.[18] Moreover, even if the new citizen had equal rights to those of the other citizens, his title was regarded as an honorary favour if he didn't live in Athens and profit from the privileges he has been granted. This seems to imply that citizenship 'is only itself when activity is added to status'.[19]

Instances of the use of the term that touch on its withdrawal confirm that the status and the participation it implies were inseparable: the deprivation of political rights (*atimia* was an *ipso facto* deprivation of citizenship). The individual who was stricken by *atimia* found himself deprived of his both belongings and political rights: he might have kept the right to live in Athens but was barred from the Assembly and courts. This proves beyond a doubt that both these modes of civic participation were at the heart of the status of citizen. Likewise, banishment from the *polis* and proscription mean exclusion from the status of citizen, as well as exclusion from the fatherland.

A third kind of usage confirms the unity of these concepts:[20] the use of the word *politeia* in less technical and more collective meanings, which could be translated in modern language by notions such as 'civic body', 'constitution' or 'regime'. From the beginning, the collective *politeia*[21] was given a number of different meanings. First, any regime could be called *politeia*; in this case the word meant 'sovereignty' (*arche*) and the ways in which sovereignty was formalised (the 'constitution'). It is in this sense that Aristotle studied the *politeiai* of 158 Greek cities. But another usage included elements specific to the city, and politeia then meant, as with Isocrates, 'the soul of the city', its laws and morals (*nomoi* and *topoi*), what we would call today the 'civic culture'. This emphasis implies that the name *politeia* should be exclusively used for a particular regime, democracy, that deserved this restrictive denomination in the eyes of its contemporaries. In it, the *polis* is consubstantial with the citizens as a whole; the citizen only derived his right of citizenship from the fact that he belonged to the community; his rights were not individual rights as we understand them today but an equal participation in collective rights: *isocratia* (the equal distribution of power), *isonomia* (equality in political participation and equality before the law), *isegoria* (equal right to speech); rights that only make sense collectively. There is besides a very clear parallel between the 'individual' and the 'collective' notion of the *politeia*: as the city in the material sense is the unity of citizens, the constitution, in the formal sense, is the sum of citizenships. Without democracy, when the *demos* is not the holder of the *arche*, when the *polis* is not merged with the *politai*, this conceptual unity is shattered and it may seem incorrect to speak of *politeia*. At any rate, the study of monarchies and aristocracies brought the authors of the fourth century BC to reserve the term for democracies.[22]

The extreme cohesion of the *polis* and of the *politeia* – in every sense of the word – is further marked by the fact that classical Athens was incapable of thinking itself as a *sympoliteia*, a common *politeia* for several cities. The political issue of inter-city relations was continuously addressed during the fifth and sixth centuries BC – when Thebes dominated Boeotia, Sparta the cities of the Peloponnese and Athens those of the Delian League – a time when pressures on small cities were strongly felt, in a world less stable than when they had been constituted. However, the first alliances had not engendered a common *politeia*, whether in the form of a 'federal' constitution or of a common status shared by all citizens of the allied cities.[23] Some considered the idea of a single *politeia* for several *poleis*, but with only aporetical intention, to demonstrate the monstrosity of a supposed unity that, even if it maintained an appearance of autonomy for allied cities, was in fact an annexation.[24] In the conceptual language of that time federalism was inconceivable: either a city was autonomous and the 'federation' that linked it to another was only an alliance; or, on the contrary, the common unit had real power but in that case the cities that made it up lost their essence.[25] The reasons for this are more than purely conceptual. The confusion of *polis* and *politeia* shows not just the unity of the abstract ideas of 'city' and 'constitution'; more profoundly, it illustrates the identity of a fatherland and of a regime. The abstract (citizen) and the ethnic (Athenian) are synonymous, a sign of the indissoluble solidarity of the 'nation' and of the 'state', even if those words do not exist yet and the idea of them remains implicit. 'The notion of *politeia* does not go without the notion of a privileged place and of ancestral heritage – unities in space and across time'.[26] Athens, mother of the *politeia*, refrained from thinking of the *sympoliteia*. For that matter Athens' successors, very much saturated by the idea of a Panhellenic race and in spite of the consciousness they had of the intrinsic limits of cities, also failed; *politeia* did not survive the disappearance of the *polis*.

The Citizenship of Philosophers

The image Greek philosophy handed down to posterity is not that of the cohesive *politeia* of the classical era. In the course of the fourth century BC democratic hegemony began to wane, its core concepts criticised by defenders of aristocracy. Amongst others, Plato[27] wonders at freedom being granted in such an equal way 'dispensing a sort of equality to equals and unequals alike' (VIII, 558b). He says of democracy that it can only be seen as a 'fairest of States' by 'women and children' (VIII, 557b), who we know very well he did not have a high regard for. The citizen's democratic freedom is a bait, an illusion; the denial of the qualities of the rich and knowledgeable man (alone worthy of engaging in politics) is an injustice. A whole generation, including Xenophon, Isocrates and Plato, find fault with the character of 'popular' influence on the city, which sent the 'good regime' astray. Plato asserts that the city was denatured because it forgot that nature does not make identical men, which implies that true equality accommodates itself to differences in status, and that true justice gives each his proper place. The oligarchic idea replaced the 'political identity' that is central to the idea of the democratic individual with a 'social identity'.[28] These convictions about the danger of the 'popular' part gaining control were widespread even before Plato; they permeated democracy itself, hence the perceived need to make sure that citizens who hold office were financially independent.

In such a climate of criticism, the *politeia* itself unavoidably saw its meaning change. Plato only uses the word in its collective sense: on the one hand, conforming to tradition, in order to designate any constitution; on the other, to name the perfect city he has created, the Republic. The ambivalence of the collective *politeia* as it existed well before Plato is found here once more. Its study would be more informative about Plato himself and about his Republic than about the evolving meaning of citizenship, so true is it that 'Plato opposes such a total refusal to his contemporary theories that, most often, he does not care to improve them, to transform them. In a sense he presents their negatives without ever betraying them'.[29]

The situation is different with Aristotle.[30] He opposes the Athenian civic tradition to Plato's ideal city. By doing so he gave citizenship an Athenian image and created the concept while even integrating its ambiguities. The *politeia*-citizenship appears in the *Politics* as the technical word it was before, referring to nationality and mostly used in the exceptional cases where this status was granted to non-citizens (cf. II, 1270aI; III, 1278aI; VII, 1326bI). But here, as well, the *status* only makes sense if it refers to the *practices* it implies and Aristotle's hostility to granting citizenship status to those who are not 'natural' citizens shows the inseparability of the title and its contents. As the *politeia*-regime is in all of Greek thought an order (*taxis*), of which the *politeia*-constitution is a specific form (*taxis tis*),[31] the *politeia*-citizenship is simultaneously a generic title and a more specific form of civic life.

At the outset Aristotle calls to mind that 'the state is a creation of nature and prior to the individual', and that 'man is by nature a political animal' (I: 1253). As he defines the city, the supreme community ordered by the unity of its goal, in contrast with partial communities (family, peoples),[32] Aristotle defines the citizen as opposed to the non-citizen. He leaves out of consideration 'those who have been made citizens', foreigners who only have a right of residence in the city, the one 'who has legal rights to the extent of suing and being sued', children and old people, and citizens sentenced to civic degradation or to exile (III, 1275aI). He concludes that the definition of 'the citizen in the strictest sense' depends on one essential feature: 'his characteristic is that he shares in the administration of justice, and in offices' (III, 1275aI). It is known that these two tracks concentrated the civic life of Athens. Moreover, contemporary historiography has called to mind the highly political role played by Athenian courts. The 'moderate democracy' of the fourth century was not limited to the deliberations of the Assembly, in which few citizens took part and that were often reduced to sparring matches between influential speakers. The courts, whose juries were drawn from citizens and whose judges were elected, also dealt with conflicts that concerned the city as a whole, finances and military strategies. Pleadings that have reached us, such as those of Demosthenes, show that leading strategists, magistrates and speakers were summoned to these courts which allowed the *idiôtai* to control the *politeuomenoi*.[33] By setting up the 'legislative' and 'judicial' powers as cornerstones of citizenship, Aristotle redefined in a clear conceptual language the ideal of merging citizens into a city: 'He who has the power to take part in the deliberative or judicial administration of any state is said by us to be a citizen of that state; and, speaking generally, a state is a body of citizens sufficing for the purposes of life' (III, 1275bI).

This perfect conceptual unity, in which the citizen only exists through the city, which is nothing other than the unity of all citizens, does not seem to be as obvious when we focus on the other meanings of *politeia*. Like his predecessors, Aristotle speaks of *politeia* in order to name, in a descriptive sense, the regime-constitution: 'a constitution [*politeia*] is the arrangement of magistracies in a state, especially of the highest of all' (III, 1278bI). A city's *politeia*, according to Aristotle as well as to Isocrates, is made up of its laws and morals, of 'the life of the city' (IV, 1295bI).

Following in the footsteps of his predecessors, Aristotle uses *politeia* in an extensive meaning to designate 'an arrangement of the inhabitants of a state' (III: 1274bI), but he also remarks that the same word means a particular regime as well: 'when the many administer the state for the common interest, the government is called by the generic name – constitution' (III, 1279aI). This ambivalence is not without influence on the meaning of citizenship: if the word *politeia* can be applied to regimes in which citizens do not take part 'in the deliberative or judicial administration' of the city, can one still speak of citizenship? Demosthenes thought not and reserved the use of the word *politeia* for cities in which citizens have power, thus maintaining the semantic identity of the constitution and citizenship under the linguistic unity of the *politeia*. Even if, in reality, there can be no doubt about the existence of 'passive citizens', this state of affairs was not formalised. Isocrates, who was far from being a proponent of democracy, was nevertheless indignant (in his *Panegyricus*) that a majority should be submitted to a small number and that some citizens should be legally excluded from the city;[34] he shows that, in his time, citizenship was not graduated, that exclusion from power was *ipso facto* exclusion from citizenship, since there was no word to name the citizen by birth (the national) who was deprived of power.

Aristotle crossed the threshold at which his predecessors had stopped: he acknowledged the fact that 'since there are many forms of government there must be many varieties of citizens' (III, 1278a). He admits in theory what was undeniable in practice: 'there are different kinds of citizens; and he is a citizen in the fullest sense who shares in the honours of the state'(III, 1278aI). Besides, this empirical observation is coherent with his normative choice: just as he acknowledges that there are different types of citizenship in practice, in theory he backs the *politeia* that is 'a fusion of oligarchy and democracy' (IV, 1293bI), 'constituted in accordance with strict principles of justice' (III, 1279aI) since it is governed 'on behalf of the common interest' and not as 'constitutions gone astray', wrecked by 'self-interest'. But if, within this constitution, 'the fighting men have the supreme power, and those who possess arms are the citizens' (III, 1279aI), and if Aristotle shares his doubts about the political capacities of manual labourers, he continuously calls citizens those who do not have that power, merely 'they are only citizens in a certain assumption' (III, 1278aI), likewise, children and old people are citizens that are 'not of age' or 'past the age' (III, 1275aI). These *archomenoi politai*, citizen-subjects or governed citizens, like metics, are deprived of the *timai* that are the core of citizenship. Thus Aristotle defines citizenship by its status and for the first time makes the distinction between the status and the practice it entails.[35] If *politeia* was not handed down to later languages, this ambivalent image of Athenian citizenship, acknowledged for all citizens but allotted to a few, is nevertheless its most certain legacy.

CIVIS AND *CIVITAS*:
THE CITIZENSHIP OF THE ROMAN REPUBLIC

The Greek *politeia* did not entirely pass on to later languages. The only Latin inheritance of this family is made up of two words. The first has a very general meaning, it is the adjective *politicus*, which qualifies all that has a link with governing; the other is very specialised and is the substantive *politia* that refers to the Republic of Greek philosophers – Plato's Republic and Aristotle's *Politeia*.[36] The etymology of *civitas* points to a very different linguistic chain than that of *politeia*. The Greek language retained the superiority of the city over the citizen (*polites* and *politeia* are derived from *polis*); Latin first recognises the citizen, from which it derives the city and citizenship (*civitas* comes from *civis*).[37] The *civis* is the compatriot, by opposition to the *hostis*, the foreigner; it marks a relation originally based on kinship and not on territory. The abstract *civitas* inherited this particular relation of reciprocity: the city is only comprehended as the whole of compatriots, as a 'collectivity and a reciprocity of cives';[38] citizenship is a status of reciprocity. This singular etymology is a sign of two major characteristics of Roman citizenship: it reveals its civic nature in the modern meaning of the term[39] and it foretells the flexibility of the status that is not, contrary to its Greek equivalent, by definition confined to the 'natural' boundaries of the city.

Civitas as the Constituent Bond of the Republic

When the Romans started to write their history, they set the emergence of the *civitas* at the very foundation of Rome. However it seems that to the royal era the conflicts connected to the enlargement of the civic body were not expressed in terms of *civitas*,[40] no more than they were after citizens had been given equal rights. As was the case in Athens, Rome seems to have felt the need for a precise way to denominate its neighbours, its foreigners. In fact it is in connection with the issue of 'nationality' that the word *civitas* came into common usage.[41]

But if *civitas* originated in nationality, its usage served a wholly different function: the array of statuses created around the *civitas* were 'successive instruments used by Rome in the unification of Italy',[42] which proceeded first of all by assimilating tribes that were ethnically and geographically close and then progressively and continuously moving farther afield, until the *civitas romana* lost all ethnic reference. As early as 390 BC, the Etruscan town of Caere, as a reward for its help against the Gauls, received from Rome a diminished form of *civitas*, so-called *civitas sine suffragio*, because it lacked participation in political power. This practice was extended to Latin cities during the fourth century after the Latin League was abolished (338 BC), and persisted in the third century beyond the boundaries of Italy. Communities that were awarded this title were called *municipes*: they benefited from the rights of Roman citizens, except for suffrage, but they also continued to honour the *munera* and *honores* of their *res publica*, in such a way that small communities coexisted within the community of status organised by Rome.

The codification of statuses in Roman law is based on a fundamental distinction between the core, the literal *civitas*, and numerous legal peripheries. Many codified and proceduralised links organise the legal mobility of communities and individuals between these two areas of law (by emancipation, naturalisation, collective concession) and draft the stages of a *cursus honorum* whose crowning moment is the acquisition of full citizenship.

The rights that are tied to each of these inferior statuses are extremely diverse and it is impossible to order them in concentric circles because the intersections are so numerous.[43] Roman citizenship alone holds all the rights: civil (relating to family relationships, property and taxation), military, and criminal and civic guarantees. 'Latin Law' defined a status with certain civil rights and criminal guarantees. Inferior statuses refer to various groups of civil rights, essentially linked to commercial and fiscal relations. Beyond this type, two sub-groups of rights can be made out, as in the *politeia*: the more or less extensive 'civil' rights on the one hand and on the other hand the political rights that only belong to Roman citizenship *per se* and are thus less generously granted.

These statuses simultaneously distinguish communities and individuals: *civitas* can be the title of a man – making him a citizen holding the rights that are tied to it – or of a community – making it a city with its own privileges. But the granting can also be differentiated: a community can receive the title of city but without all its inhabitants attaining citizenship, as was the case in certain colonies whose elite were made citizens whilst the inferior social classes profited at best from the title of *incola* (foreign resident benefiting from certain civil rights). These statuses show to what extent Rome either substituted itself for the pre-existing authority or let it be. When integrating a community that already had efficient administration and jurisdiction, and laws similar to Roman Law, Rome gave the title of city and granted strong autonomy. After conquering a 'barbarian' territory, Rome would deprive it of political independence and administered it directly with Roman laws, institutions and magistrates. Thus was constituted around Roman citizenship a string of secondary statuses (*civis, Latinus, civis sine suffragio, socius iniquo foedu*) that were all approximations of Roman citizenship.

Territories that were granted the capacity of cities kept their original citizenship, more or less extensively according to the degree of autonomy granted them. Some kept only the name but others maintained their own laws regulating private relations and political institutions, and had very intense municipal civic lives. However, this autonomy was legally limited: for example, Roman governors could always decide to ban a local custom that went against Roman laws. Duality was only tolerated subject to a very strict hierarchy. In the sphere of collective representation, this statutory situation was, or, ideally should have been, compatible with a 'constitutional patriotism' that Cicero[44] defined in this way:

> We consider too to be a fatherland where we were born. But of necessity that one takes precedence in our affections whose name 'commonwealth' belongs to the entire citizen body, on behalf of which we have an obligation to die, to which we should give ourselves entirely and in which we should place and almost consecrate everything we have. But in our affections the one that bore us stands almost as high as the one that received us; and so I will never deny that this is my fatherland, while recognising that the other one is greater and that this one is contained within it ... as two citizenships but think of them as one citizenship. (*De Leges* II, p. 5)

The multiplicity of statuses is further complicated by the numerous types of alliances between cities (synœcisms, sympolities, contributions), which engendered the superimposition of citizenships. The same man could be a citizen of Rome and of various local cities, sometimes making it impossible to define the law to which he was submitted in his family or commercial relations, his military or fiscal obligations. The genius of Roman citizenship lay in the unity it produced while letting an important variety of laws and institutions tied with local citizenship remain. This was only made possible by a subtle legal codification whose keystone was the legally and factually acknowledged superiority of the Roman city-citizenship over its constitutive entities. In modern terms this meant that sovereignty was Roman and that local citizenships only coexisted within it by an act of sovereignty – Rome determined the cities' autonomy.

Holders of such a citizenship seem to have harboured inconsistent feelings towards it. On the one hand they were assured of the legal protection inherent in the status of citizen and a certain number of military and commercial benefits. On the other hand, the benefits that were granted might sometimes have seemed inferior to the burdens they had to carry. However, Roman citizenship remained for a long time a valued status. Not only because it gave a certain amount of legal and political privileges but also, and mostly, because it remained the sign of a civilisation that thought of itself and was thought of as superior.

Civitas as a Form of Republican *Libertas*

If *civitas* labels members of a community compared to what is exterior to it, it also permits the ordering of this community from within. From the fourth to the second centuries BC at least, it served as an organising principle of Roman society, giving each citizen a personal status matched with precise 'rights and duties'. The *civitas* was the matrix of the Romans' 'collective mentality', aggregating their dominant civil and political conceptions.[45] First of all, the status permitted the distinction of citizens from all the other categories of individuals who did not enjoy legal and political capacity: foreigners, of course, even if they lived on Roman territory, and slaves. It also drew a distinction – by virtue of the *status familiae* – between those who were citizens by right (*civis optimo iure*), such as the *pater familias*, and those who had only a legal capacity on the basis of their link to a citizen, such as wives, children, freed slaves and 'clients'. For example, the *filius familias*, who was a male citizen of age but still under the authority of the head of his family, had commercial rights (*ius commercii*), he could marry (*ius conubii*), obtain certain public offices (*ius honorum*) and take part in the decisions of assemblies (*ius suffragii*), but he was deprived of numerous rights that today would be called civil rights, such as the right of ownership of goods and slaves (*dominium*), the right to free slaves (*manumissio*), to establish a family cult, to inherit or to bequeath.

Although the *civitas* was defined with meticulous care, one must not go as far as to see it as a stable and coherent judicial-political construction. The rights of citizens were slowly codified from their customary origin and citizenship always remained fragmented and implicit. It is only retrospectively that it represents a 'diagram, a theoretical and ideal model, towards which (...) institutions tended, but that they never reached'.[46]

The logic of this principle lay in the balance of the political offices that it established. On the one hand the *civitas romana* was a formally egalitarian status, in virtue of which citizens enjoyed equal rights. On the other hand *civitas romana* organised participation in the activities of the common *civitas*, the city, in a geometric way.[47] To account for these separate and interdependent elements of the *civitas*, it is necessary to examine it in the conceptual context to which it belonged at its peak, the Republican era, and particularly to put forward the connection of the *civitas* and of *libertas* – clearly apparent in the common expression *civitasque libertas* and in the relation of the *jus civitatis* and the *jus libertatis*.

The freedom of the citizen is firstly defined as a state of non-subjection, which makes it possible to enjoy the protection of the law. Only citizens have their mutual relations governed by 'civil law', i.e. the law of fellow-citizenship. For them, freedom, an attribute of citizenship, is legal equality. Equal freedom of citizens (*aequa libertas*), equal rights (*aequum ius*) and equal laws (*aequae leges*) are synonymous.[48] This 'civil' dimension of citizenship resulted in the judicially guaranteed respect of the life and property of the citizen. The protection of the citizen was also stated with regard to public power, i.e. the power of magistrates, against which several recourses existed: either the intercession of the tribunes, or the right to refer a question to the people (*provocatio ad populum*), or yet again, codified and public legal procedures. This 'negative freedom' of the citizen, according to the modern philosophers' expression, or this 'kind of early *habeas corpus*',[49] was considered by its holders as a privilege of which they made great use and that they jealously preserved. Moreover, it would progressively become increasingly important with the deterioration of the republic.

The *civitas* and the *libertas* are not reduced to the subjection to law and to a negative relation to power. At the republican time at least, both concepts also evoked a certain form of organisation of power, of which the people were considered to be the source and the measure. In the middle of the first century BC, at the twilight of the Roman Republic, Cicero gave the most systematic outline of Roman 'political law' to have reached us. At the end of an already long political career, he offered to write for his peers a treatise on the Republic and one on its laws, to record the legacy of the Republic and to ward off its deterioration.[50] A vigorous panegyric of the Republic at the dawn of its decline, *De Republica* and *De Legibus* are the theorisation of the 'common sense' politics of his contemporaries and gave posterity an account of the republican conception of the elite, at the time when 'we preserve the commonwealth in name alone but have long lost its substance' (*De Republica* V, p. 2).

In this conceptual edifice, the *civitas* holds a special place. Cicero, as his contemporaries, sometimes uses the term in an undetermined way, as a synonym of 'state', of the republic, or even of the people. But he sometimes makes the word *civitas* and its correlatives match more rigorously defined concepts: 'What is the state if not the association of the citizens under law?' (I, p. 50). And he specifies that there is no city without law, which is 'the bond of civil society' and the principle of common law; which implies that 'the rights of all who are citizens of the same commonwealth ought to be equal' (I, p. 49). Citizenship, which Cicero seldom evokes as such, is therefore a status of equal participation in the common city, a legal identity.

This is the level of the most general concepts that Cicero defines without wanting to take sides, and the real meaning of citizenship only shows when he defends the republic. Contrary to what certain ambivalent passages can lead us to think, the republic is not reduced to the generic concept of the city or of a legal society. For only the city, where 'the people holds to its own rights', the city where 'they are masters of the laws and the courts, of war and peace, of treaties, of the status and wealth of every citizen' is 'the only one [commonwealth] properly so named' (I, p. 49).

Regarding freedom, 'in no other state that in which the people has the highest power does liberty have any home – liberty, than which nothing can be sweeter, and which, if it is not equal, is not even liberty' (*De Rep.* I, p. 48). The republic is therefore a particular form of city, where the law proceeds from the people, which is free, so much it is true that freedom 'does not consist in having a just master, but in having none' (II, p. 42). One can then suppose that there are also specific forms of citizenship, and in particular a republican citizenship. If one follows the nuance that Cicero establishes between the city in general, and the Republic, invested with political value, one can assert that citizenship in a republic is an identity of freedom, an equal participation in the power of the people.

However, one must keep in mind how much these general and abstract statements are rhetorical. Rome was not Athens, and if its constitutional theory gave all authority to the people, its institutional system did not. The conceptual constellation in Latin of what we call in contemporary language 'power', or more legally 'sovereignty', is a first sign of this. The people was supposed to be the holder of *potestas*, which tribunes of the plebeians exercised on its behalf. But this concept of power is not the whole 'sovereignty', it was only a power, in a political space where it competed with the *imperium* exercised by the magistrates and the *auctoritas* held by the Senate.[51]

Potestas, *imperium* and *auctoritas* were always competing and together gave the Republic its laws, even if the balance leaned sometimes in favour of the one and sometimes in favour of the other, definitively inclining towards the *imperium* monopolised by the Prince and then the Emperor after the fall of the Republic. In the political conceptions of the elite, the people was perceived as a minor subject, incapable of giving themselves their own laws and which, for this reason, had to be assisted by 'major' bodies, acting as tutor. The *civitas* is, along with the people, the Senate – in accordance with the famous formula *Senatus populusque romanus*. The same idea becomes apparent in the significance of the *res publica*. There cannot be a *res publica* without a people submitted to the same law and to a common interest, and even without a law adjusted in the interest of the people; however the participation of the people in the legislative function was not necessary for the definition of the *res publica*.[52] The freedom of the citizen was guaranteed by law, it is even obedience to the law, but it does not appear as clearly that citizenship was *defined* by participation in the power of enacting the law. The whole organisation of the Republic contributed to depriving the citizen of this power, while maintaining the fiction.

The main tool of this configuration was the *census*: a process which counted and classified citizens and allowed the distributing of military, fiscal and political charges and prerogatives between the orders of the civic body. Its principle was not that of universal equality, confined to civil law, but that of the geometrical equality of the aristocratic mentality: distribution according to citizens' recognised value and fortune. This was the key to social equilibrium and the source of the consensus around it: the rich carry the fiscal and military burdens in exchange for political responsibilities, of which the poor agree to be deprived in exchange for their immunity as regards taxation and war. This census organisation allowed the preservation of the principle of the power of the people while neutralising it.

Various institutions contributed to this.[53] Firstly, the 'voice of the people' only expressed itself within skilfully organised frameworks set up by the leading elite: the magistrates called the meetings, by distinguishing auspicious days from adverse days: if necessary, an excuse to defer a meeting in unfavourable circumstances. The people's only power was to pronounce on decisions prepared by governors: either to vote for a law they did not initiate, that they did not write and of which they had no possibility of discussing or, *a fortiori*, of amending; or to elect a magistrate nominated by Senators. Voting procedures themselves diminished the people's weight: upstream, censors had the power to draw up the registers of citizens, thereby validating or invalidating the citizenship of an individual. In the voting act itself, citizens were divided into groups according to their rank, and although the laws were called *leges populi romani* they were actually *leges curiatiae*, *centuriatae* or *tributae* (curia, centuries and tribes). The laws and the election of the magistrates resulted from a vote that was organised to favour citizens of the higher classes. Finally, in practice, as in Athens, the lower classes had much more difficulty in finding the leisure and income to participate in meetings, the venues of which seldom made it possible to welcome more than 10,000 people, while Rome counted more than 100,000 citizens and Italy more than one million in the first century BC. The legislative and electoral powers of the people were thus significantly framed by the elite. If the mass of citizens wanted to contest policy on collective issues, such as its collective survival or of the division of wealth during wars, or maintaining freedom by law, it had to do so outside meetings, in public manifestations of dissatisfaction that were beyond procedural frameworks or the formal ways of citizenship.

Cicero gave this duality between the formal statement of citizens' equality and the true organisation of their hierarchy a principled basis. He was influenced by representations of the 'classical natural law',[54] which postulated a homology between the structure of the city and that of nature. He believed, along with Plato and his contemporaries, that inequalities were natural and that the 'good city' aimed to balance them.

> And what people call equality is in fact very unfair. When the same degree of honour is given to the best and the worst (and such must exist in any population), then equity itself is highly inequitable. But that is something that cannot happen in states that are ruled by the best citizens. (*De Rep.* I, p. 53)

To plan this harmonious city, Cicero, following the Greek tradition imported by Polybius, established a typology of three regimes, according to whether only one, several or all had power. He added immediately that any regime could be defended in theory but that each one tended to corrupt itself in practice when individual interests came before common welfare. Therefore they should be overlooked in favour of a 'a government that is balanced and compounded from the three primary forms of commonwealth' (I, p. 69). In this mixed constitution, the principle of formal equality is moderated so as to avoid the risk of popular despotism. Cicero endeavoured to preserve the myth of formal equality while making an oligarchic principle prevail. He summarises this in the following ambivalent formula: 'The liberty should consist in this, that the people are given the power of honourably pleasing the respectable citizens' (*De Leg*. III, p. 38).

Such a reasoning only has meaning because, for Romans, the law was not the expression of the general will that it later became but the translation of a natural law, independent of men's fluctuating wills: 'law is a power of nature, it is the mind and reason of the prudent man, it distinguishes justice and injustice' (I, p. 19). The divinity endowed man with reason and, since the law is none other than straight reason considered in its injunctions and its prohibitions, to be free, to obey the law, is to obey the injunctions of those which have wisdom: the good citizens. From there come all the institutions that Cicero catalogues and praises and according to which 'the people have power and the Senate has authority' (III, p. 28). Citizenship, in the dominant ideology that Cicero describes and which is shared by the people,[55] is a status of legal identity that gives its holder judicial guarantees, and equal freedom, proclaimed in theory and stolen in practice.

This became all the more true at the end of the second century as the 'structural balance', as Claude Nicolet described the republican *civitas*,[56] deteriorated. The military and fiscal charges of the richest citizens were lightened, so that the position of citizens less fortunate and more deprived of power seems relatively disadvantaged. A new balance was ensured when, starting in 133 BC, public land as well as wheat was distributed and, subsequently, other advantages. In comparison, the situation of Allies and Latins became less and less enviable: they remained tied by the obligations of their charters with Rome but the new benefits were reserved for citizens. They also continued to be unequally treated in the face of fiscal and political charges and military privileges, without being granted either the judicial protections of *libertas* or new material advantages.

The Dilution Of The *Civitas Romana*

The fall of the Republic confirmed Cicero's concerns *a posteriori*. Under Caesar, Augustus and their successors, the word republic still existed but 'the thing no more'. The same is true of the *civitas*. Its history during the Empire is that of a continuous extension to non-Roman people and of dilution of its contents, the progressive obliteration of the *munera* and *honores* of the Roman citizen. The oligarchic character of the *civitas romana* becomes increasingly patent, and the equality of right of citizens' less and less credible. Citizenship tended to be reduced to a status of civil right, to all the *iura* which determined the citizen's private life. The *ius suffragii* and the *ius honorum*, which, under the republic, were undeniably constitutive of citizenship, even if they remained primarily formal, ceased to be essential to its definition.

Caesar and Augustus firmly re-established the old practice of extending citizenship to provincial areas. During their reigns, this policy remained prudent: only the regions of old Italian immigration received full citizenship, the others being granted a *ius Latii*, which was only a legal periphery of citizenship.[57] With this first phase of extension came an alteration in the meaning of citizenship: whereas Caesar had clearly maintained citizens' obligations, in particular military obligations, these tend to be eroded under Augustus and more still after him. After an incubation period that enabled the Empire to assimilate this new population of citizens, Claudius considered it useful to proceed in the way traced by his predecessors. He was among those who believed that the greatness of Rome was due to the openness of its political community, by opposition to Greek sectarianism. Tacitus[58] argues the fact in these terms:

> What other cause brought about the end of the Lacedaemonians and of the Athenians, who had major military power, other than the fact that they refused to accept the defeated, regarding them as being from another race? (...) but our founder, Romulus, shows such wisdom that he regarded the majority of people, on the same day, as enemies then as citizens. (XI, XXIV, p. 4)

Moreover, the historian reports the opinion of the elite who were hostile to Claudius's projects:

> Was it not enough that Venets and Insubres errupted in the Curia, without one making a crowd of foreigners enter, like a group of prisoners of war? ... They certainly can enjoy citizenship; but that the Fathers' Insignias, the honours of public office be not given to anyone. (XI, XXIII, p. 3–4)

Tacitus thus shows that the universality of Roman citizenship was not uncontested, even if it finally triumphed. He also confirms the impoverishment of citizenship under the Empire; citizen participation in the honours of public office is, increasingly openly, ruled out. The *civitas romana* did not disappear but was reduced, and increasingly clearly so until the fall of the Empire, to a status of private law in the modern sense of the expression. At the same time the meaning of *libertas* altered. It still expressed the survival of the ideal of republican freedom, on whose behalf Caesar was assassinated and which Nero fought against. But in the first and second centuries of the first millennium *libertas* merged increasingly with *securitas publica*, in the eyes of the elite concerned with their private freedom. It was reduced to respect for citizens' life and property, which was no longer even judicially guaranteed.

The Caracalla edict in AD 212 is the height of this trend towards the dilution of citizenship: giving it to all, native or not, member of the Roman cultural sphere or not, without even a condition of service rendered to the city; one is consequently a 'Roman citizen simply because one is a free inhabitant of the civilised world'.[59] The question of belonging to the city no longer arises and one now only speaks of *civitas* to designate this city of universal claims. Moreover, during the fourth century the term *Romanus* tends to replace the word *civitas*. Used as much to qualify people as territories, it designates the Empire as a whole. Especially, it makes it possible to name by opposition barbarians, the threat of invasion by whom strengthened the meaning of 'Roman-ness'; if not strictly political or legal, neither was it purely ethnic. To be Roman was to belong to a higher civilisation; once Caracalla extended the *civitas*, to be part of the civilised world was to be Roman.

NOTES

1   M. I. Finley, *Politics in the Ancient World* (Cambridge, Cambridge University Press, 1983), p. 89.

2   *Cf.* B. Manin, *Principles of Representative Government* (Cambridge, Cambridge University Press, 1997).

3   E. Benveniste, *Les institutions indo-européennes* (Paris, Editions de Minuit, 1969), vol. 2, pp. 367 and 309.

4   Herodotus, *Histories*, translated by Aubrey de Salincourt (Harmondsworth, Penguin Books, 1972).

5   *Cf.* J. Bordes, *Politeia dans la pensée grecque jusqu'à Aristote* (Paris, Les Belles Lettres, 1982), p. 19.

6   *Cf.* R. Sealey, 'How citizenship and the city began in Athens', *American Journal of Ancient History* 1983, pp. 97–129.

7   *Cf.* W. Beringer, 'Freedom, family and citizenship in early Greece' in J.W. Eadie and J. Ober (eds), *The Craft of the Ancient Historian* (London, Lanham, 1985), pp. 41–56.

8   *Cf.* Sealey, 'How citizenship and the city began', pp. 116–23.

9   P.B. Manville, *The Origins of Citizenship in Ancient Athens* (Princeton, Princeton University Press, 1992), p. 156.

10 *Cf.* Sealey *How Citizenship Began* pp. 98–9.

11 J.P. Vernant, *The Origins of Greek Thought* (Ithaca NY, Cornell University Press, 1982), p. 99.

12 Manville, *Origins of Citizenship*, p. 198.

13 *Cf.* R.K. Sinclair, *Democracy and Participation in Athens* (Cambridge, Cambridge University Press, 1988), p. 89. Sinclair gives the following numbers for the year 431: 30–40,000 metics, 100,000 slaves and 160–170,000 Athenians, of whom 40,000 were citizens.

14 *Ibid.*, p. 14.

15 Finley, *Politics in the Ancient World*, p. 68.

16 *Cf.* C. Mossé, *Politique et société en Grèce ancienne, Le 'modèle' athénien* (Paris, Aubier, 1995), particularly chapter three, 'Le fonctionnement de la vie politique', pp. 121–78.

17 *Ibid.*, p. 21.

18 Bordes, *Politeia dans la pensée grecque*, p. 57.

19 *Ibid.*, p. 62.

20 *Cf.* V. Ehrenhed, *The Greek City State* (London, Matnahm, 1960), pp. 39–43.

21 The expression is from Bordes, *Politeia dans la pensée grecque*. This paragraph is largely based on her work.

22 Isocrates opposed *politeia* to monarchy in his *Panegyric*. Still more radically, Demosthenes offered to consider as 'enemies' those who 'destroy the *politeiai* to set up an oligarchy' (*Pour la liberté des Rhodiens*, § 20). These examples given by J. Bordes, 'La place d'Aristote dans l'évolution de la notion de politeia', *KTEMA* 1980, 5/2, pp. 249–56.

23 *Cf.* M. Hammond, *Aristotle and World-State in Greek and Roman Political Theory until Augustus* (Cambridge MA, Harvard University Press,), pp. 28–38. This does not mean that there were no partial reciprocal rights between cities, according to a gradation which calls to mind the rights and privileges of citizens that Athens granted to deserving foreigners.

24 *Cf.* Bordes, *Politeia*, pp. 71–2.

25 The contemporary notion of citizenship is still marked by such an exclusive alternative, which makes it difficult to envisage a transnational citizenship. *Cf.* P. Magnette, *La citoyenneté européenne*, (Brussels, Editions de l'Université de Bruxelles,)

26 *Ibid.*, p. 77.

27 Plato, *The Republic*

28 *Cf.* K. R. Raaflaub, 'Democracy, oligarchy and the concept of "free citizen" in late fifth-century Athens', *Political Theory* 1983, 11/4, pp 517–44.

29 Bordes, *Politeia*, p. 435.

30 Aristotle, *The Politics: The Constitution of Athens*, edited by S. Everson (Cambridge, Cambridge University Press, 1996).

31 Both these expressions are borrowed from L. Bescond, 'Remarques sur la conception aristotélicienne de la citoyenneté' in *Cahiers de philosophie juridique et politique de l'Université de Caen* 1983, no. 4, pp. 25–34.

32 Aristotle equally refuses to consider a 'beyond' the city. He certainly broaches the idea of a constitutional unity for the 'Hellenic race' (VII: 1327bI), but refuses to consider that military alliances and commercial agreements form a city (III: 1280aI). On these aspects see E. Lévy, 'Cité et citoyen dans la *Politique* d'Aristote', *KTEMA* 1980, 5/2, pp. 223–48.

33 *Cf.* M. H. Hansen, *The Athenian Democracy in the Age of Demosthenes* (Oxford/Cambridge MA, Blackwell, 1991), pp. 178–224.

34 *Cf.* Bordes, 'La place d'Aristote dans l'évolution de la notion de politeia', p. 254. Also C. Mossé, 'La conception du citoyen dans la *Politique* d'Aristote', *Eirene* 1967, 6/1, pp. 17–21.

35 This division is reinforced by his use of another close term, *politeuma*. Before Aristotle, this word meant 'political acts' (*cf.* Bordes, 'La place d'Aristote', pp. 225–6 and Lévy, 'Cité et citoyen', pp. 239–40. Aristotle refined this linguistic usage. Sometimes he uses the word *politeuma* as a synonym of *politeia* (III: 1279aI), at other times he gives it the more limited meaning of 'political body' or 'holder of sovereignty' (V: 1305bI). In this sense *politeuma* indicates all the 'complete citizens' commanding and using the *timai*. Consequently, citizenship and constitution are no longer intertwined; all citizens are holders of the former but only a portion of them are holders of the *politeuma*-sovereignty.

36 Contrary to Greek, Latin does not acknowledge a single word to refer to, on the one hand, what modern languages mean by 'citizenship' and, on the other hand, 'constitution-regime'. The Latin *civitas*, like the Greek *politeia*, encompasses an individual meaning (citizenship) and a collective meaning (city). But Latin makes a difference between the form (*civitas*) and

organisation of the latter (*constitutio*); it also draws a distinction between the homeland and the city. Besides, it divides the terms in half, alternating *civitas* and *res publica* when it is a question of designating the city, without it being possible to tell them apart from the context.

37 *Cf.* Benveniste, *Les institutions indo-européennes*, pp. 335–7 and E. Benveniste, 'Deux modèles linguistiques de la cité' in *Échanges et communications, Mélanges Claude Lévi-Strauss* (Paris, 1971), pp. 589–96.

38 Benveniste, 'Deux modèles linguistiques', p. 593.

39 *Cf.* J.F. Gardner, *Being a Roman Citizen* (London, Routledge, 1992) and M. Villey, *Le droit romain* (Paris, PUF, 1975).

40 *Cf.* J.-C. Richard, 'Variations sur le thème de la citoyenneté à l'époque royale', *KTEMA* 1981, 6/1, pp. 89–103.

41 On this aspect of the *civitas*, *Cf.* A.N. Sherwin-White, *The Roman Citizenship* (Oxford, Clarendon Press, 1973 [1929]).

42 *Ibid.* p. 58.

43 *Cf.* F. Jacques and J. Scheid, *Rome et l'intégration de l'Empire, tome I: Les structures de l'Empire romain* (Paris, PUF, 1992 [1990]), pp. 209–50.

44 Cicero, *De Republica, De Legibus*, edited by J. E.G. Zetzel (Cambridge, Cambridge University Press, 1999).

45 See E. Cizek, *Mentalités et institutions politiques romaines* (Paris, Fayard, 1990).

46 C. Nicolet, *Le métier de citoyen dans la Rome républicaine* (Paris, Gallimard, 1976), p. 28.

47 *Cf.* G. Crifò, 'Remarques sur les problèmes de l'égalité et de la liberté à Rome', *KTEMA* 1981 6/1, pp. 193–210.

48 *Cf.* C. Wirszubski, *Libertas as a Political Idea at Rome during the Late Republic and Early Principate* (Cambridge, Cambridge University Press, 1950).

49 Nicolet, *Le métier de citoyen*, p. 34.

50 Cicero, Marcus Tullius, *On the Commonwealth: On the Laws*, edited by J.E.G. Zetzel (Cambridge, Cambridge University Press 1999).

51 *Cf.* M. David, *La souveraineté du peuple* (Paris, PUF, 1996), pp. 8–12; and M. David, 'Les racines athéniennes et romaines de la souveraineté du peuple', *Revue française d'histoire des idées politiques*, 1996, p. 3.

52 *Ibid.*

53 *Cf.* Finley, *Politics in the Ancient World*, pp. 130–44.

54 In the sense of L. Strauss, *Natural Right and History* (Chicago, Chicago University Press, 1953).

55 *Cf.* above the discussion on geometrical equality and also Nicolet, *Le métier de citoyen* and Finley, *Politics in the Ancient World*.

56 Nicolet, *Le métier de citoyen*.

57 M. Humbert, 'Le droit latin impérial: cités latines ou citoyenneté latine?', *KTEMA* 1981, 6/2, pp. 211–26.

58 Tacitus, Cornelius, *The Annals of Imperial Rome*, translated and introduced by M. Grant (Harmondsworth, Penguin Books, 1956)

59 Sherwin-White, *Roman Citizenship*, p. 287.

chapter two | the eclipse and renaissance of the concept of citizenship

The social theory of Christianity, which dominated Europe until the democratic revolutions of the eighteenth century and often beyond, did not amount to as complete a rupture with Roman language and syntax as is often thought. If it ruled out the concept of popular sovereignty essential to republican thought, it nevertheless borrowed some elements from the *civitas romana* and thus, indirectly contributed to its survival.

The doctrines of Saint Paul illustrate this affiliation. As a Roman citizen, he still invoked the privileges of his citizenship when he was arrested, making the claim '*civis romanus sum*' ('I am a Roman citizen') to avoid being tried by a foreign law and jurisdiction. The *civitas*, understood in this context as the protection of *habeas corpus*, remains strong. But with Saint Paul came a new theory which undermined the substantive content of Roman citizenship while continuing to make use of the political language inherited from declining Roman civilisation. One can note, firstly, that Christian theology expressed the division of nature and faith through an analogy with Roman concepts. Saint Paul insisted that a metamorphosis of man was achieved by baptism: the man of nature (*homo animalis*), the man of flesh (*homo carnis*) was reborn as a Christian (*christianus*). As in the Roman ideology, an 'abstract' identity replaces the 'natural' person. And, as in Roman thought, the Christian individual existed only as a member of a community. The linguistic analogy of *fidelis/fidelitas* with *civis/civitas* makes the heritage obvious: the *fidelis*, that is, the individual Christian, existed only by virtue of the *fidelitas*, the corporation of the faithful, which was conceived only as the unity of its elements. The Church wanted itself to be a community of men linked not by rights but by a shared belief, which prepared them for the advent of what St Augustine would call, three centuries later but still in Roman vocabulary, 'a celestial city' (*civitas*). The cement and the purpose of the 'city' were different but the matrix of reasoning was borrowed directly from Roman grammar.

FIDELIS AND FIDELITAS:
THE PERSONAL STATUS IN CHRISTIAN DOCTRINE

Like the Republic, the Church would have to face the problem that its faithful's loyalties were torn between multiple memberships. The members of the *fidelitas* also lived in human, secular communities, and the delineation of these two memberships would be ceaselessly debated from the third to the thirteenth century and even beyond. The evangelical precept seemed to be univocal: it postulated that God and Caesar have separate fields, and Paul, a Roman citizen, exhorted Christians to submit to temporal power. But in reality things were not so simple. Far from confining itself to the field of spiritual belonging, which allowed previous civic ties to remain, over the centuries the Church tended to merge with the secular power. This hegemonic tendency was inherent to Christian theology: since the universe was conceived as a whole governed by the divine principle, temporal power lost all autonomy. It was only one manifestation of Providence, among others. '*Nulla potestas nisi a Deo*' ('there is no power except from God') theologians would say after Saint Paul. Consequently, relations between the state and the Church or, in the words of the time, between the *regnum* and the *sacerdotium*, would become the central concern of medieval political thought.[1] Under the Roman republic the question had not arisen, because the 'laws of nature' were inherent in the concept of the city. Conflicts became inevitable from the moment when the Church claimed more autonomy from the republic, when religion became, in a sense, a specialised 'function' separated from, and claiming primacy over, other human activities.

Faced with this perpetual fight for supremacy, Christian thinkers tried to interpret the presence of a secular power as an integral part of the holistic cosmology of Christianity. The conceptual solution that was found at the end of the Roman period consisted of assimilating the *christianus* to the *romanus* and in seeing the Empire as an instrument providentially created by God to spread Christianity. Having accepted the new religion, the secular power tried to use it as a basis for its authority, by presenting itself as the realisation of Providence's plans. Under these conditions, there were not two opposing structures but a single entity, indissolubly political and religious. Christianity had replaced 'classical natural law', but remained within Roman political thought.

This conception became incoherent after the fall of the Empire under successive waves of 'barbarian' invasions. A new doctrine was then necessary: how could God have willed the destruction of the Empire if it was the means of achieving his reign on earth? Political change having outdated doctrine, Saint Augustine (354–430) endeavoured to rebuild it.[2] In doing so, he continued to borrow from the Roman language, if not concepts then at least words (*City of God*, I, V, p. 17).[3] To prevent the Empire taking religion with it as it fell, the two worlds had to be separated. Acknowledging the new political situation, Augustine denied the intertwining of the Roman and the Christian, and the Empire as a worldly expression of the divine project. Augustine wrote that there are two cities (*civitas*) in the universe, one of God, the other of men, which are the objects of two different kinds of human love (*caritas*).The structure of the argument is directly borrowed from Roman syntax as synthesised by Cicero. Only the cement of the city changes: it is love, rather than law, which connects Christians and defines their obligations. Augustine was so immersed in this language that he could not think of religion without it, thus the metaphor comes almost naturally. But nothing in this doctrinal development was fortuitous. The separation of cities tended to reverse the relation of authority; it involved establishing that the worldly *civitas* was only a pale image of the celestial ideal as well as stating the moral primacy of Christianity over secular power.

For this purpose, the separation cannot be total. The opposition between both *civitates*, worldly and celestial, is not dualistic: if the 'ultimate loves' of both cities are radically opposed, Augustine adds that the 'intermediate loves' of men can be reconciled and serve as a base for the foundation of a worldly society which is not the negation of the divine community. Men are moved by a common passion, shared by even the 'most malicious', for tranquillity and peace, and they can agree on their common aim of defending their material survival and safety. These are sufficient bases on which to build an earthly city. It remains sullied by sins, but it is not the antithesis of God's city. Although still imperfect, the earthly city contributes to the progressive advent of the celestial purpose:

> The heavenly city, therefore, while in its state of pilgrimage, avails itself of the peace of earth, and, so far as it can without injuring faith and godliness, desires and maintains a common agreement among men regarding the acquisition of the necessaries of life, and makes this earthly peace bear upon the peace of heaven; for this alone can be truly called and esteemed the peace of the reasonable creatures, consisting as it does in the perfectly ordered and harmonious enjoyment of God and of one another in God. (XIX, p. 17)

Human law was not considered to be a manifestation of the natural-celestial order, it was only human and infested with sin but, in spite of its limits, it also answered to Providence and endeavoured to contain the effects of evil. Augustine had a double aim in saying this: on the one hand he could clear God of the responsibility for terrestrial misery, since this was not his direct work; on the other hand, he could prescribe a teleological aim for the earthly city and order it to organise itself in view of the celestial city. This implies that it was subject itself to Christian morals, whatever the political form it chose. This reinterpretation skilfully strengthened the religious doctrine: it allows itself to pass judgement on the faults of the terrestrial city and to show it the right way.

The Roman matrix was still structured around this conception. Admittedly the celestial city was separated from the terrestrial city while Romans perceived an inseparable totality. But in one as in the other case, human law appears to be a manifestation of immanent laws, which Romans thought to be 'natural' while Christians described them as 'divine'. In addition, Christianity borrowed its universalism from the Roman republic, through the metaphor of the *civitas*.⁴ A religion of conquest, like the ethos of the Roman Republic, Christianity claims to be the foundation of a community of wills and principle, without ethnic components.

> The heavenly city, then, while it sojourns on earth, calls citizens out of all nations, and gathers together a society of pilgrims of all languages, not scrupling about diversities in the manners, laws, and institutions whereby earthly peace is secured and maintained, but recognising that, however various these are, they all tend to one and the same end of earthly peace. (XIX, p. 17)

By using the language of Rome, Augustine also reaffirmed his universal ambitions. *Mutatis mutandis*, the 'Christian city' was a community of values, a civilisation, which surpassed political groupings, while leaving them the leisure to cultivate their difference.

In the absence of borders between the temporal and spiritual, or of a clear primacy of one over the other, the privileges of both remained the subject of conflict. The fundamental axiom remained uncontested: there was no power which did not emanate from God and men's only right was to obey. Christian doctrine buried politics in an all-encompassing cosmology that temporal power-holders adopted. It is significant that the word *politicus* had disappeared, that the power was no longer called 'state', 'republic' or 'city' but simply *regnum* or *gubernatio*, which relates back to the administrative and judicial *office*, but no more to a separate *entity*. Whatever the methods, politics were diluted in religious morals.

An anthropomorphic metaphor, which persisted throughout the Middle Ages, reflected this cosmology. It simultaneously made possible the reconciliation of spiritual and temporal powers and the justification of the monarchical form taken on by the *regnum* from the ninth century. Saint Paul had already compared the assemblies of the faithful to a human body in the expression *corpus Christi*, still used today in the ritual of the Roman Catholic Church. This organicist image of the Church not only reflected the subordination of the faithful, of the *fidelis* to the *fidelitas*, but also the submission of the whole to the 'head', i.e. to the supreme authority of the church. It made it possible to recall that everyone was required (*vocatus*) to fulfil a precise task, like the organs of the human body.⁵ The metaphor was sometimes pushed to the point of making the Pope, 'in whom, like all members in the head, all orders of the Church are united'⁶ into a collective person, of whom every one of the faithful was an emanation.

The organicist representation was also applied to temporal power, thus putting forward the unity of Church and royalty. John of Salisbury (c. 1115–80)⁷ drew the most explicit picture of this, in what is alleged to be a letter of Plutarch to Trajan. In book V of *Policraticus*, finished in 1159, he starts by recalling that

> just as the soul has rulership of the whole body so those who are called prefects of religion direct the whole body.

He continues by specifying that,

> The position of the head in the republic is occupied, however, by a prince sub-ject only to God and to those who act in His plan on earth, inasmuch as in the human body the head is stimulated and ruled by the soul.

He pushes the exercise further by matching every institution with a body part: 'the place of the heart is occupied by the senate', 'the duties of the ears, eyes and mouth are claimed by the judges and governors of provinces. The hands coincides with officials and soldiers'. As to the persons responsible for the treasury and accounts they

> resemble the shape of the stomach and intestines; these, if they accumulate with great avidity and tenaciously preserve their accumulation, engender innu-merable and incurable diseases so that their infection threatens to ruin the whole body.

The people are not forgotten in this depiction: 'the feet coincide with peasants per-petually bound to the soil, for whom it is all the more necessary that the head take precautions' (V, II, p. 67). Medieval organicism reconciles the spiritual and tem-poral powers by presenting one as the soul and the other as the head. Additionally, it sets the hierarchical principle of political organisation. The social body is not composed of individuals but of ranks and orders to which men are assigned and on which their status, rights and obligations, in short their collective existence, depends. The names given to different ranks are numerous: *status*, *honor*, *ordo*, *gradus*, *dignitas*. There is no abstract individual: man (*homo*) only exists as a member of an order: *fidelis*, *civis*, *subjectus* or simply *quisque*.

The citizen has not completely disappeared: Augustine still spoke of the *civis*, and made it out to be a synonym of *subditus*. In the seventh and eighth centuries royal speeches were sometimes addressed to the *cives*. But these are only excep-tions in which the term *civis* has become extremely vague; in the texts of theolo-gians and the jurists, the citizen is completely absent. The domination of Christian organicism provides a first explanation of this absence: all power being consid-ered to be of divine origin, the freedom of the people is reduced to a misconcep-tion. The eminent specialist of the middle ages, Walter Ullmann, wrote that the expansion of Christianity replaced the 'ascending principle' of the Roman repub-lic, where authority was considered to come from the civic body, by a 'downward principle' according to which all power, emanating from God, was imposed on men.[8] And yet the *civitas* had survived the fall of the republic, had remained a cen-tral institution of the Principate and of the Roman Empire. Why couldn't a new meaning of *civitas* emerge, removed from the idea of popular sovereignty and implying only men's membership in the political community? In this sense there actually is an Augustinian *civitas*, a modelling of Roman vocabulary on to the new Christian domination. But the Church did not manage to impose its community to the point of subordinating all others completely. Over the centuries, citizens' frames of reference were duplicated, their loyalties split. The absence of an ultimate political bond and the presence of many different ones made the concept of citizenship aporetic, as if the citizen belonged to several different communities.

THE FRAGMENTATION OF COMMUNITIES AND STATUSES

Undeniably, the Church tried to assert itself in the face of temporal powers, either to integrate them or to appropriate their strength. These dreams of total domination never really disappeared; endemically, ambitious popes dreamed of rebuilding a denominational Empire from Rome. But they had to take into account the claims of kings and emperors. During the twelfth century Frederick Barbarossa hoped to rebuild the Roman Empire from the German monarchy and to transform the *imperium romanum* into a *sacrum imperium*, governing his territories in spite of papal protests. During the thirteenth century, Dante Alighieri, Englebert of Admont and John of Viterbe pleaded for the rebuilding of a European Christian empire. From the ninth century, monarchs had been opposing this idea by endeavouring to have their borders recognised and by imposing a single currency and a legal and administrative apparatus within their territory.[9] Ultimately it was the royal institution, the *regnum*, which would establish itself as a figure of what was starting to be perceived as a polity. And yet, the assertion of royal power, its theoretical recognition and its progressive codification, did not permit the establishment of a frame of univocal reference. The king owed his success to his central position within the tangle of feudalism. A complex network of relations of reciprocal dependence, based on vassalage and vows of allegiance, subtended the royal power. As the specialist of the Medieval Ages, Ewart Lewis writes:

> When the political rights were attached to the personal statute and were diffused by subinfeodation, when the supreme king in England was a vassal in France, when noblemen had simultaneously vowed allegiance to various kings for largely scattered possessions, when the ocean of the royal jurisdiction was strewn with islands of immunities of all kinds, the geographical definition of political communities was completely unthinkable, and impossible in practice.[10]

This vagueness, accentuated by the centrifugal tensions of the papal and imperial claims, makes citizenship inconceivable, even without political privilege. Men do not only come under the ministry of these vertical relations to lords, kings and dignitaries of the clergy, they are also committed to multiple horizontal networks that define their status and their 'rights'. In villages and rural communities, spontaneous and informal collective codes of conduct, later described as customs, ruled the lives of peasants.[11] The cities formed during the eleventh and twelfth centuries also enacted their own rules, often codified in charters and recognised by the royal jurisdiction. Professional corporations (guilds) were also, along with rural communities and cities, forms of voluntary association based on vertical relations with their own hierarchies. The profusion of this type of community is attested by the wealth of the vocabulary that they are associated with: *societas, communitas, corpora, universitas, multitudo, congregatio, collectio, coetus, collegium,* so many words, often formed on the root *cum,* that reflect the luxuriance of social links.[12]

In medieval Europe, men were related to different collective entities which varied in nature and size: the universal Church, the Empire, the kingdom, the feudal field, the local Church, the city or the village, guilds, corporations and confraternities. This was also true, albeit to a lesser extent, in ancient Greece and Rome; but both had managed to build a political community which transcended these individual memberships, to which a central part of the community could be attached via citizenship. Such a thing did not exist in medieval Europe, where the polity was diffuse and fragmented; citizenship could not emerge from the multiplicity of social links.

THE RETURN OF ROME

The word citizenship reappears in first half of the fourteenth century, in the works of Italian lawyers and in particular of Bartolus and Baldus of Ubaldis. Two centuries of political and intellectual transformation made possible the exhumation of the Roman concept of citizenship. The rediscovery of the citizen in the twelfth and thirteenth centuries, through the glosses of Roman law and Aristotelianism, was the preamble without which one cannot understand the re-appropriation of citizenship by men of the Renaissance.

Starting in the eleventh and twelfth centuries, the emergence of a royal doctrine had led a growing number of theologians, lawyers and specialists of public law to pay close attention to issues of power. No one spoke of 'state', 'polity' or 'citizen' but a number of specific questions were approached, which, the following century, would be integrated in the corpus of what would then be called the *scientia politica*. The king's duty to look after his subjects' wellbeing was asserted from the eleventh century in the bosom of Christian theology, which judged human actions by the yardstick of the higher morality of the celestial city, claiming the right to define the limits of temporal power and determine its specific character.

At the same time, the issue of the origins of power was being discussed with increasing freedom towards existing dogmas. The rediscovery of Roman law played a crucial role: indeed the power of the Roman Emperor was considered, by virtue of the *lex regia*, to find its source in the authority of the people. The relations between the practice of royal power, laws and customs became the central concerns of jurists. Various normative systems had appeared in the practice of feudal Europe within corporations and guilds, by means of the cities' institutions. During the twelfth century these were increasingly understood as customs, the validity of which theorists tended to recognise. The monk from Bologna, Gratian, in his famous *Decretum*,[13] stated that the laws emanating from the Prince had to be 'virtuous, just, possible according to nature and according to the customs of the country... and written, not for private advantage but for the common utility of the citizens' (I, IV: Lewis edition p. 34). But Gratian also said that in spite of the general validity of customs, 'In dignity the natural law prevails absolutely over custom and statute' (Lewis edition, p. 35). The English jurist 'Bracton'[14] expressed himself on the same lines by saying around 1250 that

> these laws indeed, when they were approved by the consent of the users and confirmed by the oath of kings, cannot be changed nor destroyed without the common consent of all those by whose counsel and consent they were promulgated. (*De Legibus*, Lewis edition, p. 40)

He added that 'custom indeed, is sometimes observed instead of law in regions where it has been approved by the custom of the users, and it takes the place of law' (Lewis edition p. 41). These remarks, which announced the development of the common law, signalled a loss of impetus in the theory of divine power and forecast the right to revoke power from its holder. Generally speaking, the rediscovery of Roman law unveiled a set of maxims and concepts through which politics were soon to be formulated. For example, the theory of the king's duty to respect the customs was found in a maxim that only needed to be recalled: *quod omnes tangit ad omnibus approbari debet* ('what touches everyone ought to be approved by everyone'). Roman law also permitted the definition of the complex corporate relations under the term *universitas*, which was to be applied as much to small groups (guilds, dioceses) as to wide communities (the Church, kingdoms, peoples) and allow them to establish mutual relations of reciprocal rights and obligations, sometimes even in the form of contracts.

This new vocabulary in itself did not express a pre-established doctrine: jurists could use it for various or even opposed ends. Thus, the advocates of royal power asserted its 'sovereignty' against that of the Emperor and of the pope by declaring *rex in regno suo imperator est* ('the king is supreme commander in his own kingdom'), while advocates of the autonomy of cities used a grammatically similar formula to promote their own ends: *civitas sibi princeps est* ('the city is a prince in itself'). The concepts that Roman law offered were a set of tools which allowed the principles of power to be thought about in an abstract way. This in turn allowed the *aggiornamento* (updating) of doctrines that were outdated in practice, not by denying them openly but by means of a subtle change in the language used to describe them.[15]

The practice of emerging cities in the north of Italy, theoretically under the rule of the Emperor although in practice enjoying a certain autonomy of government, was defended by Azo, a lawyer from Bologna, with the help of principles of Roman law. He conceded that 'the very highest *iurisdictio* rests with the *princeps* alone'. But basing himself on the observation of facts, he immediately added that 'any magistrate in a city has the power to establish a new law'; he concluded from this that it must be recognised 'that it must be lawful for *merum imperium* to be wielded by these other powers as well'.[16] In other words, if the doctrine conflicts with the facts, doctrine must give way.

Continuing in the same vein, Azo formulated the principle of popular 'sovereignty' in a new way from a reinterpretation of the *lex regia*. Regarding the Emperor, he recalled that his power to make laws 'was assigned to him by the people' and added that 'the power to make laws, if it was a power the people possessed before that time, is one they will continue to possess afterwards', for 'it is not the people who are excluded from the power to make laws by the *lex regia*, but merely the individuals who make up the body of the people. They are indeed excluded, but not the people considered as a *universitas*'.[17] The Roman law allows this subtle distinction: the people is not consubstantial with the individuals who constitute it, it is endowed with a fictitious personality that sets it apart. One can thus reaffirm the principle of popular sovereignty at the legal level, while recognising its exclusion in fact. The Roman idea of 'popular sovereignty', which carried the concept of citizenship, thus regained favour through the rediscovery of its language. The return of the *civis* a generation later would be made clearer still by the rediscovery of another vocabulary, that of Aristotle.

THE REDISCOVERY OF THE CITIZEN OF ARISTOTLE

The diffusion of Latin translations of Aristotle's *Ethics* and *Politics* in the second half of the thirteenth century gave greater conceptual precision to these ideas of an autonomous *civitas*, independent from the divine will. Moreover, the translation of William of Moerbeke gave Aristotelianism a specific orientation: he turned the Greek word *politeia* into the Latin *politia* and the distinction between *politeia* and monarchy into an opposition between the monarchical system and a 'political' government. Consequently the adjective 'political' (*politicus*) was not a generic concept that could be applied to all forms of regimes but, on the contrary, indicated an individual form of regime, characterised by equality of rights and the popular origin of power – what the ancients called a republic.[18] The vocabulary of Aristotle not only made it possible to apprehend politics as a separate sphere of human activity, thus showing the obsolescence of Christian cosmology, it also gave the new *scientia politica* a particular inflection, marked by a normative preference for the republican system.

The rediscovery of these conceptual constructions and the emergence of clarity in their terms and definitions constituted a major cultural event of thirteenth century: in the space of one generation, over half a dozen commentaries on the *Politics* were written by those that history remembers as the most important theorists of the end of the century: Albertus Magnus, Peter of Auvergne, Siger of Brabant, Giles of Rome and Thomas Aquinas. These comments all brought the word 'citizen' back into the heart of vocabulary – Thomas Aquinas dedicates practically a third of his commentary to it. However, on the whole, these works use a rather formal vocabulary: commentators are satisfied with reporting Aristotle's argument and putting forward his argumentative methods, and if they do use his language, they do not really make it their own. Aristotelianism penetrates the thought of the end of the Middle Ages more 'as a language and not as a doctrine'.[19] The use that theologian-jurists of that time make of it in other texts where they present their own doctrines reveals the partial inadequacy of this vocabulary to which no suitable concept of their time corresponds. Thomas Aquinas (1224–74), in his *Summa Theologica*,[19] uses for his own purposes the Aristotelian representation of the city and of the citizen: man is pushed by nature to live in society; beyond their separate activities men belonged to the same city which preceded them and that was defined by the law it gave itself. Walter Ullmann saw in this act of faith a radical rupture with the holistic medieval representation, which did not recognise man as a political being, but only the total man.[21] But if the citizen existed again in theory, Thomas Aquinas subordinated it to his Christian conception. For him, the law as the bond that created the city, was a very broad concept, incorporating the eternal law and the natural law, as well as the human law; any law, in whichever form it took, was the expression of God. 'The law is nothing other than a certain dictate of the practical reason in the prince who governs some perfect community. But it is evident...that the whole community of the universe is governed by divine reason' (Lewis edition, p. 49). Consequently, even if citizens gave themselves their own law, it would have 'the nature of law in so far as it accords with right reason; and in this it is clear that it is derived from the eternal law' (Lewis edition, p. 52). The issue of the form of the city consequently becomes secondary, and Thomas, by following Aristotle and all the ancient tradition, is satisfied with pleading for a mixed regime in which social forces are balanced.

The ancients' 'classical natural law' also saw a concordance between the laws of men and the laws of nature. But the power relation was different: it was up to political institutions to draw up the law that was supposed to reflect natural law. The assimilation of both forms of legislation, human and providential, amounted to using providence to the governors' profit. In the thought of Thomas Aquinas the relation is reversed: human law is subordinated to divine precepts. Only the theologian has authority to interpret the divine law. This is where Thomas Aquinas departs from Aristotle: it is no longer the *polis* which uncovers the natural law through its civil law, but the community of wise men whose aim is to elaborate the theology which states the natural law and imposes it on the temporal power.[22] Hence, citizenship is reduced to following the evangelical precepts that theologians set up as law.

Another Italian lawyer completed the rupture. The vocabulary of Aristotle abounds in the work of Marsilius of Padua (1275–1342),[23] but his allegiance was not solely formal, he was also faithful to Aristotle's concepts, which enabled the Paduan lawyer to legitimate the Italian cities' claim to 'sovereignty', as Azo did by using Roman concepts. He writes that the origin of the city is not divine, as had wrongly been said for centuries, but secular. It was because men were sociable by nature, because they needed one another, that they had spontaneously united in political communities. Similarly, the law that controlled these cities could only have secular roots. It proceeded from the city itself, of its people. Marsilius established this fact by adding up three central arguments. Paraphrasing Aristotle, he first recalled that the people taken as a whole had more wisdom than the wisest of individuals; the first justification of popular sovereignty was of a cognitive nature. Anticipating the utilitarian reasoning of the modern liberals, he added that the law of popular origin avoided the risk of arbitrariness, 'because no one knowingly harms himself'. A third argument was added to these two: the law enacted by the people was not only more intelligent and more just, it was also more effective than one emanating from a monarch, because it would be 'readily observed and endured by every one of the citizens, because then each would seem to have set the law upon themselves, and hence would have no protest against it, but would rather tolerate it with equanimity'. Marsilius's rigorous line of argument, based only on logic, anticipating and answering future criticisms of the risk of redundancy, left little doubt as to its conclusions. 'Sovereignty' belonged to all the citizens, the *universitas*, which the lawyers of the twelfth century had endowed with a personality of its own, separate from that of its components.

Marsilius was not, however, a radical democrat, advocating that the social distinctions found in the re-emerging city should be overlooked. Like all his contemporaries, he accepted the limitation of the civic body to the higher social categories and, like the ancients, left women, foreigners, children, peasants and servants aside. Additionally, he even established within the circle of citizens certain status distinctions that he maintained with the same logical rigour as the principle of popular sovereignty. While rejecting the aristocratic idea according to which 'the wise can discern what should be enacted better than can the whole multitude', he supported a form of mixed government close to the republic of Aristotle or Cicero. He wrote that the crowd is useful to legislation, 'when it is joined to those who are more learned and more experienced. For although the crowd cannot by itself discover true and useful measures, it can nevertheless discern and judge the measures discovered and proposed to it by others'. The making of the law first supposes that 'those who are prudent and experienced' are entrusted the task of 'the investigation, discovery, and examination of the standards' before these future laws 'be laid before the assembled whole body of citizens for their approval or disapproval' (I, XIII, pp. 51–5).

What's more, the Marsilian definition of citizenship reflects this shift with regards to the text of Aristotle: 'A citizen I define in accordance with Aristotle ... as one who participates in the civil community in the government or the deliberative or judicial function according to his rank' (I, XII, p. 45). As faithful as this appears to be at first sight, this borrowing is not completely neutral. Marsilius adopts the Aristotelian definition textually but, while doing so, he uses a dazzling shortcut in the last words: 'according to his rank'. Not that this nuance does not appear in Aristotle's work, but it is cross-cutting: Aristotle first defines the citizen in an egalitarian way and it is only later, after lengthy hesitations, that he adds an oligarchic reference. On the contrary, reflecting the elitist spirit of his time, Marsilius puts the oligarchic nuance at the heart of the definition.

The Marsilian concept of citizenship borrows its features from ancient citizenship, as it was defined by Cicero in particular: a collective and theoretical holder of a power which, in practice was entrusted to the *pars valentior*. This elitist shift was important because it clarified the transformation of the meaning of citizenship which occured at the time when men of the early Renaissance were drawing on old concepts for their own purposes. By demonstrating the elitist character of citizenship, Marsilius started to identify the implicit concept of representation within it. Like the Romans, he stated that citizens could legislate by themselves, but added that the magistrates they elected could also do so on their behalf. This idea was unknown to the Romans, for whom magistrates exercised a power that was delegated, the *imperium*, but separate from the *potestas* of the people. Representation was for them only a pictorial method, or a fiction accepted in the legal field, but which was not used in the political field. On the other hand, Marsilius outlined the idea according to which the power of elected magistrates 'represented' the power of the civic body; he thought out a form of 'representation-delegation'[24] that prefigured the modern idea of citizenship, founded on the temporary and conditional transfer of the power of the people to its agents. The concept was not complete, although the constituent components were there: the idea of an abstract 'personality' of the people and of a mandate. It was only two centuries later, when the representatives of boroughs and cantons, assembled in a Parliament to inform the king of the complaints of his subjects, regarded themselves as making up a fictitious body which 'represented' the real body, that the idea of political representation would be conceptualised. But Marsilius had the intuition of it. In any case, by strongly affirming the self-foundation of cities against papal claims, he swept away the intellectual obstacles that had made the formation of citizenship inconceivable. On these foundations, to take into account the political nature of the cities of Northern Italy: other jurists would erect a concept of citizenship for which they would invent a new name.

CIVILITAS: THE BUILDING OF CIVIL STATUSES

The doctrines of Azo and Marsilius show the will of the cities of Northern Italy – which developed between the twelfth and fourteenth centuries and obtained increasingly autonomous institutions – to base their legitimacy on new theories of power. What's more, this new discourse was not the privilege of jurists. As early as the twelfth century, magistrates and diplomats praised the *libertà* of their cities, designating, as the Latin ancestor of the word (*libertas*) did, both their independence with regards to external powers and their republican form of government. This wording remained fragile as long as the interpretation of Roman law by commentators who recognised the supremacy of the emperor continued to dominate. But a new ethos was asserting itself.[25] It was accompanied by a diffuse patriotism, echoed by poets who praised, especially in Florence, the *patriae amor*, the attachment of a people to its fatherland.

The progressive shift in ordinary political language confirms the emergence of a new political paradigm. At the end of the thirteenth and the beginning of the fourteenth century, the inhabitant of a city was increasingly referred to as a citizen (*civis*). John of Viterbe went as far as to see the city as a synonym for a citizen's freedom. He wrote in the first pages of his *Liber de Regimine Civitatum*:[26] '*Civitas* is also called *libertas civium*', which can mean 'citizenship is the freedom of the citizens' or 'the city is the freedom of the citizens'.

The crystallisation of the modern concept of citizenship responded first to a practical need. As each city developed its own institutional mechanisms, enacted its codes in matters of trade and magistrates' prerogatives, it became essential to determine which law a citizen lived under. In Genoa as early as 1143 the ship owner Opizo of Piacenza swore allegiance to the city and received in return the right to invest 100 Lire each year 'to trade on seas as a citizen of Genoa'; a document dating back to 1312 attested to an identical privilege for a native of Padua with regard to Venice; in Mantua, Florence, Arezzo, Orvieto and Viterbe the same issues arose and similar arrangements were found.[27] Differently from one city to another, but in the same spirit, citizen statuses were created, of which jurists endeavoured to define the contents in terms of 'privileges' and 'obligations' and to which the criteria for access were codified. In Siena, for example, one was a citizen by birth, or by decree of the council adopted by two-thirds of the vote and more than one foreigner was thus 'truly and legitimately received as a citizen of the city of Sienna',[28] according to the official Latin formula. Citizens alone were entitled to take part in political functions within the city and to benefit from its jurisdictions. They had to serve in the military along with the non-citizens but, while there, enjoyed the privileges of free medical care and allowances if they were wounded. A negligible minority of those under the city's jurisdiction were included in this category of citizens. The citizens themselves were divided into *cives antiqui*, *veri* and *naturales* (old, true and natural citizens) and *cives assidui* ('continual' citizens). At the same time the whole panoply of legal statuses was gradually elaborated to give everyone a particular position within the legal apparatus of the city. As within the framework of the Roman republic, individuals were divided into separate groups, with their own privileges and obligations, more or less close to those of citizens; they were called *districtualis*, *municeps*, *incola*, *subditus* or *habitator*.

Most often the official wordings avoided naming the status of citizens and used paraphrases such as 'making a citizen' or 'accepting as a citizen'. Sometimes a new term, *civilitas*, was used, which immediately had a very specific meaning: it designated the codified status which made the citizen and determined his prerogatives.

Over the decades, the definition of *civilitas* became a political issue of increasing importance. The *cives originarii* kept their privileges jealously and sometimes protested against the liberality of the council, as in Florence in 1316:

That foreign-born persons, under false colours and not with true causes alleged, are found to have been made citizens of Florence... especially so that as citizens they may pay less taxes at the gates of the city; which taxes paid by those foreign-born should often be greater, because higher taxes are paid by Florentines in their cities.[29]

In Sienna, a rule of 1333 instigated a survey of all new citizens during the six years that had to elapse following the granting of this title, before they were regarded as 'true and ancient' citizens. As W.I.M. Bowsky showed in his study of the texts of this city, rules concerning the title of citizen were closely connected with immigration policies: the preference granted to certain categories of individuals (teachers, judges, notaries, lawyers, physicists and so on) for immigration was reflected in the standards which governed access to citizenship.[30] The *civitas romana* was also part of the rules on immigration but was collectively allotted to certain populations whose integration was supposed to strengthen the power of the 'state'. A sign of the time, Italian cities only granted *civilitas* to individuals whose personal competencies were seen as beneficial to the city. In the eyes of the leaders, in a context of commercial and intellectual rivalry between cities, it was no longer the masses but great men who were the strength of a city.

This re-emerging concept of citizenship was empirically built up over the decades. Each city defined, on a step by step basis, according to its interests and convictions, the rules of accession to its civic body, a panel of privileges and obligations for the members of its elite. In addition, these successive codifications were not done easily. They had to reconcile competing interests and conceptions. Jurists were often called upon to decide on individual cases, which would not be subsumed under the generality of established customs and rules. It is from this body of specific decisions that a coherent doctrine of citizenship emerged at the end of the fourteenth century. And it is probably not accidental that this was the work of jurists, who were not only technicians but also political theorists and, in particular, advocates of the doctrine of 'popular sovereignty'.

Bartolus of Sassoferrato (1314–57) was the first of them. Like his predecessor Azo, he based his argument for the 'sovereignty' of cities on a methodological shift: he directly admitted, following commentators on Roman law, that the *imperium* belongs *de jure* to the emperor for matters related to the temporal power, and to the Pope for those related to the spiritual power. But he also announced 'it should not be a matter of surprise if I fail to follow the words of the Gloss when they seem to me to be contrary to the truth, or contrary either to the truth or to the law'.[31] However, this truth to which the Gloss could be contrary was what was *de facto* in the Italian cities of the fourteenth century. Bartolus noted that these *universitates*, these entities endowed with their own legal personality, shaped their own customs whose validity was not disputed and whose strength equalled (*paris potentiae*) that of the 'statuses' enacted by the Emperor. He deduces from this that cities *de facto* give themselves their own law and that accordingly they 'possess *merum Imperium* in themselves, having as much power over their own populace as the Emperor possesses generally'.[32] In other words, if he recognises in theory the power of the Emperor and of the Pope, he states by plagiarising the proverb at the base of the 'sovereignty' of kings, (*rex in regno suo imperator est*) that in practice the city is its own prince, *civitas sibi princeps est*. However, this is not an unconditional doctrine of 'popular sovereignty'. Indeed, borrowing the vocabulary of Aristotle, Bartolus specifies that this concept is valid only for small 'states', the others being monarchies or aristocracies. He adds that in these cities the lower classes, and even the magnates, must be excluded from serving as judges.[33]

Additionally Bartolus is the author of the first modern doctrine of citizenship. However, although he went over it several times, it was only a secondary issue in his work, only connected implicitly to his concept of 'sovereignty'. He approached it from two aspects related to issues raised by specific cases: can the city create citizens and are these equal to citizens by birth? Bartolus answered both questions in a definitely affirmative manner by a single argument:

It ought to be known that someone cannot be considered a citizen by an act of nature, but by the civil law, which is obvious. First, from the name of citizen itself, inasmuch as *civis* is derived from *civitas* [*sic*]. Secondly, because the *civitas* was not created by natural law, and one does not become citizen by being born. It is, therefore, the rule of civil law which makes someone a citizen, either because of place of birth, rank or adoption… Wherefore it must not be said that some men are citizens under natural law, some under civil law. On the contrary, all men are citizens by virtue of the civil law.[34]

Bartolus laid down two fundamental maxims of the modern doctrine of citizenship: *civitas sibi faciat civem*, the city creates its citizen and *cives civiliter sunt*, one is citizen by virtue of the civil law. Thus, he gave an abstract definition of citizenship, which exists only as a legally codified political act. He even went so far as to falsify etymology to that purpose – as we have seen, historically it is *civitas* which results from *civis*. But if, in specific cases, he occasionally evoked the rights related to the *civilitas*, he did not go as far as giving a substantial definition of it. For Bartolus, citizenship was a status which determined the connection of an individual to a city, but nothing in his work allows one to state that he meant citizenship as the instrument of citizens' participation in the 'sovereignty' of the 'state'. He stayed focused on specific questions of his time, and limited himself to formally stating that the title of citizen was a legal creation. One does not find in his work a finished judicial-political conception of cities, which would connect the idea of sovereignty to that of citizenship.

Like him, his disciple Baldus of Ubaldis[35] defended the idea of the 'sovereignty' of people by legally defining a *de facto* situation. He acknowledged that 'formerly there was an emperor who looked after the authority and general good of the commonwealth' but he noted that 'now, however, there is not the same bond of good faith between emperor and subjects, with the result that things have of necessity gone from one extreme to the other'. He deduced from this state of things that 'cities which in reality do not recognise superiors and appropriate regalian rights for themselves do this by custom, and what they have always had as an established custom should not, it seems, be changed at all' (Canning edition, Latin p. 249; English p. 114). This doctrine was more precise in Baldus' work, when he combined the corporatist theory of the city already used by Bartolus with the Aristotelian idea of politics. Like that philosopher, he assimilated people and city and confused them both with the whole body of citizens:

> If the natural man is considered in a congregation he is political and the people is created by uniting several men. This people is sometimes surrounded by walls and inhabits a city, and as such is properly called political, from 'polis' which means city. (Canning edition, Latin p. 249; English p. 114)

But Baldus, like Azo and Bartolus, also thought in corporatist terms and thus introduced a distinction into the Aristotelian conceptual tool:

> separate individuals do not make up the people, and thus properly speaking the people is not men, but a collection of men into a body which is mystical and taken as abstract, and the significance of which has been discovered by the intellect. (Canning edition, Latin p. 249; English p. 114)

Baldus, prefiguring the Moderns, endowed the people-city with its own legal personality, which distinguished it from the individuals who constituted it. This collective personality also differentiated the city from the one who, if necessary, embodied it temporarily, be he a king or a magistrate:

> Every collection of people, corresponding to one man, is to be regarded as a single person ... It is also a corporate person which is understood as one person, but consists of many bodies, like the people ... and this person similarly is regarded as corresponding to one man and is considered to be an individual body.... It is clear therefore that this word, 'person', is sometimes used for an individual, sometimes for a corporation and sometimes for the head or prelate. (Canning edition, Latin p. 265, English p. 189)

The modern concept of the state is prefigured here, simultaneously separate from those which constitute it and from those (or the one) which embody it, and endowed with a power which has no master.[36] But, like all his contemporaries, Baldus conceded that insofar as this sovereignty rests on a resignation by the emperor, which could be revoked, this 'state' remained conditional.

Baldus continued in Bartolus's steps when he tried to define a concept of citizenship. Like his master he was consulted on the question of knowing if 'someone can prescribe the citizenship and citizen privileges of some place'. His answer was also positive and is expressed at a high degree of legal abstraction:

It seems that he can, with the exception of origin which cannot be prescribed. But the advantages of origin can certainly be prescribed, and he (the new citizen) will then be at one and the same time a true citizen and a fictive original one. ... For no art or ingenuity of man will in the case of someone lacking native origin be able to make him a truly original citizen, but will be well able to produce in him the fictive likeness of such a citizen. (Canning edition, Latin p. 262–3, English pp. 172, 176)

Since the concept of citizenship is legal and not natural, and citizenship existed only by virtue of its definition by law, it existed as soon as the law constituted it.[37] Baldus confirmed this fundamental axiom of Roman civil law and thus restored the concept of citizenship as a legal category. He even went so far as sometimes to give a definition of citizenship which went further than the formal question of its attribution and even studied its contents 'I argue that citizenship entails obligations both ways ... for just as they are to be protected as duty requires, so also they are bound to obey and submit to the bound of our citizenship' (*Consilia, Lucca* 358, Canning edition, Latin p. 263, English p. 178) . Elsewhere he confirms that in the laws of the Italian cities of the Renaissance, as in those of the Roman republic, the concept of citizenship was closely connected with that of freedom:

Anyone who on account of his merit is made a citizen by statute fully obtains the freedom [*licentia*] even of native citizens, because he now belongs to the society of citizens, and is one of their number and an addition to it, and of the same citizen-body and corporation actively or passively. (*Consilia Bresia* 3, 299; Canning edition, Latin p. 264, English p. 181)

In a way, these references to citizenship prove that the word *civilitas* covers a concept defined by the enjoyment of freedom and the passive or active membership of the civic body, and tends towards the idea of 'sovereignty'. But one should not underestimate the fact that these definitions emerge from specific cases and are not, contrarily to concepts of the 'sovereignty' of the city, the subject of theoretical developments. Nowhere does Baldus define the *civilitas* as the form of the *licentia*. Nowhere does he write with the same precision he uses to define the abstract entity of the 'people', holder of the power, that the *civilitas* is the subjective form of this power. This seems to show that a concept of citizenship had emerged at the beginning of the fifteenth century in the north of Italy, but that it was not central to reflection on politics.

Outside Italy, citizenship did not get even this recognition at the end of the Middle Ages and at the beginning of the Renaissance. It is true that royal charters in France and in England were sometimes addressed to citizens; in certain cities, like London as early as the thirteenth century, registers of citizens were drawn up and rules for the attribution of privileges were elaborated.[38] But as Max Weber underlined, the cities of northern Europe never were city-states, they were never able to affirm their power on the surrounding country and their political prerogatives remained limited. As early as the thirteenth century, power was concentrated in the king's hands and soon the districts were assembled in Parliaments, thus depriving them of the possibility of political independence.[39] The developing state was not yet obvious enough to assert its direct relation to individuals, but its existence deprived cities of the very appearance of independence; citizens could be attached exclusively neither to one nor the other.

As new political entities asserted their autonomy and refused to acknowledge a master, a concept of citizenship was slowly forming. Two types of change prepared the way for this conceptual innovation. At the intellectual level, the rediscovery of the political nature of man, in particular through Aristotelian language, questioned the Christian idea of his submission to the theological precepts stated by the Pope or the Emperor. At the political level, the emergence of cities which claimed in the language of Roman law to have the *right* to give themselves their own law because they did so in *fact*, made it possible to understand the political nature of man in reference to a univocal political framework, the city.

The fact that citizenship was built empirically, by the work of jurists who considered specific cases, is revealing: it testifies to the fact that this concept, which was then specifically qualified (*civilitas*), mainly designated an individual's membership of a particular *civitas*. Today, this would be called nationality. However, this did not imply that it was a strictly formal concept lacking in political content. Indeed, it only appeared in autonomous, or 'sovereign' cities, and was only codified by jurists whom history remembers as the forbears of the modern idea of sovereignty. It is true that the doctrine did not make explicit the concepts of citizenship and sovereignty. It did not describe citizenship, as one would be tempted to do in contemporary terms,[40] as an active participation of citizens in the exercise of the sovereignty of the city. This link appeared only in a tangential, almost fortuitous way, when concrete cases forced consideration of which privileges were part of the title of citizen. This lack of theoretical development reveals that citizenship remained mainly a nationality concept. Indeed, politics were thought in the general terms of the *imperium*, which was under the rule either of the *imperator*, or of the *rex*, or of the *civitas*; the *civis* only had a role in certain types of cities, where he only existed by virtue of the collective being of the city.

The conceptual tool of this pivotal period, forged from Roman law and Aristotelianism, is, however, much more complex than the one of the antiquity. In Athens, the word *politeia* covered five concepts that modernity has separated: the regime, its form (constitution), a specified form of regime (republic), the civic body and citizenship. Democratic Athens confused the whole of the citizens and the city, and citizenship remained inseparable from this collective concept. In Republican Rome, admittedly the city (*civitas*) and its specific shape (*res publica*) were distinguished, but the assimilation of the civic body with the city (*civitas* in both cases) remained and, similarly, citizenship remained hidden in this collective concept. In both these ancient civilisations, the privileges of citizens were defined as an equality of rights, linguistically marked by a prefix (*iso -*) or by a qualifier (*aequus*). It was between the twelfth and fifteenth centuries that this unity was

broken: as Baldus said, echoing Azo, Marsilius, Bartolus and most of their contemporaries, the city-people was indeed the whole of the citizens from a material
point of view, but it also existed on its own as a collective personality separate
from the all the individual personalities. Marsilius and Azo called it *universitas
civium* while Bartolus and Baldus called it *persona*. In both cases a mediation took
place between the physical mass of the people and the city as an abstract collective being. A theoretical concept of a collective entity, separate from its constituent
components and from those which embodied it, became clearer, prefiguring the
modern idea of the sovereign state. Citizenship also acquired an existence apart
from the word *civitas*. This is linguistically marked by the invention of the derivative *civilitas*, resulting from the adjective *civilis*: citizenship is 'civility', a status
of political right. The privileges that it covered were no longer flanked by collective qualifiers: in the language of Baldus, the citizen simply has *iura* and *officiis*,
which were the form of his *licentia*. Citizenship is not yet a status of individual
rights, but is no longer the characterisation of strictly collective rights.

CITTÀ; CIVILITÀ: THE REBIRTH OF THE CIVIC IDEAL

Shortly after Bartolus and Baldus defined a legal concept of citizenship, a new
political language asserted itself within Italian cities, and Florence in particular, to
defend the autonomy of republic-cities. Those who have been called 'civic
humanists',[41] simultaneously writers and statesmen, discovered the rhetorical
defence of the freedom of the cities that had been developing for two centuries.[42]
Coluccio Salutati (1331–1406)[43], a humanist and the Chancellor of Florence,
replied to one of his detractors who supported the Duke Visconti:

> Perhaps you have never known, in Italy or elsewhere, a freedom, freer and
> purer than Florentine freedom; which could, I do not say precede, but even be
> compared with our freedom? And the tyranny of which you are the slave is
> perhaps such that you could have the audacity to call Florentine freedom tyran-
> ny. (*Invectiva*, pp. 14–17).

These authors' assurance rested in their confidence in Roman history, from which
they drew their doctrine of civil freedom. Salutati defined this freedom as 'the life
governed by law' or 'obedience to the laws that rule all things in the fairest equality', as opposed to the tyrant who 'rules everything by the arbitrariness of his will'
(*Invectiva*, pp. 32–3). The reference to the Roman idea of citizenship defined by
its right and the equal status of its members, of which Cicero was the herald, was
perfectly explicit, so much so that Salutati could exclaim: 'What does it mean, in
fact, to be a Florentine, if it is not to be by nature and by law a Roman citizen, and
consequently to be free and not enslaved?'(*ibid*.). One can hardly conceive a more
faithful rebirth of the concept of citizenship of the Roman republic. Leonardo
Bruni[44] (1369–1444) amplified this praise of Florence, by defending also the

equality of its citizens:

> All our laws go in the same direction, that there should be *paritas* and *equalitas* of citizens in their relations among themselves; in that consists the pure and true freedom .... Our laws endeavour as much as possible to reduce the overpower [*supereminentiam*] of individual citizens and to reduce it to parity and to moderation [*mediocritas*]. (Baron edition, p. 413)

This is the condition that Bruni described as 'popular government', whose essence lay, in his eyes, in equality of right, but which also promoted citizens' participation in power:

> The hope of attaining honour and raising oneself up is equal for everyone, so long as they make the effort, possess talent and have an approved, serious way of life. Our city requires virtue and honesty in a citizen; whoever possesses these is considered sufficiently noble to govern the state.[45]

If it seems indubitable that the civic humanists adopted the Roman concept of citizenship,[46] it must be recognised that their tone is as emphatic as their arguments are elusive. Faithful to the canons of rhetoric, the humanists declaimed without bothering to support their arguments and behind their speech there was little institutional thinking. No more does one find there an explicit definition of citizenship. They do not use the word, and if the concept were to be deduced from their texts, it could be modelled on Roman citizenship, as an equality of rights and access to the *cursus honorum*, without going beyond that. The weight of good citizenship in the work of the humanists and their influence on their time are moreover liable to polemic and it must be admitted that their language remains too evasive for one to determine a concept of citizenship which gives an account of Florentine policy:

> Specialist in discourse, the humanists did not articulate a new and compelling full-scale analysis of the new and dangerous political world that they inhabited. They praised, they blamed, they concealed; the classical themes and ideas they revived more often proved a template to be imposed on obdurate facts than a lens through which to inspect them more closely.[47]

By the turn of the century, when the republic had collapsed, been restored (1494) and collapsed again (1512), the certainties of the humanists of the *quattrocento* had vanished and a more sceptical vision of political life had taken their place. But the republican ethos remained, and freedom continued to be praised as the people's happiness. This moment in the history of political thought was interpreted by J.G.A. Pocock as the era of the rediscovery of a concept of 'active citizenship'.[48] He argued that, from 1494, those who presented themselves as the *ottimati* ('the best') tried to define the relations that linked them to the new power and resorted to a humanistic vocabulary that, whether they wanted it or not, 'restored the ideal of universal citizenship in the Florentine vocabulary'.[49] The term 'citizenship' appeared only marginally in the texts of the main authors of this period but the concept that it covers was present: the authors of the *quattrocento* and of the beginning of the *cinquecento* restored the credibility of the idea, criticised for almost two thousand years, of 'popular participation' in political life.

Compared to the one caused by jurists during the previous century, this second rebirth of republican thought was characterised by a more complete rupture with medieval representations but, and at the same time, also by the forsaking of the abstract and precise political syntax of Roman law. One cannot avoid being struck by the contrast between the semantic and conceptual clearness of the jurists of the thirteenth and fourteenth centuries and the inaccuracy of their rhetorician-successors of the fifteenth and sixteenth centuries. In the intellectual climate of Renaissance Italy, the idea of a benign Providence lost its normative strength and history was increasingly perceived as an inextricable chaos. This seemed to be demonstrated by the sequence of revolutions, in echo to the old theory of a cycle of regime types. The concepts of fortune and necessity also found in the Roman tradition were exhumed to make sense of this seemingly untameable history. In the allegories of the time, men were represented with their feet and hands attached to a wheel that the goddess of fortune span in one direction or another according to her whims. But by her side appeared a virtuous prince (*virtuoso*), likely, if not to tame fortune, at least to master it in part. The literature of the turn of the century conceived the *vita civil* as the art of predicting and countering the risks of chance.[50] Man was no longer the plaything of a history already written against which he could do nothing; he became its author.

Hence, popular civic culture was of cardinal importance: as piety was necessary for a society dominated by the idea of Providence, civic engagement was essential to a society understood as a permanent fight against chance, which required courage, devotion and harmony. This idea belongs, in its generality, to the time, which revered the cardinal qualities of the virtuous citizen, as devoted to his city as the soldier was to the defence of the fatherland. Moreover, both dimensions, civic and martial, were closely dependent: the freedom of the *città* depended as much on its strength with regard to external dangers as on its determination to eradicate, or at least to neutralise, internal dissensions. But, like in Rome, exaltation of civic virtue, which reversed the 'downward principle' of authority and went back to an 'ascending principle', based in man and in him alone, did not lean without reservation towards the people, which should have institutions intended to check it. All the authors of the time conceded that the freedom of the city supposed a balance of social powers.

However, the elitism of the men of the Renaissance had nuances which reflected political circumstances as much as authors' personal preferences. With his prophetic republican thought going against the patrician prudence of most of his contemporaries, the Dominican friar Savonarola[51] (1452–98) was perhaps the only one to have dared radical populism. In the denunciations with which he bombarded the Florentine people, massed within the cathedral to hear him, the heretic monk mixed, in a strange blend, the moral rigour of Christian orthodoxy with the exaltation of civic grandeur. Drawing on contemporary Aristotelianism, he recalled that man is a social animal condemned by nature to live in a city. Reflecting his contemporaries' social pessimism, he added that man is subject to ambitions so that as 'everyone would want to be the head that governs and controls the others, to control and not to be controlled ... dissension and discord among citizens' inevitably occur (vol. I, *Novembre–Dicembre 1494, Predica terziadecima, 14 Dicembre 1494*, pp. 182–183). He gave a theological explanation for this political anarchy: if the worst kind of moral corruption prevailed, it was because God had inflicted tyranny upon the Florentines and then, in his mercy, set them up against it. Once the penance had been suffered, it was time to straighten out the morals 'by passing laws against the unhealthy vice of sodomy' and by suppressing 'poetries, tavern games and women's bad clothing habits'. And with the same moral fervour, Savonarola defended civic virtues: 'I tell you, devote yourself to the common good of the city and if there is one who wants to be chief, may he be deprived of all his goods' (*ibid.*, p. 193). In his strange political theology, man is called upon to reconcile himself with God by penitence and a righteous civil life.

Solely concerned with admonishing his audience, Savonarola did not elaborate precise institutional mechanisms. At the most he gave a few, elementary and at times contradictory republican-sounding pieces of advice: 'Citizen, if you want to be a good citizen, do not seek power [*stato*], nor public office [*officii*], if they are not given to you. And if they are given to you, use them for public and common good and not for your own' (*ibid.* p. 193). The Friar contented himself with exposing tyranny to public contempt and with repeating 'no one should be made chief, if you want to live in freedom' (*ibid.*, p. 195). At times he speaks of the constitution of Venice, very much praised by his contemporaries for the serenity it seems to draw from its mixed regime – the balance between the Gonfaloniere (a top-ranking civil magistrate in the communal government), the Doge and the people – and states that there

> is no better and you should take example on it while ridding it of certain things which are not relevant and which we do not need. Like the institution of the Gonfaloniere. ... And it will neither be beside the point to choose the higher magistrates by election and the others by drawing of lots. (*Ibid.*, p. 195)[52]

Savonarola's anti-oligarchic enthusiasm undoubtedly called upon the people to govern itself, but only at the price of a high level of abstraction. The preacher stayed within a confused republican vocabulary, crossed with scholasticism: 'I tell you, no one will be able to resist God's will, and I say that the will of God is that the city of Florence be governed by the people and not by tyrants' (*Predica ottovadecima, 19 Dicembre 1494*, p. 275). His institutional opinions are unclear, even though he suggested the removal of the Gonfaloniere and the nomination of magistrates by lot, which seems to imply that his republic was eminently 'democratic', rid of its oligarchic institutions. There was a strong paradox in that, unlike his contemporaries, he legitimates a democratic form of government by linking it to divine will.

With his paradoxical humanism, Savonarola was an exception, his contemporaries being less trustful of Providence and more wary of the people. The diplomat and humanist Francesco Guicciardini[53] (1483–1540), member of a large Florentine family, left in his '*Discorso di Logrogno*' (1512, Scarano edition pp. 247–296), written at the twilight of the Florentine Republic, a very elaborate image of the city's institutions and vocabulary. Like many of his contemporaries who were attached to the republican heritage of Florence, he feared that the city 'if God obviously does not help it, will lose its freedom and its power [*stato*]'. The invocation of divine support seems to be only conventional because Guicciardini looks for the reasons for this decrepitude in quite human facts: the military and financial weakness of Florence and also that 'our regime [*vivere civile*] is very removed from the constitution [*vivere ordinato*] of a good republic, as much as regards the form of the government as our other customs' (Scarano edition, p. 249). The diplomat goes on to say that the remedy lies in rebuilding a proper and stable army and treasury, and especially in thinking about institutional reforms.

On this last issue, Guicciardini was guided by his conviction that the main threat to the city's harmony was the complex game of citizens' ambitions, which must be cajoled by subtle institutional mechanisms that were needed to strengthen the republic. The dominant feature of the Italian city-republics since the thirteenth century had indeed been the perpetual war between popular and aristocratic factions, the extreme rivalry of families and clans. All the authors of the time were obsessed by these internal struggles, which threatened the harmony of the city, and their political science was in search of a principle of equilibrium that would contain these quarrels.[54] Guicciardini refused outright the simplistic solution taken up by some of his contemporaries that consisted purely and simply in entrusting the government of the city to a limited but strong power.[55] This expedient solution was out of the question, said Guicciardini, 'because freedom is intrinsic and natural in our city' (Scarano edition, p. 255). Like his humanistic predecessors of the beginning of the *quattrocento*, he defined freedom by reference to Roman doctrine: 'it is nothing other than the primacy of public laws and institutions [*legge* and *ordini*] over the appetites of individual men.'

He went on to specify the implications of this imperative: 'To establish freedom a popular government [*vivere populare*] is necessary, the spirit and base of which is the *consiglio grande*, which distributes the city's honours and public offices [*magistrati and dignità*]' (Scarano edition, p. 255). Guicciardini even went so far as to justify this choice: he approved of the exclusion from the *Consiglio grande* of 'those which in the past did not take part in government, in order that it is not a council composed only of the plebs and the peasants', but he defends however the *larghezza* (inclusiveness) of this council, aware of the risk that 'many uninformed and malicious persons and some idiots will take part' but convinced nevertheless that it is better 'to live thus with some disorder, than to see all good and all evil in the hands of only one' (Scarano edition, p. 256). He also added that this large council would have to be balanced by a Gonfaloniere and a restricted council. Laws would only come before it after they had been examined by the restricted council and major decisions would be withdrawn from it. This balance reflected the republican practice of the time. The city-states of the Italian Renaissance were not 'democracies' governed by the people, but regimes built so that the people, without exercising power itself, remained its permanent keeper. This 'people' was moreover limited to the citizens of the 'middle classes', natives or long-standing residents of the city who paid a certain amount of taxes. The Italian Renaissance was no exception to the prejudices that excluded women, children, foreigners and the poor from civic life. Reduced to these dimensions, the people is nevertheless the measure of power. It elected the *Consiglio grande*, a kind of parliament of the city. And the *Podestà*, a magistrate with executive, legal and military powers, came from this council, was elected for a very short period, and was required to consult the council and to give it an account of his actions at the end of his mandate. The logic of power 'delegation' to restricted bodies does not prevent the people of these cities from conceiving themselves as 'sovereign' because they perceive themselves as the source and the measure of power, of which the magistrates are only the temporary and subordinate expressions.

Guicciardini put all his trust in a balance of powers, in conformity with the ancient idea of a 'mixed regime' that would satisfy the ambitions of the people[56] and the powerful without letting them run free. He tried to institutionally reproduce the alchemy of social passions, in order to neutralise their tensions. This formula is not in his eyes 'a perfect constitution of a republic, but it is at least more than mediocre; if one wanted to carry it higher, the roots of our souls' weaknesses and limpness should be tackled' (Scarano edition, p. 293). Customs and spirits would have to be transformed but these are extreme solutions that this moderate man refuses.

Guicciardini's institutional vocabulary is complex and precise: a first category of terms names the regime, the government in a general meaning, applicable to *any form of government* (*vivere, modo di vivere, stato*). In a second category one can gather the qualified terms which designate a *'constitutional' form of government*, subjected to laws and institutions and not to the arbitrary (*vivere civile, vivere sotto le legge, vivere ordinato*). Finally a number of terms designate a form of government which is not only 'constitutional' but also 'popular' (*vivere popolare, libero governo, governo largo, governo della repubblica*). The expressions by which Guicciardini unambiguously designated a concept of citizenship were part of this third category: *partecipare nel governo, partecipare nello stato, partecipazione*. He confirms this when he properly names this concept, evoking the Romans who 'gave citizenship [*città*] *cum iure suffragii*' (Scarano edition, p. 257).

Guicciardini carefully defined what he means by 'participation' and 'citizenship': the issue was not to give everyone the right to vote for laws, nor even to elect or be elected a magistrate, but to give the people the right to elect its magistrates and to the best of its members the right to obtain these public offices. For

Guicciardini, participation was only conceived in relation to the election of magistrates and not as direct deliberation: 'To keep this type of government intact it is necessary to maintain the law which forbids deliberation by popular acclamation [*fare parlamento*] which can easily dissolve popular government' (Scarano edition, p. 285). In the election of magistrates the people is not mistaken (Scarano edition, p. 258) but if one 'deliberated with the crowd' the result would be a 'popular solution' the 'ignorance' of which would make one fear the worst outcome (Scarano edition, p. 260–1). He explicitly distinguishes the *città* from the *degnità della città*; the first was granted to all and the second refused to 'men deficient by ignorance and by malice' prevent the entry into government of 'men who know nothing about it'. In 'popular government', therefore, 'each one must take part according to his rank (Scarano edition, p. 262–3).

The spirit of oligarchy remained powerful in this 'Renaissance concept of citizenship'. As with Aristotle, Cicero and Marsilius, the power of the citizen was consistent with elitist mechanisms. Only Niccolo Machiavelli (1469–1527) was a partial exception to the spirit of the time. The poet and Florentine diplomat never had the chance to benefit from the *degnità della città* and his modest social origins perhaps explain why he was more trusting of the people's virtues than Guicciardini. In his political writings, after the fall of the Florentine Republic, Machiavelli was more tormented and less methodical than Guicciardini but also more favourable to the extension of public offices to the common people. Like his predecessors he was convinced of the corruption of the republic and of all political life in Italy. He believed, like Guicciardini, that the weakness of the army and the unbridled passions of the powerful and of the people were its first causes[57] but the prince's and the republic's incapacity to adapt to variations of fortune, and the weakening of the moral tone of public life – towards effeminacy and away from worldly life – as a result of the weight of the Christian religion, bore their share of responsibility.[58] This time the rupture with Christianity is definite; Christianity is no longer ignored but held responsible for political decay.

Since these bodies, these organisms that were republics and principalities, would perish if they were not renewed, they had to be submitted to a salutary cure (*Discourses*, III, I and II, V).[59] Machiavelli wrote that this would come to them necessarily either from an external threat or from an internal revolution, either as the result of the agency of a man or of an institution (III, I).[60] Machiavelli disliked the first solution, the salutary war, which was likely to wash away the 'state', and judged the advent of a supreme legislator too random in a republic to be trusted.[61] Other means were needed to modernise the republic. The Roman precedent, so revered by his contemporaries because it provided the example of a city which regenerated itself unceasingly, which found in itself the strength to modernise whenever it appeared about to perish,[62] showed the way. Indeed, if one despaired of finding a supreme legislator able to give men a perfect constitution, one could only try to substitute for it the political rationality inherent to social confrontation. According to Machiavelli, Roman history showed that political rivalry and battles generated specific institutions which were invented as problems arose, the whole of which constituted a valid approximation of a good constitution. Better still, the dynamics inherent to political opposition never came to an end, and this 'organising turmoil' guaranteed the regime's permanent adaptation to the variations of fortune. Conflict went from being an unavoidable evil for his contemporaries to the condition of the permanent regeneration of the republic for Machiavelli. He firmly believed in the deep unity of the principle of a healthy republic: 'For as good customs have need of laws to maintain themselves, so laws have need of good customs so as to be observed.' (*Discourses*, I, 18, p. 48). However, both had no other source than political life itself, the eternal opposition of the powerful (wealthy) and of the people, so that in a republic:

> There are so many examples of virtue; for good examples arise from good education, good education from good laws, and good laws from those tumults that many inconsiderably damn (I, 4, p. 16).

Machiavelli followed in Guicciardini's footsteps when he tried to think about the conditions in which citizens' ambitions would best be put to profit for the defence of the republic, but he accepted the turmoil that resulted from it to a much larger extent.[63] However, if there is no doubt that Machiavelli trusted 'the people' to guard freedom, it is less easy to determine up to what point he gave it the right to participate in the exercise of power. On the one hand he ensures that

> a prudent man should never flee the popular judgement in particular things concerning distribution of ranks and dignities, for only in this does the people not deceive itself at some time, it is so rare that a few men who have to make such distributions will deceive themselves more often (I, 47, p. 483 see also I, XX, p. 434).

The historical proof given by Machiavelli is in the least ironic, he notes, 'for coming to the creation of these tribunes and being able to create all plebeians, the Roman people created all nobles. ...So, ashamed of them [the men of the plebs], it had recourse to those who deserve it' (I, 47, p. 81). The people can easily be misguided 'if it is not made aware that that is bad and what the good is, by someone in whom it has faith' (I, 53, p. 106), only 'such coloring over is easily recognised, and especially by prudent men' the 'people are often deceived in it' (III, 12, p. 248). Machiavelli does not say it explicitly, but he seems to agree with Guicciardini that the people should only be entrusted with the right to elect its magistrates. Nor did he think that eligibility was universal:

> In Republics, when men that have only the experience of manual labour are assigned to a public office, they are not capable of commanding like leaders, since they have only ever learned to serve. Thus, to command, one must choose men who have never obeyed, except to kings and laws; citizens that live from their own revenue, for example. (*Discourses, Sentenses diverses*, p. 718)

What distinguished Machiavelli from Guicciardini on the issue of popular participation was that the former kept public offices for talented men when the second, without acknowledging it, adopted a more traditional selection criterion, centred on socially recognised value.[64] The talent or *virtù* of Machiavelli was the capacity to dominate fortune, what would be called today 'political sense' and which is in no way subordinated to 'age or birth' (III, LX), so true is it that 'titles do not give lustre to men, but men to titles' (III, XXXVIII, p. 297). Like his contemporaries, Machiavelli saw politics as a power struggle between antagonistic groups and sought to neutralise these tensions so that they involuntarily worked towards the general interest. However, he does not believe that this requires the exclusion of certain social categories; he highly esteems civic virtue, to the point of having it prevail over social origin and the passions that it induces.

Unlike Guicciardini, Machiavelli did not invent sophisticated institutional constructions. We can only deduce them from the scattered references he makes throughout his writing. If he had a concept of citizenship, it is concealed behind this fragmentation. The word was known to him but he seldom used it. To name citizenship three times in the *Discourses*, he used three different words (*città*, like Guicciardini, *civilità*, like the jurists, or a circumlocution: *che fosse cittadini*, 'that they be made citizens') (II, 23, p. 57; III, 49, p. 309). Every time, this was a reference to the *civitas romana*, which clarifies the meaning that Machiavelli gives to this word. He recalled that the granting of citizenship to the Privernates was accompanied by this formula: 'That people who care for nothing in the world except their freedom were worthy to become Romans'. He also said, in conclusion of his *Discourses*, that it is because it had granted its citizenship to foreign families that Rome saw them have 'so much share in the votes that the government began to vary' (*ibid.*). All this testifies that for Machiavelli citizenship held political power. But that he so seldom evoked it by name, and under such various names, shows that this idea did not occupy a central place in his conceptual construction, one may even say that he had only a vague notion of it. If he had defined it, he probably would have limited it, like Guicciardini, to a voting right, keeping the right to hold public office for another concept (*degnità*), even if he agreed to open it to all who were worthy of it. One can acknowledge, following Pocock and Skinner, that the Florentine authors of the *cinquecento* enhance the political role of popular participation but, if they are given the paternity of a modernised idea of citizenship, it must be remembered that no formally stated concept of it is to be found.

For all the thinkers of the beginning of the *cinquecento*, politics could only be thought about through the dominant anthropology, which was man as a being driven by his ambitions – which varied according to his social membership – and the risks of discord which were perceived to result from it. Praise of the city's freedom had two aspects: its independence from external powers and its harmony against the threats of factions and popular rebellion. The political theories of the *cinquecento* tried to think out the conditions in which these ambitions could be controlled and maybe even be made to reinforce the city. Authors diverged on some points but all proposed some form of institutional balance that could counter abuses by the people, the powerful and leaders. They also all drew from the same conceptual sources: the certainties of the Roman republic, seen as a synthesis of the first three regimes – democracy, aristocracy and monarchy – and a language borrowed from texts of Aristotle and of Polybius, also articulated around this trilogy. The Roman influence was particularly marked in the definition of citizenship: if it was not the subject of explicit developments, it was at least associated with the imperative of the rule of law and of the equality of citizens, which was for Cicero and his contemporaries the cornerstone of the republican *civitas*. The word citizenship itself is copied from Latin: Guicciardini and Machiavelli speak about citizenship in terms of *città*, which is also the city and the word *civitas* also covered both meanings. However, the men of the *cinquecento* differed from their Roman ancestors when they clearly differentiated the *città* and the *degnità*. In Rome, the *civitas* was access to the *cursus honorum*; in Florence the exercise of the right of vote was dissociated from access to public office.

The difference between Romans and Florentines was also seen in the scope of this suffrage: in Rome the people was considered to be the author of laws; in Florence it was strictly elective. Thus, the men of the Renaissance seemed to replace the principle of *social representation* which *implicitly* supported Roman citizenship by a principle of *explicitly political representation* – even if, in practice, it tended to entrust power to the same social groups. Though they were prefiguring the concepts of the modern concept of citizenship, they had not yet fully developed them.

NOTES

1   *Cf.* J.P. Canning, *A History of Medieval Political Thought* (London, Routledge, 1996).
2   St Augustine of Hippo, The City of God: De Civitate Deo, edited by R.V.G. Trasker (London, J.M. Dent 1962). For an historical interpretation of Saint Augustine, see R. A. Markus, 'The Latin Fathers' in J.H. Burns, ed., *The Cambridge History of Medieval Political Thought*, c. 350–c. 1450 (Cambridge, Cambridge University Press, 1988), pp. 92–122.
3   See also the numerous comparisons that Augustine draws between the *munera* and the *honores* of both *civitates*, terrestrial and divine, in V: 18.
4   *Cf.* P. G. Geary, *The Myth of Nations: The Medieval Origins of Europe* (Princeton, Princeton University Press, 2002).
5   *Cf.* W. Ullmann, *The Individual and Society in the Middle Ages* (London, Methuen, 1967), pp. 40–43.
6   Augustine of Ancona, (c. 1270), quoted by M. Wilks, *The Problem of Sovereignty in the Later Middle Ages* (Cambridge, Cambridge University Press, 1963), p. 37.
7   *John of Salisbury, Policraticus*, edited and translated by C.J. Nederman (Cambridge, Cambridge University Press, 1990)
8   W. Ullman, *Principles of Government and Politics in the Middle Ages* (London, Methuen, 1961), especially pp. 19 n. 26. This thesis of the two principles appears many times in

Ullman's writing but is most clearly developed in this work.

9   See J. Nelson, 'Kingship and Empire' in Burns, *Medieval Political Thought*, pp. 211–51. See also A. Black, *Political Thought in Europe*, 1250–1450 (Cambridge, Cambridge University Press, 1992) particularly chapter 3, pp. 85–116, 'Empire and Nation'.

10   E. Lewis, *Medieval Political Ideas* (London, Routledge and Paul, 1954), p. 34.

11   *Cf.* Ullmann, *The Individual and Society*, pp. 56–8.

12   *Cf.* A. Black, 'The Individual and Society' in Burns, *Medieval Political Thought,* pp. 588–606.

13   Gratian, *Decretum Gratiani* (c. 1148), in Lewis, *Medieval Political Ideas*, p. 34

14   Bracton, *De Legibus et Consuetudinibus Angliae* in Lewis, *Medieval Political Ideas*.

15   On the general issue of the role of Roman law in the twelfth and thirteenth centuries, see K. Pennington, 'Law, legislative authorities and theories of government 1150–1300' in Burns, *Medieval Political Thought*, pp. 424–53.

16   Quoted by Q. Skinner in 'Political Philosophy' in Q. Skinner, C.B. Schmitt, E. Kessler and J. Kraye (eds), *The Cambridge History of Renaissance Philosophy* (Cambridge, Cambridge University Press, 1988), pp. 389–452, *cit.* pp. 392–3.

17   *Ibid.*

18   *Cf.* N. Rubinstein, 'The history of the word *politicus* in early-modern Europe' in A. Pagden (ed.), *The Languages of Political Theory in Early-Modern Europe* (Cambridge, Cambridge University Press, 1987), pp. 41–56.

19   A. Black, *Political Thought in Europe*, p. 10.

20   Thomas Aquinas, *Summa Theologica*, in Lewis, *Medieval Political Ideas*.

21   Ullman, *The Individual and Society, op cit.*

22   *Cf.* M. Villey, *Le droit et les droits de l'homme* (Paris, PUF, 1983).

23   Marsilius of Padua, *Defensor Pacis* (1324), translated by A. Gewirth (Toronto, Toronto University Press, 1980).

24   J. Quillet, 'Souveraineté et citoyenneté dans la pensée politique de Marsile de Padoue', page 80, in *Actes du colloque sur la citoyenneté et la souveraineté*, pp. 73–85.

25   *Cf.* Q. Skinner, *The Foundations of Modern Political Thought*, vol. 1 *The Renaissance* (Cambridge, Cambridge University Press, 1978), pp. 3–12.

26   Quoted by Q. Skinner in 'Pre-humanist origins of republican ideas', in G. Bock, Q. Skinner and M. Viroli (eds), *Machiavelli and Republicanism* (Cambridge, Cambridge University Press, 1990), pp. 121–41, *on page* 134. John of Viterbe's formula is *civitas autem dicitur civium libertas*.

27   *Cf.* P. Reisenberg, *Citizenship in the Western Tradition* (Chapel Hill, University of North Carolina Press, 1992), pp. 134–9.

28   Decree of 1312 (*Recipi in verum et legitimum civem civitatis senensis*), quoted on p. 197 by W.M. Bowsky in 'Medieval citizenship: the individual and the state in the commune of Sienna, 1287–1355', *Studies in Medieval and Renaissance History* 1967, IV, pp. 192–243.

29   *Ibid.* pp. 203–4.

30   *Cf. ibid.*, pp. 205–7.

31   Quoted by Q. Skinner in *Foundations*, p. 9.

32   *Ibid.*, p. 10.

33   *Cf.* Black, *Political Thought*, pp. 126–9.

34   Bartolus of Sassoferrato, *Consilia* 1. 62 in *Opera Omnia*, quoted on p. 699 by J. Kirshner,

'*Civitas sibi faciat civem*: Bartolus of Sassoferrato's doctrine on the making of a citizen', *Speculum* 1973, XLVIII/4, pp. 694–713.

35 Baldus of Ubaldis, *Commentaries on the Digest*, I. 8, quoted by J. P. Canning, *The Political Theory of Baldus de Ubaldis* (Cambridge, Cambridge University Press, 1987).

36 See the definition of the concept of the modern state established by Q. Skinner in 'The state', in T. Ball, L. Farr and J.A. Hanson (eds), *Political Innovation and Conceptual Change* (Cambridge, Cambridge University Press, 1988), pp. 90–131.

37 About these issues see J. P. Canning, ' A Fourteenth-century contribution to the theory of citizenship: political man and the problem of created citizenship in the thought of Baldus de Ubaldis', in B. Tierney and P. Linehan (eds), *Authority and Power* (Cambridge, Cambridge University Press, 1980), pp. 197–212.

38 *Cf.* P. Reisenberg, *Citizenship*, pp. 112–17.

39 M. Weber, 'Citizenship', in *General Economic History* (London, 1927), pp. 332–4.

40 J.P. Canning, for example, permits himself to extrapolate this definition from the remarks of Baldus, but he acknowledges that 'clearly Baldus' remarks here have a somewhat restricted meaning because he is only considering the corporation of citizens in its corporeal form in congregation, and also manifestly has a non-sovereign city in mind', in Canning, *Political Theory*, p. 200.

41 *Cf.* H. Baron, *The Crisis of the Early Italian Renaissance* (Princeton, Princeton University Press, 1966 [1955]).

42 *Cf.* Q. Skinner, *Foundations*, vol. I, pp. 69–112.

43 Coluccio Salutati, *Invectiva in Antenium Luschum Vicentinum*, in E. Garin (ed.), *Prosatori italiani del Quattrocento* (Milano/Napoli, Ricciardi, 1952), pp. 7–37

44 L. Bruni, 'Epistolary Description of the Florentine Constitution', in H. Baron, *Humanistic and Political Literature in Florence and Venice* (Cambridge MA, Harvard University Press, 1955).

45 L. Bruni, *Funeral prayer*, quoted by A. Black in *Political Thought in Europe*, p. 134.

46 *Cf.* Baron, *Crisis*, pp. 430.

47 *Cf.* A. Grafton, 'Humanism and political theory', in J.H. Burns and M. Goldie (eds), *The Cambridge History of Political Thought 1450–1700* (Cambridge, Cambridge University Press, 1991), pp. 9–29; p. 29.

48 J.G.A. Pocock, *The Machiavellian Moment* (Princeton, Princeton University Press, 1975). Pocock uses the term 'citizenship' very frequently throughout his book and on pp. 184–5 he seems to indicate that he uses this term to name what Guicciardini and his contemporaries called 'participation' or *virtù*. Q. Skinner, *Foundations*, also uses the expression 'active citizenship' to describe these authors' concepts.

49 Pocock, *Machiavellian Moment*, p. 102.

50 *Cf.* F. Gilbert, *Machiavel et Guichardin, Politique et histoire à Florence au XVIe siècle*, translated into French by J. Vivies (Paris, Le Seuil, 1998), chapter III, 'La crise des fondements de la politique', pp. 92–128.

51 Girolamo Savonarola, *Prediche italiane ai Fiorentini*, edited by F. Cagnasso (Perugia/Venezia, La Nuova Italia, 1930).

52 Savonarola continues without a transition, which testifies to the singular character of his republicanism: 'In addition, it is necessary to make laws, as I said before, against the sin of

sodomy and infamous persons and that all sin should be excluded from the city.'

53 F. Guicciardini, *Opere*, edited by E. L. Scarano (Torino, UTET, 1970).

54 *Cf.* Q. Skinner, 'The Italian City Republics', in J. Dunn (ed.), *Democracy, The Unfinished Journey* (Oxford, Oxford University Press, 1992), pp. 57–71.

55 *Cf.* J.G.A. Pocock, *Machiavellian Moment*, pp. 114–55.

56 At that time, 'people' meant the 'civic body', that is all those who were represented in the Council, as opposed to the plebs, who remained excluded. The principal political conflicts in Florence at that time were between the rich and the middle classes, while the *vulgo*, the plebs, were ignored. *Cf.* F. Gilbert, *Machiavel et Guichardin*, chapter I 'Idées, problèmes et institutions politiques à Florence à la fin du XVe siècle', pp. 15–47.

57 See in particular N. Machiavelli, *The Prince*, translated by G. Bull (London, Penguin, 1999). chapter XXIV.

58 See *The Discourses*, edited by B. Crick (Harmondsworth, Penguin, 1970), book II, chapter II.

59 One can note the relationship between the language of Machiavelli and of Savonarola who readily uses organicist metaphors and calls for a new *form* for corrupted *matter*. Compare *The Prince*, chapter. XXVI and III and Savonarola, *Prediche*, in particular pp. 109 and 185.

60 On the 'dilemmatic method' of Machiavelli *cf.* F. Chabod, 'Metodo e stile del Machiavelli', in *Scritti su Machiavelli* (Torino, Einaudi, 1964).

61 See Chapod 'Metodo e stile', and *Discourses*, I, XVII, p. 427, I, IX, p. 405 and *The Prince*, VI.

62 *Cf.* E. Garin, *L'umanesimo italiano* (Bari, Laterza, 1952), chapter 2 'La vita civile', pp. 47–94.

63 See F. Guicciardini, *Discorso*, p. 256 and see also the comment by Guicciardini in which he condemns this tumult on pp. 615–17 of his 'Considerazioni sui "Discorsi" del Machiavelli', in *Opere*, pp. 605–77. Guicciardini regards these disorders as necessary evils but not as conditions of freedom, contrary to Machiavelli.

64 This means 'healthy and experienced men' (*Discourses*, p. 259), 'the flower of the city' (p. 260), men 'of quality' (p. 261), the 'best of the city' (p. 276), the 'best and healthiest men of the city' (p. 293).

chapter three | modern citizenship: between rights and state

Nothing better reveals the advent of political modernity in the first years of the seventeenth century than the complete overhaul of the vocabulary of political science. The terms 'contract', 'pact', 'consent', 'representation', 'obligations', 'status' and 'rights' – all borrowed from legal science and formerly confined to 'private' affairs – would henceforth apply to relations in the public sphere. In this context, citizenship was redefined in terms which still mark us deeply.

The innovations of the Middle Ages, which, nevertheless, could not get beyond providentialism, and the concepts fathomed but not explicitly defined during the Renaissance became clearer in the modern era. This conceptual development is explained as much by political events as by a methodological revolution. Modern rationalism, borrowing its deductive methods from the physical sciences and its abstract language from the law, generated a general theory of the state constructed around the organising concept of sovereignty. All doctrines relating to the articulation of authorities and to the status of the individual were redefined within this intellectual framework.

Modern political thought is based on a major conceptual rupture: what is generally called 'the birth of individualism'. The Moderns' 'natural law' substituted atomist representations for the Middle Ages' organic conception of society: it no longer saw the social body as an arrangement of organs but as a sum of individuals. This upheaval in representations contributed to the development of the language of rights: where the Ancients thought in terms of collective functions, Moderns saw personal, individual and subjective rights. Where the ancients and the thinkers of the Middle Ages expressed their idea of the 'just life' in the form of a natural 'law', a general, objective rule, binding communities, the moderns individualised the concepts, expressing them as 'natural rights'. It is within the framework of this double intellectual revolution, the definition of the sovereign state and the theory of subjective rights, that the old concept of citizenship was redefined and adopted the modern meaning it still has.

CITIZENSHIP AS THE RULE OF LAW:
BODIN, GROTIUS AND HOBBES

The advent of the modern theory of the state is partly explained by the political situation of Europe during the sixteenth century: the wars between nations that tormented Machiavelli called for the constitution of a rapid and efficient executive power. Rivalry between families, factions, social groups and constituted orders called for a referee who could be above dissension. The king of France set the example. He was able to use the social divide in order to establish his authority: by protecting the middle class from the attacks of the nobility he ensured the support of a new and powerful class. On this basis, he gradually built a supreme authority, by claiming the 'marks of sovereignty' (legislation, justice, taxation, army, administration) and by establishing himself as the incarnation of the country's unity. Still, these gains rested on a series of compromises: the king was forced to concede the survival of the privileges of a large number of corporate bodies and to submit himself to doctrines which limited his sovereignty.

Following in the steps of medieval theories, the first doctrines of royal power endeavoured to justify both the statement of the king's pre-eminence and the defence of the limits to his authority. A contemporary of Machiavelli, the French jurist Claude Seyssel (c. 1450–1520), a lawyer, diplomat and bishop of Marseilles, gave a completed version of this doctrine in 1515. In the first book of his treaty *La Monarchie de France*, he tried very hard to show that 'royal dignity and authority' are not 'totally absolute, nor too restricted, but regulated and ordered by good laws, prescriptions and customs, which are established in such a way that they can hardly break and disappear'. He used all his energy to defend these 'brakes by which the absolute power of the kings of France is regulated',[1] which were religion, justice and police. Like most of his contemporaries, Seyssel used two arguments. On the one hand, using the argument of efficiency, he tried to convince kings that their power would be all the more respected if it was limited. On the other hand, using the dominant morals, he showed the limitation of power as a duty: the good king is one who, unlike the tyrant, does not govern arbitrarily but with measure and in the respect of customs established over time. This doctrine was the continuation of those of the end of the Middle Ages, and met a very broad consensus among specialists of public law during the sixteenth century.

It was only a half-century later that the doctrines of the state began to be freed from medieval theories. The French jurist Jean Bodin (1529/30–1596),[2] remembered historically as the author of the first modern theory of sovereignty, is part of a generation that claimed to break with moral precepts. As a man of the Renaissance, he turned away from scholastic discussions and returned to history, to inquiry and to comparison. According to Bodin, this 'scientific' approach made it possible to break a lengthy tradition: 'we will leave to the Philosophers and Theologians the moral discourse and will take Politics' (I, III, p. 52) and by taking it 'neither do we wish to picture an Ideal Republic without effect, such as Plato and Thomas More, Chancellor of England imagined, but we will be satisfied with following the *political rules* as closely as possible' (I, 1, p. 31, emphasis added). Neither empirical description, coarsely translated into moral precepts, like Seyssel, nor an ideal republic, like More, in *Les Six Livres* Bodin tried to bring to light the principles of real republics, to conceptualise the new means of power which was constructed in Europe during the sixteenth century, and in France particularly. This was a broad analytical ambition but also, inevitably, a normative work: the monarchy would find in these doctrines the arguments which would legally enable it to shore up the legitimacy of its sovereignty – despite their claims to scientific methods, legists knew this full well and, basically, wished it.

The ideas in opposition to which Bodin constructed his famous doctrine of sovereignty were, of course, political: the 'intention' which drives him is the invalidation of the theory of legitimate resistance to royal power, which was developed in the sixteenth century by the Monarchomacs, French Protestant thinkers who opposed the absolute power of the sovereign. Bodin blamed this doctrine for the disorders within France of which the Massacre of Saint-Bartholemew was the culmination.[3] But, more than his political motivations, it was the methodical rigour and semantic precision Bodin required of himself that explained how he managed to rebuild the European political language. Bodin immediately states in the *Les Six Livres* how important methodological rigour – and in particular the art of definition – is to him. It was of primary importance that the definition be attached to the essence of its object: 'one must fix not on accidents, which are innumerable, but on essential differences of form'.[4] Moreover one will have to proceed in a deductive way: after the general definition has been set, one will endeavour to deduce 'the parts in great detail' from it (*Six Livres*, I, 1, p.27). Hence, for his object, after having defined the republic, which is the whole, one will proceed to the parts 'starting with the family, holding forth on each member of the republic, that is to say the sovereign Prince, and of all types of republics, then of the senate, of officers and magistrates, of corporate bodies and colleges, states, and communities, of the power and duties of each' (I, Foreword, pp. 10–1).

This method, which Bodin prided himself in opposing to the mistaken ideas of those, from Plato to Machiavelli, who came before him in political science, had been establishing itself over the years in humanist anti-Aristotelian circles. In his *Dialectic*, Pierre de la Ramée suggested 'the provision of the various things, deduced from the general principles to the singular parts' and gave three criteria to the art of definition: 'need' (or universal validity), 'homogeneity' (or necessary connection between the parts) and 'property' (or reciprocal convertibility of the terms).[5] The political science of Bodin, starving for scientific method and nourished by his fascination for mathematics and the harmonic rules of music,[6] leads to the construction of a system of primary definitions, based on broad empirical surveys and from which the secondary definitions are deduced.

As announced, *Les Six Livres* begins with a definition of the general category: a 'Republic is a legal government of several households and of what is common to them, by sovereign power' (I, 1, p. 27). By this definition, a republic is quite different from what Aristotle claimed. According to Bodin, Aristotle lacked the definitions of the 'three principal points' that are 'the family, sovereignty and what is common', while he had added, without it being necessary, that the republic exists so that citizens might live happily (I, 1, p. 30).

Only its essential elements can be used to define the republic, starting with its constitutive entities: families, or households, or homes. This statement has often been used to attribute to Bodin an organicist, pre-modern vision of politics. Indeed, unlike the Moderns, he did not see the state as a sum of individuals but as the articulation of constituted bodies. However, Bodin seems, at least, to prefigure these atomist conceptions, often evoking the republic as a group of citizens rather than as organic groups: for example he writes that 'A Republic is made up of several citizens when they are governed by the sovereign power' (I, 1, p. 30). Furthermore, the two statements – that the republic is made up of families or of citizens – are not contradictory, because the republic only acknowledges the head of the family. The *domus* escapes public authority; it is subjected to the *pater familias*. But 'when the head of the household has just left his house where he commands, to deal and negotiate with the other heads of households, about what concerns them generally, he then loses the title of master, leader, or lord, to become a companion, peer and associate with others, and instead of lord, he is called citizen' (I, 1, p. 112). In the public sphere, the citizen is the basic component of the republic.

This distinction between domestic and public status points to the republic's second characteristic: its limitation to 'what is common' to households, or to what is, in other words, public. Republics 'are planned by God, to render to the Republic what is public and to each his own' (I, 2, pp. 44–5). Therefore, the field of the state is, by definition, limited. Finally there remains sovereignty. Sovereignty is the 'primary cause' that Bodin sought for so eagerly: 'the republic without sovereign power, which links all its members and parts, and all the households and colleges in a body, is no longer a republic,' just as a ship, if deprived of reinforcement, is only a heap of wood (I, 2, pp. 41). Sovereignty is not just an essential characteristic but the most essential, subsuming the other characteristics and expressing their essence. Bodin defines sovereignty with more care than any other term. In his *Methodus* he had already noted that 'this supreme power that Aristotle calls the sovereign civil authority, a sovereign command, and where lie the majesty and form of the Republic, is defined nowhere'.[7] In Chapter 7 of the first of *Les Six Livres*, the jurist from Angers, clearly aware of his invention, provides this definition: 'Sovereignty is the absolute and perpetual power of a commonwealth' (*On Sovereignty*, I, 8, p. 1). He claims that it is this principle which makes 'the state of the republic' (*ibid.*, II, 1)[8] what it is. To use the anthropomorphic metaphor he often draws upon, one could say that sovereignty is the soul of the body that is the republic. As he had promised himself, Bodin inferred the principle of sovereignty from the analysis of the 'marks of sovereignty' of public authorities (such as declaring war, examining appeals of a last resort, naming and discharging magistrates, taxing or exempting subjects, minting coins and so on). Behind these separate forms of authority he saw a common principle which is the 'power to make and repeal laws' under which 'all the rights and prerogatives of sovereignty are included' (I, 10, p. 58). The act of legislation is the form of sovereignty.

By defining the republic and sovereignty, Bodin created a work of analysis. He named something he observed, he defined reality. To say that 'sovereignty is perpetual' is to note that it lasts beyond the succession of generations, that it has a reality and a personality independent from those of the families or citizens who constitute it. This is also expressed by the saying 'the King is dead, long live the King', which opposes the mortal person to the perpetual title. To say that 'sovereignty is absolute' is to ascertain that in the state all power derives from a single principle. However, the republic is not by definition an absolute monarchy, monopolising all forms of power. On the contrary, Bodin distinguishes the 'state' of a republic, from its 'government'. The latter can be monarchical, aristocratic or democratic, but sovereignty is still absolute, meaning that all authority is exerted on its behalf. The conceptual function of sovereignty is to organise authorities: only the powers exerted on behalf of the republic are legitimate. For example, Bodin observes that, in a monarchy, if 'estates' verify royal edicts, it by no means implies that they have autonomous power; put simply, they 'make sure they are kept' (I, 8, p. 30) and the king could very well do without them. No more do officers, such as (III, 2) magistrates, whose power 'is left pending 'in the presence of the king' (III, 4), nor corporations and colleges (III, 7), which can act only within the limits fixed by the king, have a part of sovereignty. Each of these statements is as much a prescription – 'this is how it should be in a republic' – as a description – 'it is so'; for if these rules are not respected, the republic is no longer a republic.

If the sovereign imposes his law on his subjects, he cannot govern arbitrarily. First, because, like 'every Prince on earth', he is required to respect 'divine and natural laws' (I, 8, p. 13.). This is a traditional argument from the end of the Middle Ages, which Bodin uses again as if it were obvious and without considering it necessary to define the nature of these higher laws. But he adds, which is more original, that the sovereign is required to observe the 'just and reasonable contracts in the observation of which his subjects in general or particular subjects have an interest' (p. 14). The sovereign imposes his law on his subjects, and he does not subject himself to it since he is its author, but he has to abide by the 'contracts':

> Law depends on him who has the sovereignty and he can obligate all his subjects but cannot obligate himself. A contract between a prince and his subjects is mutual; it obligates the two parties reciprocally and one party cannot contravene it to the prejudice of the other and without the other's consent (p. 15).

This concept of conventions prefigures social contract theories. As to content, Bodin only calls to mind, as jurists had been doing since the twelfth century, that the king was required to comply with customs. But he says it with new words, which borrow their logic from legal science. In doing this he anticipated how contract theories would see customs as norms that, owing to their popular origin and to their recognition by the sovereign, could be regarded as contracts.

Bodin's theory of the state inverted the prospect: it brought together, within the unity of a concept, what the Middle Ages saw to be dispersed. It inevitably involved a revision of the status of the individual, a redefinition of citizenship. Already in his *Methodus*, Bodin had criticised Aristotle regarding the definition of the citizen: Aristotle suggested that what makes the citizen is the 'power to dispense justice, to hold public office and to take part in deliberations' but he admitted that 'this definition is only appropriate for popular government'. However this restriction is a contradiction in terms 'since a definition has to be universal' (*Methodus*, p. 350). Aristotle's error was methodological, said Bodin: it derived from the fact that he tried to establish his definition on accidental features:

> Privileges do not make subjects more or less citizens, there is no commonwealth in which the bourgeois has so many privileges that he is not also the subject of some charge... And if the prerogatives and privileges that some have over others made the citizen, then allies would be citizens because foreigners and allies are often given the right of citizenry as an honour and without any subjection (*Six Livres*, I, 6, p. 130).

According to the precept of Ramée, a definition only needs to hold the necessary characteristics of its object, of which privileges are not one. If one used the latter as a basis for 'the definition of the citizen, there would be fifty thousand definitions of the citizen' (p. 141), concluded Bodin, slightly excessively. If, on the other hand, one sticks to basics, the citizen 'is nothing else than the free subject of the sovereignty of others' (p. 112). Every word matters in this pithy formula. The exemption distinguishes the citizen from the slave. Only the first is 'free of all constraint', while the second 'in legal terms is counted for nothing' (p. 116). Neither can the subject be confused with a foreigner. Bodin is very careful to specify whether the subject is a native or naturalised citizen, what the conditions are to be a native citizen – born from one or two citizens – how the 'letters of naturality' are obtained and how legally binding they are – while stipulating, for example, that 'If the foreigner who has been granted the "letters of naturality" outside his country, does not wish to stay, he loses the right he claims, because a double fiction cannot be acknowledged by law' (p. 134 and 139–40). By doing so he defined strict rules of nationality as a *sine qua non* of citizenship.

Nationality is not the only condition. When Bodin defined citizenship as subjection he also meant the relation to sovereignty. If the republic is defined by sovereignty, membership in the republic is, by definition, submission to sovereignty. But submission is not constraint. Bodin stresses the fact that this relation is reciprocal, which makes it close to being a contract: 'privileges do not make the citizen, but the mutual obligation of the sovereign to the subject, to whom, in exchange for the faith and obedience he receives, he owes justice, comfort, aid, protection: all of which are not owed to foreigners' (p. 131, see also p. 141).

Accordingly, he seems to define citizenship in contractual terms, his expressions are sometimes very close to those that contractualist theorists would use during the following century: the citizen is the one who does not live under natural freedom which is 'to be, after God, the subject of no living man, and to tolerate no other command than from oneself' (I, 3, pp. 51–52) and having thus left 'something of his freedom, to live under the laws and command of others' (I, 6, p. 112) receives from the Prince in return 'the safety of his person, assets and families' (I, 7, p. 151), i.e. protection. Citizenship is understood as the benefit of the law of the sovereign, as opposed to a private condition which subjects men to the domination of non-official authorities – to the orders of their masters for example. To be under the authority of the law is to benefit from it, to have access to 'civil rights' (which Bodin calls rights and freedoms; I, 6, p. 114) as well as to judicial protection, which foreigners are deprived of.[9] In this case citizenship covers a concept very close to the Roman *civitas*, seen as a form of their *libertas*.

Bodin is more hesitant however when he tackles the 'rights and privileges' of the citizens who take part in 'the bodies and colleges'. He could rule the question out by stating that those are contingent elements of citizenship, the absence of which would not eliminate the concept. This is what he seems to say when he points out that 'there was never a Republic, i.e. true or imaginary, or even the most popular one that one can think of, where citizens were equal in all rights and prerogatives, but still some have more or less than others' (I, 6, p. 150). In other words, there are various forms of citizenship but they have in common the fact of being an 'honest subjection to sovereignty'. However, Bodin seems uncertain about separating these rights and privileges from the essential core of citizenship. This is proven by the distinction he uneasily makes between the citizen and the bourgeois, although he often seems to use these terms as synonyms elsewhere. He also declares, with a hesitation unusual in his peremptory discourse, that 'this word citizen has a *je ne sais quoi* more special to our eyes than the word bourgeois, and it is the natural subject, that has a right of corporation and of college, or some other privilege that are not given to the bourgeois' (p. 117). Bodin seems to understand that his minimal definition is unsatisfactory because it could result in confusing citizenship and other forms of legal subjection, such as 'bourgeoisie' – membership-title of a city endowed with certain civil rights – unobtainable for foreigners or slaves. But he cannot go as far as keeping the title of citizen for those who participate, in one way or another, in the exercise of sovereignty. This is politically impossible since these ideas were not common at the time. But it was also impossible from a strictly logical viewpoint: if he stated that political privileges were essential to the definition of citizenship, then, as he said himself, he would be forced to see fifty thousand different kinds of citizenship. To avoid settling this dilemma by choosing between a too-precise definition that results in reserving citizenship for a few free subjects and one too vague that does not clearly separate citizenship from bourgeoisie, his definition remains incomplete.

This ambivalent position makes Jean Bodin a pivotal author between traditional royalist theories, handed straight down from medieval dogma, and contractualist theories marked by the idea of natural law that would follow. The whole heritage of medieval political thought is refracted through Bodin, under the effect of a method of hypothesis and deduction, and the result is precursory to elements of modern theory, albeit still in disarray. The advance of political science in later decades would free his inventions of their ambiguities.

For the generation of philosophers that followed Bodin, the issue of the relationship between the method of knowledge and the science of politics became more important still. Pierre Charon (1541–1603) embodied radical scepticism in the twilight of the sixteenth century: any knowledge, any perception was related to the subject who experienced it, and no criterion makes it possible to establish the general veracity of a fact. All truth is individual and one must not believe that it is possible to proclaim an undeniable rule, be it in physics or ethics. Politics does not avoid this indeterminacy: when they speak of the destiny of cities, Montaigne (1533–1592) or Justus Lipsius (1547–1606) only acknowledge one irrefragable imperative, the preservation of civil peace, and they exhort the prince to have no scruples in pursuit of this end. Since one doubts the possibility of setting up the 'political rules' that Bodin claimed to have exhumed, one cannot go beyond the maxims of pure politics and 'raison d'état'; as if by the swing of a pendulum, the Stoics and Machiavelli reappear on the horizon of the seventeenth century.

The bold successes of the physical sciences soon opposed a clear denial of this Pyrrhonism. Around 1620, a new generation of philosophers, scientists and jurists sought out epistemological foundations capable of, if not denying, at least going beyond the ambient pessimism. For these men who were scientists – astrologers, physicists – as well as scholars – moralists, philosophers, lawyers – mathematics and geometry offered, if not the answers to ethical and political questions, at least a method of investigation. The analytical – or resolutive – and synthetic – or compositive – method, the power of which Bodin had foreseen before Descartes theorised it, would be these young men's line of conduct, so decided were they to give ethics and politics their letters of scientific nobility.[10] And this methodological revolution would in turn produce the spectacular change in language that, from the beginning of the seventeenth century to modern days, placed subjective rights at the centre of political theory.

It is not by chance that the foundations of this new approach were laid down by specialists in the law of nations: scepticism could recognise the irreconcilable diversity of the rules of human societies but this observation condemned to silence those who speculated about the relationships between nations and about the 'rights' of an individual in a nation other than his own. The very essence of the law of nations required that one be able to define valid rules beyond the borders of historical communities.[11] It was one of the notable merits of the Dutch jurist and scholar Hugo Grotius (1583–1645)[12] to state that this difficulty could only be overcome with the weapons of the 'new method':

Just as the mathematicians customarily prefix to any concrete demonstration a preliminary statement of certain broad axioms on which all persons are readily agreed, in order that there may be some fixed point from which to face the proof of what follows, so shall we point out certain rules and laws of the most general nature, presenting them as preliminary assumptions which need to be recalled rather than learned for the first time, with the purpose of laying a foundation upon which our other conclusions may safely rest. (*Prolegomena*, p. 7)

Anxious to avoid giving the sceptics any basis that they could refute, Grotius drew from the same source: he reduced the fundamental axiom on which all human actions rest to a minimum anthropological characteristic, selfishness. If man is taken as he is, said Grotius, such as God created him, one must recognise that 'love, whose primary force and action are directed to self-interest, is the first principle of the whole natural order'. (p. 9) From there, and in accordance with the line he set himself, Grotius inferred two 'precepts of the law of nature', the contents of which were so undeniable at the time that there was a broad consensus about them, among 'the Stoics, the Epicureans and the Peripatetics' and the 'members of the Academy'. These two seminal principles are stated as follows:

It shall be permissible to defend (one's own) life and to shun that which threatens to become injurious; secondly, that it shall be permissible to acquire for oneself, and to retain, those things which are useful for life (pp. 10-11).

These laws were formulated in contemporary terms as the right to life and property and did not seem to say more than what the common meaning and philosophers' opinion acknowledged at the time. In fact, they introduced a radical innovation: the laws of nature gave men *rights*. The relevant concept was no longer, as with Aristotle and his successors, general characteristics of the natural order but properties inherent in the individual. 'Right, narrowly understood, is the relation which exists between a reasonable being and something appropriate to him by merit or property'.[13] A right, in the meaning of Grotius, is not the *ius* of the Roman, which belongs to the individual in relation to others, but the *dominium*, which belongs to him in his own right. The law is a 'body of rights', the principle of attribution of these 'moral qualities of a person, which enable him to have or to do something legally', 'attached to a person' and which 'depends on none other than the one which is entitled to a certain thing' (*De Jure Praede*, Prol., p. 14). The individual is no longer defined solely as a member of a community; he exists in himself, and his 'nature' can be formulated as rights. This conception has become so common since the seventeenth century that it is difficult to understand its novelty but, in Grotius' time, it was revolutionary. It was to trigger, among his successors, a complete reformulation of the political language.

Grotius was aware that these two seminal maxims alone did not make it possible to conceive harmonious human societies, because selfishness would prompt men to quarrels. He resolved, in order to complete his doctrinal construction, to lay down a second axiom resting entirely on the authority of religion: God cannot have created a man strictly egotistical, unless he had no care for the safeguarding of his creation, which is inconceivable. It must therefore be admitted that he endowed his creatures with the faculty to care about the well-being of their fellow men. 'Love, therefore, is double; love for oneself, and love for others' (p. 11). Sociability is the second fundamental instinct of man, competing with selfishness. Grotius can, yet again, deduce from this second axiom two more fundamental precepts, which complete the first two: 'That no one inflicts damage on his fellow' and 'That no one takes possession of what belongs to another' (p. 13). The duty to respect the physical integrity of other men corresponds to the right to life, as the duty not to violate the propriety of others corresponds to the right of property.

In this way Grotius lays down the fundamental method of modern political philosophy: the modern natural law was a number of normative precepts deduced from rational research. It resembled a theology, insofar as these precepts were understood as manifestations of the divine will and were imposed on men. However, this theology was triply freed from Christian dogma. First of all it was secularised, since these precepts remained valid even when they went against the laws stated by theologians; secondly it was subjected to a formal logic, to the rules of hypothetico-deductive reasoning; and, finally, it was subordinated to the imperative of social usefulness, these rules having no other object than to render a harmonious society conceivable.[14]

Natural sociability was the condition, necessary but insufficient, of social life. Grotius had harboured enough of the doubts of the Sceptics to avoid simply substituting one transcendent principle (nature) for another (Providence). He knew that in the state of nature such as he defined it, 'numerous persons (because such is the evil which results from the corrupted nature of certain men) either do not honour their obligations, or even plague fortune, not to say the lives of others' (p. 19).[15] The normative strength of natural law was not sufficient to ensure it was obeyed; it supposed an authority able to guarantee its implementation. However, history has indicated the way out of this state of insecurity: empirically one can observe that men assemble in societies sufficiently large to ensure their own defence and to provide for their needs. Having measured their own interest, men agreed to strip themselves of their original power to enforce the laws of nature themselves and punish those who violate them, and they transferred these powers to a common entity they created to ensure the safety of all; this artificial social unit 'is called republic; and the individuals who constitute the republic are called citizens' (p. 20). The whole world is made up of these forms of 'states' (*civitates*), because such is God's desire and such are men's wishes.

History indicated that men had passed a 'civil pact' among themselves to transform their original society, where the laws of nature were permanently threatened with being violated, into a civil society the *raison d'être* of which was to consecrate these laws. This pact did not leave natural law untouched: 'it seems', said Grotius, 'that it comprises specific rights' derived from the first laws and which stretched beyond them: civil laws which added to the natural rights and duties of men the political rights and duties of citizens.

> Individual citizens should not only refrain from injuring other citizens, but should furthermore protect them, individuals; secondly, citizens should not only refrain from seizing one another's possessions, whether these be held privately or in common, but should furthermore contribute individually to both that which is necessary to other individuals and which is necessary to the whole (p. 21).

The constitution of the republic 'civilised' the natural order and required particular discipline on the part of the citizens, which was the price of the safety they could find in it. Insofar as he has 'agreed to this arrangement' any citizen was held 'to match his will to that of the others. The will of all, when it is applied to all is called law (*lex*). ...What the republic acknowledged as its will is its right (*ius*) and concerns the whole body of citizens' (pp. 22–23). This meant that accession to the civil state, accession to citizenship, involved a change in the status of man and thus a change in his rights:

> for even though people grouped as a whole and people as private individuals do not differ in the natural order, a distinction has arisen from a man-made fiction and from the consent of citizens (VIII, p. 107).

Does the change in their status mean that the rights and duties of citizens replace those of the natural man, or do right and duties accumulate? Does society eradicate nature; does man die by becoming a citizen, or do these two orders of reality coexist? To these questions, which would be discussed at length by the theorists of natural law, Grotius brought only rough answers: he did not admit that civil right abolished natural law but he conceded that the establishment of a republic seemed at least to require natural law to be put in parentheses.[16] For example, the basic right of men to resist tyranny in the natural order was abolished in the civil order.

> By nature all men have the right of resisting in order to ward off injury, as we have said above. But as civil society was instituted in order to maintain public tranquillity, the state forthwith acquires over us and our possessions a greater right, to the extent necessary to accomplish this end. The state, therefore, in the interest of public peace and order, can limit that common right of resistance ...If, in fact, the right of resistance should remain without restraint, there will no longer be a state, but only a non-social horde.[17]

Grotius seemed to say that natural and civil law were not in contradiction, that the citizen was not the denial of the man. By becoming a citizen, man relinquished his natural freedom to a degree that varied from one society to another. The issue of the extent of the pact, of the depth of the change in the social order and individual status that it involved, would deeply divide natural law thinkers throughout the seventeenth century. But they would all continue to reason according to the terms set by Grotius. In the second half of the seventeenth century it became common to speak about the 'rights' that man had by nature and to look for their origin in human reason rather than in divine intention; just as frequently, these rights were defined as the source of authority. The dualistic philosophical pattern outlined by Grotius became the matrix of republican political law, from which the modern concept of citizenship sprang. All the authors of the classical era make use of this contractualist language and perfect the idea of the social contract, which replaces the quarrelsome natural order by a pacified artificial order; the egotistical and savage man replaced by the virtuous and obedient citizen.

Born five years after his famous Dutch contemporary, the English philosopher Thomas Hobbes (1588–1679) faced the same doubts regarding the possibilities of human knowledge and the prospect of enacting ethical and political rules. Like the Sceptics, he equated the truths of the scientist with those of the ordinary person: if the theoretical certainty of the former are based upon his understanding and can claim no general validity, practical convictions are no longer universal. From the first version of his great philosophical work, perpetually revised, Hobbes had already outlined the question which would concern him his whole life:

> In the state of nature, where every man is his own judge, and differeth from others concerning the names and of things, and from those differences arise quarrels, and breach of peace; it was necessary there should be a common measure of all things that might fall in controversy; as for example: of what is to be called right, what good, what virtue, what much, what little, what it and of, what a pound, what a quart, &c. For in these things private judgements may differ, and beget controversy. This common measure, some say, is right reason: with whom I should consent, if there were any such thing to be found or known in rerum naturâ. But commonly they that call for right reason to decide any controversy do mean their own. But this is certain, seeing right reason does not exist, the reason of some man, or men, must supply the role thereof, and that man, or men, is he, or they, that have the sovereign power.[18]

Hobbes followed in Grotius' footsteps in defining the fundamental precept of his political science: he recognised that all the workings of human passions rested on man's selfishness. The human being is in love with himself, a prisoner of his desires and particularly the desire for glory. But Hobbes did not believe in a propensity to sociability. In this he distanced himself from Grotius and gives his work its originality. According to him, Grotius was wrong when he saw altruism where there was in fact only a reasoned form of selfishness: 'We do not therefore by nature seek society for its own sake, but that we may receive some honour or profit from it; these we desire primarily, that secondarily' (*De Cive*, I, II, p. 111.[19] In the natural state in which they found themselves before the republic, men were equal – each having, at least, as weak as he might be, the right to kill his neighbour[20] – and perfectly free. In this theoretical state, every man had an inalienable right, a natural right, which 'is the Liberty each man hath, to use his own power, as he will himself, for the preservation of his own Nature; that is to say, of his own Life' (XIV, p. 91 ; *cf. De Cive*, I, 10, p. 117). The state of nature is a perpetual battlefield, where competition, suspicion and the desire for glory cause the 'war of all against all' to reign. No sociability brings order to it.

Hobbes did not give in to pure scepticism, however. Anarchy was not inevitable, because righteous reason inclined man to recognise the sterility of this state. It dictated the 'law of nature' to him and showed him how to safeguard his life. If the *natural law of man* led him to war, the *natural law of humanity* convinced him to seek peace (*Leviathan*, XIV, pp. 91–2). There is rationality within the universe that the philosopher can bring to light. Using reason, one could realise that, if the world was made up of men having the same unlimited right over all things, and if chaos came from this, there was only one way to avoid it, by giving up this right, as much as was necessary for the establishment of peace, and in the exact same measure that others relinquished theirs (*ibid.*).

Hobbes took up the Grotian idea of the social pact and radicalised it. All must refrain from doing what they think to be just and right and agree on a common definition of these terms. It is Hobbes's total epistemological scepticism which makes the institution of the state necessary in his eyes. He greatly fears eloquence and the manipulation of the crowd by the power of words. Thus, he justifies the existence of the state by the need to define and ensure the application of a common language: 'before the names of Just, and Unjust can have place, there must be some coercive Power, to compel men equally to the performance of their Covenants, by the terror of some punishment, greater than the benefit they expect by the breach of their Covenant' (*Leviathan*, XV, p. 101). The structure of the argument is identical to that of Grotius: it is the incapacity of isolated men to enforce the laws of nature which makes necessary the erection of a private authority superior to men, and prevailing against private volitions. The difference lies in the degree: since he does not believe in the sociability of man, Hobbes makes absolute the contract, the provisions of which remained relative with Grotius. He wants to give nothing up to their free will; all that will remain out of the state's reach will be still likely to rekindle the 'war of all against all'.

Man completely stripped himself of his natural right by this contract with his fellow men. He became a subject, or a citizen, which is the same in Hobbes's language: 'I call subjects of the one which exerts *sovereignty* all the citizens of the same city' (*De Cive*, II, V, XI, p. 145). The social contract involved a much clearer change of man's status than with Grotius. The private man became a subject; his freedom lost all its natural power, it 'lieth therefore only in those things, which in regulating their actions, the Sovereign has praetermitted' (*Leviathan*, XXI, p. 148). To be free is to obey the law. The Leviathan is not an external authority imposed on man and oppressing him; on the contrary, it is the force which represents him, the power which is exerted on his behalf, which makes common reason dominate individual passions.[21] To be a citizen was to be free from constraints, to belong to no one save to the republic.[22] Indeed, it was to be doubly free: first because man was shielded from the private sovereignties which characterised patrimonial forms of authority; secondly because he was diverted from his illusory freedom, which was only blind passion and led him to lose his real freedom. For Hobbes the state was the rational form of social life, governed by law, as opposed to the irrational form of the state of nature which was dominated by passions. In the same way, citizenship was understood as a submission to law, which was only the submission to one's own reason, as opposed to all the private constraints of natural man, subject to his passions and of those of his fellow men.[23]

HUMAN RIGHTS AND THE CITIZEN: PUFENDORF, LOCKE AND SPINOZA

After Hobbes had rigorously defined the sovereign republic and the contract it stemmed from, his political vocabulary and syntax became paradigmatic. His atomist representations of society, reduced to a crowd of isolated men; his dual anthropology, in which man was divided between his passions and his reason; his idea of a contract and of the abstract personality of the republic were constantly revised, reinterpreted and reused. From one author to the next, in the second half of the seventeenth century, the nuances are what separate Hobbes from Grotius: faith in the social awareness of man. Later political philosophers questioned the Hobbesian theory of the total transfer of their rights by individuals and its corollary, the absolute character of sovereign power. This involved, in other words, rebalancing the rights of man and those of the citizen.

This is largely because of political development in Europe in the middle of the seventeenth century. When Hobbes was endeavouring to establish a rigorous science of politics, the question which preoccupied him was still the one that was faced by Machiavelli and Bodin, i.e. how to ensure the exclusiveness of sovereign power and the general validity of its laws in order to avoid anarchy. The answer was simple: the subject had to be placed under the exclusive jurisdiction of an indisputable law. The situation he saw in Europe, particularly in England, encouraged this idea: Parliament's attempts to counter royal power – in fiscal matters especially – the Stuart kings' defiant scorn of the rights claimed by Parliament and the descent into revolution, civil war and finally restorations because rival doctrines of legitimacy conflicted, an unequivocal criterion had to be found which could quell quarrels and nip the civil dissension they fuelled in the bud.

In the second half of the century, the problem in England took on a new shape. A new claim came to light, put forward by the middle and lower classes: the Levellers demanded that privileges be extended more widely; the struggle between Parliament and the king was fuelled by the old issue of judicial protection against royal arbitrariness; revolutionary ideas abounded and modernised the old idea of a contract between the king and the people and, by following in Hobbes' footsteps, made it the founding and legitimising act of sovereign power.

The 'Glorious Revolution' of 1688 made a subtle compromise between these divergent tendencies: William of Orange was declared King of England by 'the lords spiritual and temporal, and commons, assembled at Westminster, lawfully, fully, and freely representing all the estates of the people of this realm' (*Bill of Rights*, 1689, I). The king agreed beforehand to recognise

> that all and singular the rights and liberties asserted and claimed in the said declaration are the true, ancient, and indubitable rights and liberties of the people of this kingdom, and so shall be esteemed, allowed, adjudged, deemed, and taken to be, and that all and every the particulars aforesaid shall be firmly and strictly held and observed, as they are expressed in the said declaration; and all the officers and ministers whatsoever shall serve their Majesties and their successors according to the same in all times to come.

Similarly, William recognised the rights of Parliament, which continued to be in session and adopted with the King this charter of the laws and freedoms of England. A balance was struck between the King and representatives of English high society and, more remarkable still, the King recognised that his authority came from the people and that it was limited by the prerogatives of the people.

Theorists of politics would henceforth have to take this inversion into account. The more so as England was not an exception: at the same time on the continent, the 'people'– as the prosperous classes symbolically identified their interests – asserted its relative autonomy with regard to sovereign authority. Hobbes' contractualist representation appears already too absolutist to describe and direct the forming of European states.

Three men born the same year, 1632, in three different European countries, would articulate a vision of politics in which the state of nature and the civil state[24] were not excluded as radically as in Hobbes, and in which the rights of man and the rights of citizens were no longer inevitably paradoxical. All three also showed, without taking their reasoning to its logical conclusion, that the contractual nature of the state was not necessarily limited to the time of its foundation: in the state built by contract, citizens were not only subjects but perhaps also holders of what would, in the next century, be called popular sovereignty.

This argument is barely visible in the works of Samuel von Pufendorf (1632–1694) but by moving away from Hobbes, Pufendorf anticipated later reasoning. All his work can be interpreted as an attempt to reconsider Grotius' theory of the republic on the basis of Hobbes' philosophical premise.[25] Pufendorf did not postulate – like Grotius – that man was inclined towards altruism; on the contrary, he kept to Hobbes' minimum premise, according to which man is selfish. Like Hobbes and Grotius he knew that men's 'vices' threatened their safety. Natural law suggested that 'men shall refrain from all infliction of injuries' but 'respect for that law cannot guarantee a life in natural liberty with fair security'.[26] Like his predecessors, he called therefore for 'each (to) submit his will to the will of one man or one assembly, in such a way that from that time whatever that man or that assembly wills in what concerns the common security be taken as the will of all and everyone' (*De Officio Hominis et Civis*, II, 6, 5, p. 136).

Pufendorf however gave a different version of this contract from Hobbes': the transfer of their rights by men was not done by a single contract that men concluded among themselves, but by two agreements and one decree. By the first agreement, men stated among themselves that they 'wish to enter into a single and perpetual union ..., that they wish to become fellow-citizens'. They then passed, still among themselves, a decree on the form of government they wished to give themselves. Finally came the second agreement, which connected the united people to its sovereign, and by which those who were entrusted with power 'bind himself or themselves to provide for the common security and safety, and the rest bind themselves to him or them' (II, 6, 7–9, pp. 136–7). By thus subdividing the social contract, Pufendorf made obvious the idea of the contractual link between governors and governed.

The relations of individuals to power and the status of citizenship are modified by this. Pufendorf admitted, after Hobbes, that 'in becoming a citizen, a man loses his natural liberty and subjects himself to an authority whose powers include the right of life and death' (II, 4, 5 pp. 132–33). But he refused the Hobbesian assimilation of the subject and of the citizen:

> Hobbes ...appears to make subject and citizen equivalent terms, so that women, boys and slaves would also be citizens. But it is my opinion that since a state is established by a submission of wills to one man or to a council, those, or their successors are primarily citizens, by whose pacts a state was first formed. And since this was done by fathers of families, it would be my judgement that the name 'citizen' belongs to these first of all, but only indirectly and through them to the women, boys and slaves of their establishment, whose wills were included in the will of the father of the family, in so far as they enjoy both the common protection of the state, and some rights by reason of that relation.[27]

Pufendorf reintroduces gradation in the status of citizenship, which Hobbes had eradicated by reducing it to subjection. He distinguishes a 'wider sense' of citizenship and a 'narrower sense', which applied only to the founders of the state and their successors, the *pater familias* (*De Officio*, II, 6, 13, p. 138). What is common to all citizens is the advantage of the rule of law, which results from the duties that the sovereign holds from the contract: safety from external aggression and civil war, written laws which came with sanctions, and even a certain material support for the poor (II, 11, 1–3, pp. 151–4). In exchange, citizens owe the sovereign absolute obedience.[28]

However, in the definition of the citizenship given by Pufendorf, who was the first modern theorist to produce such a definition explicitly, the reference to the initial assent expressed in the social pact is clearer than in Hobbes' work:

> Citizenship, or the right of citizenship, includes, to their largest effects, the actions that are the prerogative of the members of the commonwealth, as well as the right to the benefits of these actions, which similarly entail a duty towards the commonwealth (*De Iure Naturae et Gentium* 2, VII, 2, 20, p. 995).

This is a clear definition of the political status of citizenship, as reciprocity of rights and duties between the citizen and the state, but it is only a formal definition. Pufendorf does not go so far as to give citizens, as subjective right-bearers, a share in the exercise or even only in the possession of the principle of sovereignty. Although he stresses the precept according to which 'consent of subjects is required to constitute any legitimate government' (*De Jure Naturae*, II, 10.1, pp. 148), he does not translate this maxim into an individual right. The idea of consent is twice limited: it is limited in practice to certain subjects, which include the will of those which are subordinated to them; and limited theoretically to an assent in principle, considered to have been obtained in the past and tacitly given by all who live under the laws of the republic.

The degrees of citizenship that he differentiates do not include more or less 'power' but, at the most, a difference in charges and honours, which hold no sovereignty. The citizens who hold these 'honours' are not 'more active' than others, according to a terminology which will be developed a century later. These distinctive signs emphasise their high position in the social hierarchy, but do not make them the holders of popular sovereignty. Like Bodin, and later Sieyès, Pufendorf considered participation in power not as a right, which would reflect the idea of popular sovereignty at the subjective level, but as a duty; the obligation that certain citizens have, which also is an honour, to assume certain political charges.

The conceptual connection between sovereignty and citizenship is outlined more distinctly in the work of his Dutch contemporary, Benedict de Spinoza (1632–77). While also drawing on the ideas of Hobbes, he looked on the relation between the citizens and the state in a radically different way. Questioned by one of his correspondents, Spinoza answered:

> As regards political theories, the difference you inquire about between Hobbes and myself, consists in this, that I always preserve natural right intact, and only allot to the chief magistrates in every state a right over their subjects commensurate with the excess of their power over the power of the subjects. This is what always takes place in the state of nature'.[29]

His ideas are those of the times: after Hobbes, he realises that the natural law of man 'forbids absolutely nothing that is within human power',[30] that he is permitted in the state of nature to do all he is able to do. 'In consequence, since all are equally bent on supremacy, they start to quarrel, and do the utmost to enslave one another' (*TP*, I, §5, p. 265). He also shares the idea of the ambivalence of human nature, torn between the passions and the arguments of reason. But Spinoza is not neutral in this assessment. Without beating about the bush, he expresses his conviction that rational control is more laudable than passionate inclination. Better still, where Hobbes defined freedom in mechanical terms, as the lack of impediment to act according to one's wishes, Spinoza defined it in moral terms: 'I call a man completely free in so far as he is guided by reason' (II, §11, p. 275). A man could seem completely free because he determined his behaviour himself; he would nevertheless be a slave if he were prisoner of his passions. This is the point of origin of his political theory: the point was to consider the conditions which enabled men to regulate their existence in accordance with the dictates of right reason.[31]

Formally, Spinoza follows Hobbes' reasoning: to put an end to the state of discord in which men exist, it was necessary to substitute a single judgement for the multiplicity of their individual judgements. This requires the institution of a 'sovereign', on whose thinking 'all its subjects had to be guided; and so it alone had the right to decide what was good, what bad, what fair, and what unfair' (IV, §1, p. 301). But a power whose word *does not make* the just and the unjust, the good and the evil. The power is produced from men's will 'to join together' and to ensure that 'the right to do everything which each had by nature should be held collectively', which is equivalent to saying that they have agreed 'to direct everything by the dictate of reason alone'.[32] While with Hobbes the purpose of the republic is effectiveness, and law is reduced to the will of the sovereign, with Spinoza the republic aims at the triumph of a rationality that the sovereign can only interpret. The Hobbesian rupture, which had completely emancipated the sovereign from natural or divine law, or from an absolute human reason, is put in parentheses: the sovereign again becomes the one who expresses rather than creates the law, as with Grotius or Pufendorf, and Locke or Rousseau.

Spinoza especially differed from his predecessors by strictly limiting the extent of the contract, according to the Machiavellian principle of force. For Hobbes, men transferred all of their rights to the sovereign, whatever the form of government, whether sovereignty belonged to only one, to several or to all. Spinoza asserted, on the contrary, that the extent of power was related to its strength. In monarchy and in aristocracy, for example, the transfer of rights never seemed to be absolute: nothing prohibited it in theory, but experience generally indicated that most often 'the individual retains his own right in many of his actions, which therefore depend on nobody's decision but his own' (*TTP*, XVII, p. 149). The extent of the contract could not be defined theoretically. It depended on the turn taken by events: 'thus a people freely transfers to a king only what it cannot wholly command itself' (*TP*, VII, §5, p. 339). This was the 'continuation of the state of nature' presented by Spinoza. He remembered the lesson of Machiavelli, which he quoted reverently: the relation between governors and governed is not based on a decision made *a priori* but on a balance of power. It is established by the capacity of both sides to maintain their natural power. The civil state is not the negation of the natural state; at the most it is the eruption of a public authority. This also means that one could not fix *a priori* the duration of the contract, since 'a contract can have no biding force but utility; when that disappears it at once becomes null and void' (*TTP*, XVI, p. 139).

Citizenship was marked by this overlapping of the civil state and the natural state. 'For citizens are not born, but made' (*TP*, V, §2, p. 309) says Spinoza, to recall that it is in fact a civil state. But he also says that, even if they are governed by the city, men cannot 'lose their human nature and assume another' (IV, §4, p. 303). Citizenship was not the antithesis of nature, any more than the civil state replaced the natural state. In a sense the freedom of man depended on his civil status, as with Hobbes:

> I call men citizens in so far as they enjoy all the advantages of the commonwealth by civil right; and subjects in so far as they are bound to obey the ordinances or laws of the commonwealth' (III, §1, p. 285).

Citizenship was interpreted as the rights that were guaranteed through obedience to the law; the subject and the citizen are only two faces of the same being. But the 'right' of the citizen, i.e., its power, in Spinoza's language, is inversely proportional to the power of the state: 'the more the commonwealth exceeds a citizen or subject in power, the less right he has' (III, §2, p. 285). Everything was resolutely based on the balance of power: the individual still had both 'citizen's rights' and 'human rights' and the supremacy of one over the other depended on the clauses of the contract.

However there was a political regime which seemed to be an exception to this rule: democracy. Spinoza specified that, in this type of government, 'everyone transfers all his power to the society. Thus it alone will have a perfect natural right to do everything, i.e. sovereign power, and everyone will be bound to obey it either in freedom of spirit or from fear of the supreme penalty' (*TTP*, XVI, p. 133). This exception to the realistic assessment of the supremacy of power in politics led Spinoza on an uncharted road. Insofar as the transfer of 'right', i.e., of power, was complete, man could seem to be, paradoxically, entirely submitted in democracy. But this was only an appearance.

> For in it no one transfers his natural right to another so completely that he is never consulted again, but each transfers it to a majority of the whole community of which he is a member (p. 137).

In monarchy or in aristocracy, man kept a share of natural freedom. In democracy, he stripped himself of it completely but, by this transfer, gained new freedom. *The Political Treaty* which presents the three forms of government was left unfinished and tells us little about what Spinoza meant by democracy. One only knows that he granted to all the 'right to vote and undertake offices of state' (*TP*, IX, §1, p. 441) and that, like all the men of his time, he excluded women and servants, children and foreigners from it. Only men apt to conform their behaviour to the dictates of reason had a say, since government was instituted precisely to this end.[33] Whatever the institutional modalities of this democracy, Spinoza outlined a new conceptual connection, a logical link between citizenship and sovereignty. In this regime, where man was completely citizen – since he gave up his natural right – the citizen was answerable only to his own law. By becoming a citizen, man became a member of a community that held sovereignty, and exercised sovereignty in the right to vote. All this is still of unfinished beauty, and Spinoza did not yet state explicitly that 'obeying to all, in fact obey to themselves,' but one finds in his thinking an assertion of citizenship as the other face of sovereignty, an idea whose full power Rousseau would develop.

The third philosopher to be born in 1632 and to give the social contract a less monolithic representation than Hobbes was the Englishman John Locke (1632–1704). From the start one is struck by a singular feature of his writings: Locke only reluctantly used the vocabulary of his predecessors. In his main work, the *Two Treatises of Government* (c. 1679), he did not once use the term 'sovereignty', preferring the expressions 'supreme' or 'legislative power'; he seldom speaks of the 'state' and refers more readily to the 'government'. Locke was aware of the connotations of words and preferred the strategy of vocabulary shift to that of semantic subversion: to struggle against absolutism, he used a different language to that of his contemporaries.

His most direct adversary, who acted as a foil for the construction of his own doctrines, was Robert Filmer (1588–1653), author of the well-named *Patriarcha*. According to Filmer, a perpetuator of the medieval conception of authority, the sovereign derived his power from divine devolution, and he must exercise it absolutely but with paternal consideration for his subjects:

> By this means are all kings, even tyrants and conquerors, bound to preserve the lands, goods, liberties and lives of all their subjects ... by the natural law of a father, which binds them to ratify the acts of their forefathers and predecessors'.[34]

Locke dedicated the whole of the first volume of his *Two Treatises* to the rebuttal of Filmer's claim that kings held their power from the property-rights and paternal jurisdiction over the world that Adam received from God. In the second treatise, the only one that is still read, he set down the principles of another vision of politics. He began by disclaiming Filmer's providential argument: power is not a divine devolution in line with God's laws but a human institution. Then Locke also opposed himself to all those who, like Hobbes, thought of power as the direct opposite to the might of individuals. He intended to show that an efficient government could be instituted without necessarily mortgaging individuals' natural freedom. And, like others who measured themselves against the *Leviathan*, he was compelled to imagine a state of nature less radically savage than Hobbes', if he wished to have the means of justifying the moderation of power.

Locke argued that, although men were undeniably free and equal in the state of nature, they were not condemned to perpetual war. The reason he gave for this is puzzling by its simplicity and dogmatism: the law of nature, which men can find by using their reason, ordered them to not 'harm another in his Life, Health, Liberty or Possessions' because 'Men being all the Workmanship of one Omnipotent, and infinitely wise Maker; All the Servants of one Sovereign Master, sent into the World by his order and about his business, they are his Property'.[35] Men, said Locke, did not belong to themselves, they are God's creatures, and accordingly have the duty to preserve 'their' own life as well as the remainder of humanity. He said no more on this point, neither on the bases of this law of nature, which can only be axiomatic, nor on the way in which men can be aware of it.[36] This is probably explained by the fact that the *Two Treatises* were addressed to the honest man rather than to the philosopher, and that thus there was no reluctance in using the preconceptions of the time.[37] Whatever the roots, the heart of the matter for his readers was that Locke developed a radically new, radically individualistic, theory of 'government'.

Insofar as men were naturally subjected to a higher law, their pre-political condition could not be as tragic as Hobbes claimed it to be. There was a

> plain difference between the State of Nature, and the State of War, which however some Men have confounded, are as far distant, as a State of Peace, Good Will, Mutual Assistance, and Preservation, and a State of Enmity, Malice, Violence, and Mutual Destruction are one from another (*Two Treatises*, II, 3, §19, p. 280).

The need for government did not disappear for all that, because, before it was introduced, the *execution* of natural law, along with the right to punish which comes with it, depended on each individual. This leads ineluctably to 'Confusion and Disorder' (II, 2, §13, p. 275). It remains essential for the safeguarding of natural law, that is, for the achievement of God's intentions, that men agree 'together mutually to enter into one Community, and make one Body Politick' (II, 2, §14, pp. 276–7). This can only be accomplished if everyone 'hath quitted this natural Power, resign'd it up into the hands of the Community' which was thus endowed with the power to make and implement laws (II, 7, §87–89, pp. 324–5). Up to this point the argument was still very conventional; it was on the subject of the contract's modalities and on the nature of the power that resulted from it that Locke moved away from his predecessors.

The contract did not aim to strip men of their natural power to the profit of an external authority, as with Hobbes and Pufendorf. It was an act through which individuals *entrusted power to themselves*. They each individually gave up the exercise of their natural right and committed themselves to exercising it jointly.

> When any number of men have consented to make one Community or Government, they are thereby presently incorporated, and make one Body Politick, wherein the Majority have a Right to act and conclude the rest (II, 8, §95, p. 331).

Individuals only fictitiously gave up their right, they could no longer make individual use of it, but they still had the option of exerting it within the political body of which they are members – the sacrifice of the minority was only a practical need without which no agreement could be obtained. The people became the authority of the freedom of individuals, the mediation through which it was carried out. This was already the case with Hobbes, since the subject was free insofar as he was only submitted to law, and protected from private exactions by law. Locke doubled the argument: citizens were free because they were obedient only to the law and not to men, but they were more so still because they *continuously* approved the laws. The citizen was invested with a symmetrical right and duty: the right to express his approval of governmental action, i.e. the faculty to give, himself or through his representatives, his free consent to the drafting of laws,[38] and the inseparable obligation to yield to the determination of the majority (II, V8, §97, p. 332).

Locke reversed the relation between the citizen and the state: it was the assembled citizens who constituted the legislative power, of which the executive was only the agent, responsible for its actions to citizens and which 'may be at pleasure changed and displaced' (II, 13, §152, p. 368). Locke clearly tried to connect the concepts of citizenship and sovereignty, although he used neither of the two words: citizenship was no longer submission to, but rather possession and exercise of, sovereignty.

Now, by definition, this exercise was only applicable to citizens, and Locke nowhere said that all men were citizens. On the contrary, like all his contemporaries, he pronounced that only reasonable men could take part in the election of the legislators. He also acknowledged that property was the best criterion by which to choose citizens from among the people. What's more, if civil society was established to guarantee property as an essential condition of conservation, it was common sense to entrust the safeguarding of it to those who would have the greatest care for it, that is, property owners themselves.

Despite these limits, which were commonplace at the time, Locke completely redefined the relations of man and citizen, and answered a question which had long remained ambiguous. Hobbes plainly delimited the rights of citizens – the civil rights established by the sovereign and even *the* right of man: the right to life – and Grotius and Pufendorf did not offer a clear formulation of this duality. As for Spinoza, indeterminacy was one of his principles: the rights of man were those that he managed not to transfer to the sovereign. Locke stated very clearly that the union of individuals only involved the transfer of their power in the measure 'necessary to the ends for which they unite into Society' (II, 13, §152, p. 368). Government was a means to ensure the protection of man, and its ends were subordinated to natural law (II, 11, §135, p. 358). Admittedly, this principle does not make it possible to draw up an immutable catalogue of the rights of man and of the citizen[39] but Locke defined their respective extents. The agreement between individuals recorded in the clauses of the contract showed the limits of government's action. And even though he did not explicitly set limits to the contract, he clearly stated that man kept the entirety of his rights at all times and therefore could always break the agreement. Not only could the people legitimately undo the executive[40] but *any individual* was also allowed to do so: '*every Man* is *Judge* for himself (...) whether another hath put himself into a State of War with him' (II, 19, §241, p. 427), whether this other is one of his fellow citizens or a holder of power. Under no circumstances, and whatever the terms of the contract, was the citizen forced passively to accept attacks upon his life and property.

Locke reconciled the most radical individualism – even acknowledging an individual right to rebel – and a collective concept of freedom seen as obedience to a law that has been agreed upon – what later will be called autonomy. The Lockean concept of law confirms this: the legislative process was not an autonomous creative act whose decisions were considered just simply by the fact that they were taken according to prescribed procedure. Rather, it was a process of revelation of natural law: 'The Obligations of the Law of Nature, cease not in Society, but only in many Cases are drawn closer, and have by Humane Laws known Penalties annexed to them' (II, 11, § 135, p. 358). 'Popular sovereignty' was inseparable from the belief in an immanent reason, that of God, who prescribes irrefragable laws. The legislative process is a *cognitive* act, which aims to uncover, but not to create *ex nihilo*, the human laws that God expressed in nature.[41] Assembled men consecrated and protected their natural rights: this was where, by the alchemy of the social contract, individuality met collective freedom, where man became citizen in order to guarantee his inalienable rights as a man. In the republic, the inalienable individuality of man was sublimated in citizenship.[42]

'What a contrast! What an abrupt passage!'[43] Paul Hazard exclaimed, reflecting on the incomparable intellectual journey that took place from Grotius to Locke. This historian of ideas dated this transition to the turn of the century (1680–1715); indeed, if no great work came out of these three decades, they were at least a period of sedimentation for the ideas promulgated by the authors of the first part of the seventeenth century. From 1680 to 1715, the educated classes of the European nations immersed themselves in the new doctrines, which would also prove to be milestones on the way to the next era. The eighteenth century would be the century of 'universal criticism'[44] but using the language of the previous half-century. The idea of natural law and the political doctrines that it initiated were widely circulated during the eighteenth century. For the literate population, which would propel the coming political revolution, natural law had become the common basis of thought; it was taught in all the European universities, its terms were quarrelled over in interminable polemics, it was referred to as a philosophical alphabet.

This strange idea that men have rights by nature before they conquer them politically by their struggles was the product of the epistemological revolution that began in the twilight of the sixteenth century. After Machiavelli and his contemporaries had demolished the medieval intellectual system, which rested on immutable dogma to which everything political was constantly referred, a science of politics which proceeded by intuitions, set down maxims and not principles, and understood politics in terms more literary than philosophical would soon be found wanting. Bodin acknowledged his ambition to re-establish political science on fundamental definitions that would give it stability and coherence. The progress of the physical sciences, and of the Cartesian method, could only strengthen this will to discover the organising principles of politics. We have seen how Grotius, Hobbes and Pufendorf expressed their conviction that human organisations could only be understood if certain preliminary axioms were established, from which all the science of politics would be deduced. This underpinned the main idea of the modern law of politics: the social contract.

State-of-nature–contract–republic: this conceptual triad is everywhere present from the beginning of the seventeenth century until beyond the eighteenth, even though it was employed by very different doctrines. Generally, this representation has the same heuristic function everywhere: by enquiring what the condition of man was before the state was instituted, a framework for a fundamental anthropology and sociology is defined. By analysing the process leading to the social contract, and the nature of the republic that results from it, one explains how a political law is articulated with these conceptions of man and society. The social contract does not aim at historical explanation: it sets down hypothetical cases, premises (the state of nature) used to determine by deduction the respective weight of human attitudes, of the power of law and of institutions to measure the fine structure of this subtle arrangement that is political life.

Words were different from one author to another but their consequences were similar: Hobbes' passionate and ambitious man could only give birth to a society of perpetual war with an absolute state as the only outcome. On the other hand, as according to Locke, man, guided by the reason his creator bestowed on him, could form a relatively peaceful society, which needed only to be corrected by the institution of a civil government. The representation of man, society and politics are always logically in phase: the more or less rational and sociable nature of man dictated the clauses of the contract. All the authors of the time believed in the existence of natural laws and rights, even if they did not give the same meaning to these words. For some they were only manifestations of the divine will, drawn out in nature; for others they were more directly set in human reason. The sovereign's autonomy narrowly depends on these conceptions: if laws were only a reflection of Providence, as they were according to Locke, the sovereign is nothing more than an exegete; if, on the contrary, they are defined in a purely civil manner, as according to Hobbes, sovereignty has no limit and all it decrees is law. In all scenarios, the authors admit that, to triumph, natural law and rights need an artificial authority which asserts and protects them. Without this paradigm, one cannot understand the forming of the modern concept of citizenship: in the state of nature the individual is a man, endowed with natural rights; in the civil state he is a citizen-subject whose rights are those that the sovereign gives him.

For all that, the rights of man and those of the citizen are not mutually exclusive; they are connected on several levels revealed by the ambivalence of the modern concept of freedom. Firstly, freedom can be, according to these authors, a natural, pre-civil freedom. In theory it disappears with the institution of the republic, but it can also remain: this is what Spinoza says when he affirms that individuals never completely give up their natural right; Hobbes says so as well when he points out that freedom deploys itself in the silence of the law.

Essentially the freedom of the citizen-subject is the negative of this natural freedom: it is his safety, guaranteed by law. This is a crucial idea of the modern law of politics, where human rights and citizen rights are supposed to meet, but which remains ambivalent. Indeed, having given up his natural rights, man made a common law which ensures his freedom as a citizen. In a sense the citizen replaces the man. At the same time the civil law only endorses the natural right to life and property; it is only an artificial form of the same principle. Therefore, there is between man and citizen a relation of exclusiveness and consubstantiality without this enigma ever really being solved: by becoming a citizen, man did not completely cease to be a man, but he was a man differently, in another capacity. This clever abstraction, which borrows the mechanism of legal logic and neglects historical evasiveness, would be, over the following centuries, the target of many criticisms, whether in the name of tradition (Burke), utility (Bentham) or 'real' history (Marx).

Protection by the law is only one side of political freedom, what is today called 'negative freedom'. The other side emerged in the seventeenth century only as a rough outline that would be refined during the eighteenth century. In Spinoza's democracy, as in the civil government of Locke, a citizen's freedom was also found in the consequence of the consent which gave birth to the republic. When the law was decreed, not by a sovereign to whom sovereignty was entrusted once and for all but by a legislative body which remained perpetually subject to citizens' will, the citizen was positively free: the law he obeyed must always have received, in one manner or another, his approval. Citizenship and sovereignty were then in a relation of completeness: citizens own and exercise collectively (which is the definition of their citizenship) the power to make laws (which is the first manifestation of sovereignty).

At the end of the seventeenth century this idea of citizenship was not widely accepted: for Pufendorf as much as for Hobbes, and for Bodin before them, the privileges which certain citizens enjoyed – voting and public office – were not entitlements to participate in sovereignty but duties that befell certain men by virtue of their social condition, which gave them honour in the social order but did not make them more powerful in the political field.

Nevertheless, it must be noted that for Locke and Spinoza, as for all their contemporaries, citizenship was subordinated to social conditions: not just women but also 'servants', that is all those who depended on others for their subsistence, were systematically excluded. The argument is long-standing and would continue for quite a while: the first theorists of popular sovereignty implied that participation in collective decision-making required a certain degree of rationality and the homogeneity of the social body. The possession of property seemed to be an objective criterion of these conditions. Political exclusion was justified by the cognitive deficiencies of the lower classes and by the threat they presented to the hierarchical harmony of a society organised around property. Later, the evolution of the philosophy of conscience would make it possible to detach political inclusion criteria from this social idea and thus to envisage the popular accession to citizenship that goes with the progress of public enlightenment. And, in parallel, acknowledgement of the growing similarity of social conditions would justify the access of all to the decision-making process. In all cases, contrary to the reappearing idea of *partecipazione* that had its origins in ancient Athens, popular sovereignty rested on a social uniformity that was thought to be an essential condition of the materialisation of a rational collective will.

THE COMPLETE CITIZEN: ROUSSEAU

Taught throughout Protestant Europe, natural law at first ran up in France against the opposition of the specialists in Roman law and the clergy. This lasted until translations by Barbeyrac and the progress of the *Encyclopédia*[45] introduced and popularised the texts of Pufendorf, Grotius and Locke and of their French-speaking disciples.

It is out of this melting-pot that Jean-Jacques Rousseau (1712–78) elaborated his own political law, steeped in theories of natural law but which 'owes more to them by what he rejects than by what he retains of their teaching'.[46] Briefly, Rousseau reformulated the whole contractual theory around two novel ideas: an anthropology which typified man by his conscience rather than by his reason and the idea that the people, as much as the state, far from being 'natural', is a creation of law.[47]

His *Discourse on Inequality* is punctuated by criticisms addressed to Grotius, Hobbes, Locke and Pufendorf at the turn of a note or of a digression. On the whole, he finds fault with the hypothesis of the state of nature for resting on a crude epistemological error: the laws that his predecessors found there are actually 'derived from a range of Knowledge which men do not naturally have, and from advantages the idea of which they can conceive of only once they have left the state of Nature'.[48] In other words, those who, before him, claimed to go back to the state of nature stopped on their way; they described an imperfect, pre-civil society, which came after the real state of nature. The projection of rational rules on to nature was a delusion, because such laws could arise only *after* the institution of society. For Rousseau, the alleged laws of nature were only 'almost arbitrary conformities' (*Discourse on Inequality*, p. 127). When observing rightly, it was obvious that natural men could not be guided by the ambitions that Hobbes attributed to them, since these resulted from social life (p. 127). There was no *natural* selfishness or jealousy since both these feelings could only arise from a social context. In his purest naturality, in his undomesticated isolation, man had only two primary tendencies: the instinct of self-preservation and compassion for others.

A priori, nothing differentiated the natural man from other animals endowed with the same instincts. But Rousseau noticed an essential distinguishing human characteristic. By birth, man has faculties 'in potentiality' (p. 150). Forced to react to situations that arise, man gradually reaches an understanding, his 'reason perfects itself' (p. 142): unlike other animals, man is 'free to acquiesce or to resist', he grants himself the faculty to choose, freedom, and 'it is mainly in the consciousness of this freedom that the spirituality of his soul exhibits itself' (p. 141).

The radical aspect of this innovation cannot be stressed too much: Rousseau shatters the Hobbesian framework and reduces the state of nature to a condition in which individuals are totally isolated and where neither war nor sociability reigns. By nature, men are neither good nor bad since these qualities can only arise in a social relation. A new anthropology develops from this: by entering into social life, man loses his original neutrality, develops his reason, his consciousness of determining his own fate and freedom.

The consequences of this singular idea are fundamental: 'Man is born free'[49] and he could do nothing to change that. His nature was to have the faculty to choose, to be endowed with consciousness: 'To renounce one's freedom is to renounce one's quality as man, the rights of humanity, and even its duties' (*Social Contract*, I, IV, p. 45); to be enslaved was to sink lower than the condition of animals. Rousseau did not deny that man could physically be deprived of his freedom but he claimed that nothing could deprive him of his faculty for choice, the exercise of his free consciousness, even if he was in chains; man could physically 'be forced', said he, but one could not morally 'compel' him.

In the *Discourse on Inequality* (1755), these premises did not take Rousseau beyond the solutions of Locke: he saw the establishment of the political body as the result of a 'true Contract between the People and the Chiefs it chooses for itself' (*Discourse on Inequality*, p. 180). This contract was discussed and revocable, because man remained at all times master of his fate. Only in the *Social Contract* (1762) did he state new 'principles of political law'. As he identified freedom of conscience as the essential feature of human nature, the issue of the constitution of the political body was formulated in new terms. The contract must guarantee not just security or property but also the first natural right, freedom. The political issue then arose in the following terms:

> To find a form of association that will defend and protect the person and goods of each associate with the full common force, and by means of which each, uniting with all, will nevertheless obey only himself and remain as free as before (*Social Contract*, I, VI, p. 49–50).

This is reconciling the irreconcilable: individual freedom and collective security. Rousseau's answer to this owes much formally to Hobbes's contract. One finds in both the same alienation by all of all their rights; the same mutuality and equality of engagement, the same juridical alchemy that has the unity of the body politic proceed from the multitude of men; the same melting of individual wills into a general will. The sole difference, and it is not slight, was that the contract did not bring forth a sovereign that was exterior to it but, by taking effect between individuals 'and the social body of which they would become members',[50] it brought about the mutation of the multitude into a people that was its own sovereign. The social contract was an act through which a shapeless multitude acknowledged itself as a people, proclaimed itself such and decided to give itself its own law. The contract no longer gave birth to a sovereign *for* the people but *to* a sovereign people. The duality between the people and the sovereign, affirmed by his predecessors, was abolished and Rousseau felt the need to redefine the whole of political vocabulary in order to translate this revolutionary concept into words.

> The public person thus formed by the union of all the others formerly assumed the name City and now assumes that of Republic or of Body politic, which its members call State when it is passive, Sovereign when active, Power when comparing it to similar bodies. As for the associates, they collectively assume the name people and individually call themselves Citizens as participants in the sovereign authority, and Subjects as subjected to the laws of the State (*Social Contract*, I, VI, p. 50–1).

The definitions are dazzlingly innovatory and it is worth dwelling on them somewhat, because Rousseau lacks 'the art of being clear to those who are not willing to be attentive' (III, I, p. 82). Generally, Rousseau's contract, like its predecessors, sets out the criterion of the state's legitimacy: he called 'Republic any State ruled by laws' where 'the public interest alone governs' and concluded on a peremptory tone that 'Every legitimate Government is republican' (II, VI, p. 67). The contract produced the negation of the state of nature: it replaced the inequality of strength or of intelligence resulting from nature by the equality of rights (*cf.* I, IX); freedom and safety replaced natural independence and the power to harm others (*cf.* I, VIII, and II, IV). The pact no longer compensated for the defects of nature, it replaced it; it no longer corrected the defects, it eradicated them. Man was no longer a man, he became a citizen.

Rousseau realised all the consequences of this: he said that the transformation 'produces a most remarkable change in man by substituting justice for instinct in his conduct, and endowing his actions with the morality they previously lacked' (I, VIII, p. 53). He took the step that only Machiavelli had taken before by stating that the republic could hold only if the citizens who make it up have it in them to dominate their private passions for the general interest.

> The first [individuals] must be obligated to conform their wills to their reason; the other [the public] must be taught to know what it wills. Then public enlightenment results in the union of understanding and will in the social body, from this union results the smooth cooperation of the parts, and finally the greatest force of the whole (II, VI, pp. 68).

In the purity of its concept, the republic is a society of men governed by collective reason, where individual passions are controlled because each citizen makes the general interest prevail in himself over his individual volition. This is the meaning of the 'general will': it is the common interest that all citizens revere when they follow their reason rather than allowing themselves to be governed by their individual passions. The right to vote laws, which is the supreme mark of sovereignty 'of which nothing can deprive Citizens' (IV, I, p. 122), does not create the general will but reveals it: 'Therefore when the opinion contrary to my own prevails, it proves nothing more than that I made a mistake and that what I took to be the general will was not' (IV, II, p. 124). The citizen filled with egoistic passions is not free, because he feels the general will to be a constraint that oppresses him; but the genuine citizen, who has eyes only for the general will, is free because, while obeying the law as an expression of the general will, he obeys only his virtuous conscience, his reason: 'the words *subject* and *sovereign* are identical correlatives whose idea is combined in the single word Citizen' (III, XIII, p. 111).

Citizenship in Rousseau's meaning was understood as personal ascetic behaviour, which aimed at the self-imposition of public virtues, at seeing the common good as one's own, and at deliberately subjecting oneself to law to avoid being submitted to it.[51] Rousseau felt acutely to what extremes he had gone for his idea of human liberty and his unyielding logic. Examining things by his criteria, he admitted that 'very few nations would be found to have laws' (*The Social Contract*, p. 115) and that the republic as he envisaged it was improbable. And this is without even speaking about democracy, which was only one of the variants of the republic, and of which Rousseau conceded, after Montesquieu, that it required so much of men that it would only be appropriate for a 'people of gods' (III, IV, p. 92). Even if one was satisfied with a republic governed by a king or an elected aristocracy, the idea that the people gave itself its own laws is far from accessible: 'it would require gods to give men laws', it would be necessary to 'feel capable of, so to speak, changing human nature' (II, VII, pp. 69), one would need to allow oneself to believe in this 'chimera' (III, XII, p. 110).

To avoid reducing his principles to a Utopia, Rousseau was forced to specify their practical scope and his conception of citizenship was defined as a result of this concession. The republic was possible only if the people enacted a small number of fundamental laws and entrusted the task of applying them to elected and controlled magistrates. Rousseau did not reduce the republic *to* the sovereign: the sovereign people needed a minister to apply its law. The people had no other choice than to set up by law a government responsible for this subordinate task: ministers and magistrates would be appointed; they would forget they were citizens for as long as they were in office and would 'pass from general to particular acts, and from the law to its execution' (III, XVII, p. 118). It goes without saying that this government remained perpetually submitted to the will of the people, which could revoke its authority to govern when it wished. It was also powerless as soon as the people met to decide by itself. Magistrates did not get any more sovereignty from their status: 'they are only fulfilling their duty as Citizens' (III, XVIII, p. 118).

Despite appearances, in Rousseau's intentions these institutional provisions were not connected in any way to the liberal mechanism of representation, 'that iniquitous and absurd Government in which the human species is degraded, and the name of man dishonoured' (III, XV, p. 114). Sovereignty was the general will, which could not be alienated, divided or represented because if it was no longer immediately itself it existed no longer. Only the implementation of laws could be delegated; if the government claimed to go beyond this, the people was dissolved because sovereignty, by which the people was constituted, was taken from it. This rigorous principle did not prevent Rousseau from acknowledging that the government had the right to decide as long as the people did not meet for that purpose: 'This is not to say that the commands of the chiefs may not be taken for general wills as long as the sovereign is free to oppose them and does not do so. In such a case the people's consent has to be presumed from universal silence' (II, I, p. 57–58). It belonged to the people, when it met, to decide what matters fell within its sovereignty and which ones could be delegated. The principles of Rousseau's political law were not those of a utopian republic, made up of virtuous citizens perpetually assembled to govern themselves; they indicated, in a manner which claimed to be realistic, which constitutional arrangements could ensure that citizens never had the feeling of losing their freedom when they obeyed the law.

In his incidental writings, Rousseau showed how one can be Rousseauian in spirit without being so literally. When he set out to try to give a constitution to Poland, for example, he recalled that laws were not good as such but that they could be as good as possible for the people for whom they are intended (cf. II, VIII); that if one did not necessarily need to leave things as they were, 'nothing should be done to them except with the utmost caution'.[52] He reviewed the laws in force and endeavoured to maintain and strengthen those which were marked by the republican spirit, which encouraged citizens' inclinations towards the general interest. He patiently sought the means of gradually educating the people to the spirit of patriotism. The most important of these means was the division of citizens into three separate classes endowed with increasing powers, a reminder of the idea he had evoked for Corsica. This was a far from absolute popular sovereignty, or direct democracy, and Rousseau shared the bias of his time against the intemperance of the populace.

It was seldom claimed that his ideas had taken institutional form but, here and there, institutions can be seen to carry the imprint of the *Social Contract*. They might have succeeded without him but the strength of Rousseau's ideas plainly contributed to their success. Even more, as we will see, it is the *spirit* of Rousseau that made an imprint on the eighteenth century: the strength of his criticism of 'modern' institutions, his exaltation of civic virtue and patriotism, the dignity he gave back to the people, had a far-reaching resonance.

It remains to be seen if, by modernising natural law, Rousseau managed to solve its ambiguity; if he managed to reconcile, as he hoped, personal freedom and collective safety. His definition of the citizen seems to affirm it: citizenship, the synthesis of sovereignty and subjection, claimed to be the instrument of men's freedom. This is what Kant, clarifying Rousseau, would call autonomy: freedom by obedience to the law given to oneself. Moreover, Rousseau put great emphasis on stating the specific character of the term citizen, which he cherished above all. He declared with nostalgia: 'these two words, homeland and citizen, ought to be erased from modern languages'[53] and vindictively said: 'As if there were citizens who were not part of the city and had not, as such, a share in sovereign power! But the French, who have thought fit to usurp the honourable name of citizen ... have degraded the idea till it has no longer any sort of meaning' (IV, note 35). They confused it, in a 'bad blunder' (*Social Contract*, I, VI, p. 51*n*) with the bourgeois, who is simply the inhabitant of a city.

There is no doubt that Rousseau gave the citizen back his republican nobility, that he recalled that the concept was linked to a constitutional order conceived in such manner that the people could be conceived as the source and measure of all authority. But, by freeing man through the state, did he not put him under the control of a new master? Liberals exploited this doubt and made it the cornerstone of their criticism. In spite of his often monolithic conclusions, Rousseau did not leave man completely powerless vis-à-vis the state. He stated several times that it was 'not permitted to break natural laws by the Social Contract',[54] and that it was appropriate to 'distinguish clearly between the respective rights of the Citizens and of the Sovereign, as well as between duties which the former have to fulfil as subjects, and the natural right which they must enjoy as men' (*Social Contract*, II, IV, p. 61).[55] But he does not say what these natural laws are. Some thought they could affirm that he referred implicitly to those rules of social life which appear to man when he reaches reason – as he leaves the state of nature but before his reason makes him lose his original pity.[56] The laws of nature were those of the 'good savage'; the general will, always right, should make it possible to find these laws and, when the general will is mute, man need only follow his conscience. But it is not enough to declare the irrefutable laws of nature; they need still to be given means of existing. And here Rousseau is quite ambiguous: he claims that the sovereign 'does not and cannot exceed the limits of the general conventions, and that everyone may fully lay out of such of his goods and freedom as are left him by these conventions' (*Social Contract*, II, IV, p. 63);[57] but since the general will prevails against individual wills, it is up to the sovereign to judge of the extent of these conventions.

Ultimately, the only guarantee that the state did not encroach on the rights of man was found in the nature of sovereignty: as the expression of the general will, the law could only consider 'the subjects in a body and their actions in the abstract, never any man as an individual or a particular action' (II, VI, p. 67). It is not sure that this avoids uncertainty: Rousseau wanted to believe that the people would reflect in civil law the precepts of natural law but he did not ensure it would be so. His political morals prohibited him from doing so for, if it pleased the people 'to harm itself, who has the right to prevent it from doing so?' (II, XII, p. 80).

In the second half of the eighteenth century republican language, which Rousseau had given its highest expression, remained marginal: the author of *Émile* and of *La Nouvelle Héloïse* was better known than the author of the *Social Contract*. But the writer nourished a whole generation with his rebellious spirit and nostalgic outbursts; beyond the abstract formulas of his political law, the simple and virtuous image of a free humanity fed fantasies (*Social Contract*, II, IV, p. 63). Diffusely but irresistibly, the republican ethos penetrated consciousnesses. This does not mean that Rousseau's influence on the modernisation of political culture was solely indirect; as a whole, the texts of the revolutionaries carry his mark. The draft *Declaration of the Rights of Man in Society* – prepared by the Committee of the Five under the patronage of Mirabeau in 1789 – had many formulas which seem directly taken from the *Social Contract*: Article 2, 'All body politic receives an explicit or tacit Social Contract, by which each individual puts in common his person and his faculties under the supreme leadership of the general will, and at the same time the body receives each individual as a part'; Article 5, 'the law, being the expression of the general will...'; Article 6, 'the freedom of the citizen consists in being subject only to the law'.[58]

Here the style of Rousseau imposed itself but, more generally, it is all the language of natural law which is popularised. Diderot, examining it in the *Encyclopédia*, reflects accurately the 'gospel according to natural law' at the end of the eighteenth century: 'The use of this word is so familiar', he warns immediately, 'that there is practically no person which is not convinced in himself that the thing is obviously known to him'. He continues by defending the idea of the original freedom of man, of the moral neutrality of his nature, and shows that the content of natural law can only be revealed by the general will, 'the general will is in each individual a pure act of his understanding that reasons in the silence of passions what man can require of his fellow men, and on what his fellow men have the right to require of him' and he self-confidently concludes that 'all the consequences are obvious for the one who reasons'.[59] Natural law is then the lay breviary of the honest man.

AGAINST NATURAL LAW: MONTESQUIEU AND SMITH

The undeniable pre-eminence of this way of thinking should not lead us to believe that it exhausts the range of pre-revolutionary political doctrines, however. Notably, during the same decades, appeared a political paradigm radically separate from the first, which we now call liberalism, and whose influence competed with natural-law theory, during and after the democratic revolutions of the eighteenth century. It was only *a posteriori*, because nineteenth century-liberals found themselves illustrious ancestors in Locke and Montesquieu, that we understand the latter as liberal authors; they did not consider themselves as such. To nineteenth century liberals, Locke and Montesquieu appeared to be the precursors of liberal thinking, insofar as they had been centrally preoccupied by reflecting on how the power of the state could be constrained, so that releasing man from the domination of corporations did not crush his personal freedom.

The theoretical unity of liberalism lies in the following methodological shift: whereas the great authors of the school of natural law had thought about the normative bases of the state as political philosophers, liberals considered the effective functioning of this power as sociologists or political scientists. They neglected hypothetico-deductive reasoning and used history, observation and comparison. And the importance they gave to history inclined them to be cautious towards utopian social visions; feeling the weight of history they realised the price paid in social upheaval for such dreams.

Montesquieu is singular in the French eighteenth century because of his empiricism and his barely veiled contempt for contractualism. In the first book of his treatise *The Spirit of Laws*, he refers laconically to the hypothesis of the social contract[60] but it nowhere structures his argument. He wrote that his intention was to challenge 'the system of Hobbes', which claimed to make 'all the virtues and vices depend on the establishments of human laws' because 'as it would prove that men were born in a state of war, and that the first law of nature is a war of all against all, he [Hobbes] overturns, like Spinoza, all religion and all morality' (*The Spirit of the Laws*, Book II). Montesquieu was among the first to see Hobbes as a representative of political positivism: he reproached him for ignoring natural laws by confusing them with the laws of the sovereign; and for regarding as legitimate only those laws enacted by the prince. Montesquieu believed there were less profane natural laws: 'there are relations of fairness prior to the positive law that establishes them' (I, I, p. 4). He believed there was an order of things that was just in itself, and which human laws should take into account.

Consequently, the philosopher's task was no longer to legitimate a state which gave itself autonomously its own laws but to examine real laws and to infer from them what they reveal of natural laws. This involves understanding how the 'general spirit' of a nation is formed, through subtle interaction in which 'climate, religion, laws, the maxims of the government, examples of past things, mores, and manners' (XIX, IV, p. 310) mingle. This consideration will suggest to the legislator the means of giving laws to the people, so that he could say, like Solon, 'I have given them the best laws they could endure' (XIX, XXI, p. 322). For if one considers that men do not make laws freely, but that they are determined by physical, social and moral conditions, their autonomy is reduced: laws cannot be enacted arbitrarily, these conditions must be taken into account; similarly, the choice of the government depends narrowly on the spirit of the people.

This observation was not new in itself: Machiavelli put much emphasis on the solidarity of laws and morals, considering that the first could not hold without the second, and Bodin undertook a broad survey of the influence of climatic, geographical and other factors on the forming of institutions. This methodological choice is not without axiological consequences: as one is seeking for laws that are adequate for reality, one no longer tries, like natural-law theorists, to think an ideal legitimate order, but rather to legitimate a realistic order.[61]

Montesquieu was convinced, at the end of his long examination of history and of distant peoples, that citizenship can only be synonymous with popular sovereignty under exceptional conditions, and that most political societies must exist in more aristocratic forms of republics. When he described historical democracy, he recalled that 'the laws establishing the right to vote are fundamental in this government' (*The Spirit of the Laws*, II, II, p. 132) and pointed out that 'the right of sovereignty' belonged to the people as a body. But, he added, this was possible only if democracy was supported by its 'principle', virtue. For a people to govern itself, in spite of its turbulence, of its quarrelsome character and of its cowardliness, its members must reach a state of 'self-abandon', the love of their country, of its laws, and the sense of public interest must have been inculcated in them. Also, there must be frugality and the spirit of equality, without going as far as egalitarianism. All this was only conceivable in a small state, whose people had kept simple mores and which was accustomed, through a lengthy education, to submitting their particular interests to the general interest. History has certainly known such peoples, and Montesquieu described their exceptional character all the more minutely as it showed how difficult, or even impossible, it was to find these conditions once more in the era of big states. It was better, to avoid disappointment, not to expect too much of men. Monarchical and aristocratic governments, based respectively on the principles of honour and moderation, were more modest. 'Honour makes all the parts of the body politic move; its very action binds them, and each person works for the common good, believing he works for his individual interests' (III, VII, p. 27). What is more, these governments had a social elite which was able to 'discuss public business' for which 'the people are not at all appropriate' (XI, VI, p. 159). The nobility, by its ancient wisdom and natural moderation, could take up this duty extremely well, but Montesquieu conceded to the people the power to choose its own representatives: 'this is quite within their reach' (XI, VI, p. 160).

Ultimately the precise form of government mattered little to him and one would find it difficult to determine which institutions he preferred. ' I say it, and it seems to me that I have written this work only to prove it: the spirit of moderation should be that of the legislator; the political good, like the moral good, is always found between two limits' (XXIX, I, p. 602). There is no legal theory of the *separation of powers* in Montesquieu's work, in the sense in which modern constitutionalists mean it, but rather a political theory of the *balance of powers*. Like Guicciardini two centuries before, Montesquieu stated that 'power must check power by the arrangement of things' (XI, IV, P. 155). His institutional creations were meant only to ensure that the same social groups did not hold both the power to make laws and to apply them.[62] Montesquieu used a wise nobility as an essential intermediary between the king and the people.[63] According to Montesquieu, the English government fended off despotism but also laid the threatening ghost of democracy; it was a modern form of the 'good regime' that the ancients sought, a mixed regime that neutralised social forces by giving them each a part of authority. The moderation he praised so much was the 'division of power between the powers',[64] the balance that institutions must establish between social forces.

Unlike the contractualists, who use universalist language to cover their elitism, Montesquieu is perfectly clear about his intentions. He even acknowledged that, in his meaning, citizenship was simply submission to the law, and he was annoyed that 'the power of the people has been confused with the liberty of the people' (*The Spirit of the Laws*, XI, II, p. 155). Political freedom was not 'popular sovereignty', it was only 'philosophical liberty' (XII, II, p. 188): it was 'the right to do everything the laws permit' (XI, III, p. 155). It was, for the citizen who benefited from it, 'that tranquillity of spirit which comes from the opinion each one has of his security' (XI, IV, p. 157). Here Montesquieu is very close to the definition of the contractualists: the citizen is free insofar as he is convinced that his fellow-citizens will obey the same laws, so that all feel safe. Citizenship is the antithesis of despotism, government without law 'where no one is a citizen' (V, XXIII, p. 67). Montesquieu broke the conceptual solidarity that, in the Roman republican tradition, in the work of the renaissance civic humanists and in Rousseau, made 'freedom by the law' inseparable from 'political participation'. Whereas for republicans, the citizen guaranteed his rights only by playing an active part in the management of the city, it was the internal organisation of power, the institutionalisation of moderation, which ensured the freedom of the citizen according to Montesquieu.

These lessons would be lengthily meditated on by the men who, in the eighteenth century, led democratic revolutions; and then by those who, in the nineteenth century, endeavoured to make viable the modern republics that the previous century bequeathed to them. The idea that democracy required too much civic virtue for it to be trusted, and that a form of mixed government was preferable, would be cardinal in the drafting of the American constitution. This was likewise true of the axiom that power must check power, subject of much work by European constitutionalists during the eighteenth and nineteenth centuries.

These teachings of Montesquieu were not fundamentally different from the precepts of the contractualists; rather they were understood as attempts to make republics viable, by defining their detailed structure and social conditions. 'Political liberalism' is an extension of republican thought. 'Economic liberalism' on the other hand, whose foundations were laid at the same time, was the most radical negation, until the advent of socialist thought, of modern political law. The British philosophers who were contemporaries of the French natural-law trend laid the foundations of the liberal doctrine of economics (David Hume and Adam Smith are at the forefront of these thinkers) and built their system in clear opposition to the idea of the social contract.[65] Generally speaking, the contract idea, from Grotius to Rousseau, considered man to be governed by his passions, trapped in social conflict and forced, in his own interest, to give up his natural freedom to allow the creation of a public power which allowed the general interest to prevail against individual inclinations. The *raison d'être* of the republic was to substitute an artificial and collective rationality for the irrationality of the multitude's natural instincts; whatever its means, and whatever its size, the republic intended to enforce political virtue upon men.

Montesquieu still thought that way. If he saw the aristocratic republic as a trick of reason, which had the effect that each pursuing his own good also contributed to collective happiness, he saw honour as being the motor of this harmony. The *Fable of the Bees* of Mandeville[66] (1723), had already outlined this argument: it intended to show satirically how, despite preconceptions, personal faults contributed to public benefit. Giving free reign to the selfishness of each made possible the prosperity of all. This axiom of economic liberalism, dazzling in its simplicity, was formulated in different ways over the following decades.

The Scottish philosopher Adam Smith was so convinced he had found in this the key to the understanding of society that he became an economist in order to represent it with all the exactness of mathematics and statistics.[67] In his examination of 'moral sentiments', he observed a natural tendency of men 'the propensity to truck, barter, and exchange one thing for another' (*Wealth of Nations* vol. 1, I, II) and had the intuition that the social problem which had been bothering thinkers for two centuries was simply non-existent. If, as he states, it is true that men's behaviour is guided only by their needs, and if it is equally true that 'man has almost constant occasion for the help of his brethren' (p. 48) social harmony can lie only in the consistency of the system of individual needs. Thus, the very principle of modern society, division of labour, produces this harmony spontaneously, as an 'invisible hand' would. Hence the famous tirade:

> It is not from the benevolence of the butcher, the brewer, or the baker, that we expect our dinner, but from their regard to their own interest. We address ourselves not to their humanity but to their self-love, and never talk to them of our own necessities but of their advantages (p. 48).

By a curious alchemy which has to be described rather than explained, everyone, by pursuing his interests, takes part in the general well-being, the needs of some being identical to the interests of others. It is not necessary to presume, as certain theorists of the social contract did, an inclination of men toward sociability, in order to attain social balance; society can support itself 'from a sense of its utility, without any mutual love or affection (...) by a mercenary exchange of good offices'.[68]

By replacing traditional psychology (which saw men as reasonable animals, inclined towards discord but able to conceive institutional means of neutralising it) by a sensualist vision, Adam Smith and his followers disowned the whole of modern political law, relegating politics itself to the rank of subordinate concerns. Since men responded only to their needs, it was useless to want to make them hear reason; it was enough to ensure that these needs were harmonised.

Liberal political economy wanted to believe in the natural identity of interests and refused artificial harmonisation of men's passions.[69] Pursuing his destruction of republican doctrines, Adam Smith went as far as saying that the state was the main cause of these tensions; the monopolies, corporations and commercial restrictions promoted by the patronising state distorted the game of civil society. This was without mentioning the 'unproductive expenditure' of the state which burdened the wealth of nations (*Wealth of Nations* IV and V).

However, Smith does not completely get rid of political functions. If the nation as he saw it was *essentially* self-sufficient, the state was required to lay down the conditions of the free game of 'civil society'. It was the public power which had to enable 'civil' society to reconstitute itself, by eradicating obstacles in the way. It is also up to the state to assume the tasks which have always been its, and which the nation was unable to manage by itself. The public power must defend the nation against foreign aggressions, administer justice and cover the deficiencies of the market. This permanent hesitation between blind confidence in spontaneous market forces and the awareness of their failings is one of the major characteristics of economic liberalism. It means that the liberal political economy could not abolish the state, even if it envisaged its natural and gradual decay. As the republic required the action of the state in education in order to instil in citizens' hearts the political virtues without which the republic could not survive, the market called for public power to teach consumers the economic rationality on which the market system rested.

Liberals aimed to have the state lose its central role, to reduce it from its constitutive power to a palliative function. In the republican tradition, the state understood in abstract terms was consubstantial to civil society; through the state, civil society existed as a community governed by laws, as opposed to in the state of nature. When laws were set, the state's only limits were the natural and inviolable rights of man. Liberal doctrine overturned this outlook: it stated the perfection of 'natural' society and the superfluous character of the state; at best it recognised, when it could not avoid noticing spontaneous tendencies towards monopoly and the rupture of free competition, a regulating role for the state. But it did not theorise the state's institutions, which were perceived as a pre-existing nuisance; to be opposed at times, a necessary evil at others. It is not surprising that there is no new idea of citizenship in this system. Postulated, in modern language, was a separation of man, who must become another (a citizen responding to public logic) in order to remain himself (a man protected in his natural qualities). Insofar as it reduced the state and laws to a residue, liberal doctrine paid little attention to the idea of citizenship; less, in any case, than it concentrated on the behaviour of individual men seen as producers and consumers. By valuing the 'private' against the 'public', 'civil society' against the state, the original liberalism devalued the very idea of political action. In its original purity, liberalism did not know citizenship. It substituted for it another human condition, which could be called 'civilness' or 'civility', and thereby gave the opposition between the private man and the citizen a new meaning that has lasted until the present day.

NOTES

1   C. Seyssel, *La Monarchie de France* (1515), edited by J. Poujol (Paris, Librarie d'Argences, 1961), I, VIII, p. 115.

2 J. Bodin, *Les Six Livres de la République* (Geneva, 1709). For a translation see *Bodin: On Sovereignty*, edited and translated by J.H. Franklin (Cambridge, Cambridge University Press, 1992).

3 *Cf.* J. H. Franklin, *Jean Bodin and the Rise of Absolutist Theory* (Cambridge, Cambridge University Press, 1973). See also the interpretation of Bodin by Q. Skinner in *The Foundations of Modern Political Thought*, vol. 1 (Cambridge, Cambridge University Press, 1978) pp. 284-301

4 Franklin, *Bodin: On Sovereignty*, book. II, 1, p. 89.

5 *Cf.* C. Vasoli, 'Il metodo ne "La République"', in *La 'République' di Jean Bodin* (Atti del Convegno di Perugia, 14–15 nov. 1980, edited by Florence, L. Olschki, 1981), pp. 3–17.

6 See M. Villey, 'La justice harmonique selon Bodin' in H. Denzer (ed.) *Jean Bodin, Verhandlungen der internationalen Bodin Tagung in München* (Munich, C.H. Beck, 1973), pp. 69–86; and P. Desan, 'Jean Bodin et l'idée de méthode au XVIème siècle' in *Jean Bodin, Actes du colloque interdisciplinaire d'Angers* (Angers, Presses de l'Université, 1985), vol. 1, pp. 119–30.

7 J. Bodin, *Methodus ad Facilem Historiarum Cognitionem* (1566), in *Oeuvres Philosophiques*, tome V, vol. 3, edited by P. Mesnard (Paris, PUF, 1951), p. 350.

8 'We have to see, in any given commonwealth, who has sovereignty in order to determine what its state is', p. 89.

9 On the 'civil rights' of the citizen as opposed to those of foreigners, *cf. Six Livres*, I, 6, pp. 142, 146–147.

10 *Cf.* A. Dufour, 'L'influence de la méthodologie des sciences physiques et mathématiques sur les fondateurs de l'Ecole du Droit Naturel moderne (Grotius, Hobbes, Pufendorf)', *Grotiana* 1980, vol. I, pp. 33–52.

11 *Cf.* R. Tuck, 'Grotius, Carneades and Hobbes' in *Grotiana* 1983, vol. IV, pp. 43–62.

12 H. Grotius, *De Iure Praede Commentarius* (1604), edited by J.B. Scott (Oxford, Clarendon Press, 1950), *Prolegomena*, p. 7

13 H. Grotius, *The Jurisprudence of Holland*, I, pp. 2–3. quoted in R. Tuck, *Natural Rights Theories* (Cambridge, Cambridge University Press, 1979), p. 67.

14 *Cf.* M. Villey, *Le droit et les droits de l'homme* (Paris, PUF, 1983).

15 H. Grotius, *De Jure Praede*, p. 19.

16 *Cf.* R. Tuck, *Natural Rights Theories*, pp. 78–81.

17 H. Grotius, *De Iure Belli ac Pacis, Libri Tres* (1625), translated by F. W. Kelsey (Oxford, Clarendon Press) 1925, vol. II, IV, II, 1, p. 139.

18 T. Hobbes, *The Elements of Law, Human Nature and De Corpore Politico*, edited by J.A. Gaskin (Oxford, Oxford University Press, 1994), XXIX, 8, pp. 180–81.

19 T. Hobbes, *Man and Citizen (De Homine, De Cive)* (Indianapolis/Cambridge, Hackett Publishing, 1991), *De Cive*, I, 2, p. 111.

20 *Cf.* T. Hobbes, *Leviathan*, edited by R. Tuck (Cambridge, Cambridge University Press, 1991), XIII.

21 *Cf.* B. Barret–Kriegel, *L'Etat et les esclaves, Réflexions pour l'histoire des Etats* (Paris, Calman-Lévy, 1979), pp. 65–91.

22 *Cf.* R. Polin, 'Hobbes et le citoyen', in C. Zarka, (ed.), *Thomas Hobbes, philosophie première, théorie de la science et politique* (Paris, PUF, 1990), pp. 327–37.

23 'The freedom of the subject is first of all the safety which results from the reign of the law. It is also, innocent freedom, the freedom to act according to one's wishes in the silences of the law' (*Leviathan*, XXI, p. 152). There is, however, with Hobbes, an exception to the absolute rule of subjection: there remains a single inviolable natural right in the republic, the only one that is logically inalienable because it is the reason for the institution of the state: the right to life. 'When therefore our refusall to obey, frustrates the End for which the Sovereignty was ordained, then there is no Liberty to refuse: otherwise there is' (*Leviathan*, XXI, p. 151). Hobbes was relentlessly logical: the rational man could not at the same time give up his freedom to ensure his survival and accept his own death sentence. His thinking was not affected by the fact that it led him to acknowledge the legitimacy of insubordination in the face of the death penalty or even the refusal to fight for one's country. The citizen-subject broke with his primary nature, replaced his natural being by a political status – safety through law – but he kept against all odds the right to life. *Cf.* L. Strauss, *Natural Right and History* (Chicago, University of Chicago Press, 1959 [1953]).

24 The expressions 'civil state' or 'civil right' are ambiguous owing to their contemporary connotations; for the authors of the seventeenth century, who generally wrote in Latin, the term 'civil' is synonymous with 'politic' and is opposed to 'nature', while we tend today to oppose 'civil society' and the political state.

25 *Cf.* I. Hont, 'The language of sociability and commerce: Samuel Pufendorf and the theoretical foundations of the 'Four-Stage Theory', in A. Pagden (ed.), *The Languages of Political Theory in Early-Modern Europe* (Cambridge, Cambridge University Press, 1987), pp. 253–76.

26 S. von Pufendorf, *De Officio Hominis et Civis*, translated by M. Silverthorm, edited by J. Tully (Cambridge, Cambridge University Press, 1991), II, 5, 8, p. 134.

27 S. von Pufendorf, *De Jure Naturae et Gentium, Libri octo*, 2 vols, edited by J. B. Scott, translated by C.H. Oldfather and W.A. Oldfather (Cambridge, Cambridge University Press, 1934), vol. 2, VII, 2, 20, p. 995.

28 Pufendorf even deprives them of the inalienable rights Hobbes had given them, tells them to give in to authority even in the most unjustifiable situations, that 'must be patiently borne by citizens'. *Ibid.*, II, 9, 1–4, pp. 146–7.

29 B. de Spinoza, 'Letter to J. Jelles, The Hague, 2 June 1674', *Selected Correspondence of Benedict de Spinoza*, edited and translated by R.H.M. Elwes (London, 1884).

30 B. de Spinoza, *Tractatus Politicus*, II, §8, p. 279 in *The Political Works*, edited and translated by A.G. Wernham (Oxford, Clarendon Press, 1958). Henceforth: *TP*.

31 *Cf.* S. Hampshire, *Spinoza* (London, Penguin 1988 [1951]), in particular ch. 5, pp. 134–55.

32 B. de Spinoza, *Tractatus Theologico-Politicus, Tractatus Politicus*, translated and introduced by R.H.M. Elwes (London, Routledge & Sons) XVI, p. 129. Henceforth: *TTP*.

33 *Cf.* TP, XI, §3–4, pp. 114–15 and A. Matheron, 'Femmes et serviteurs dans la démocratie spinoziste' in S. Hessing (ed.), *Speculum Spinozarum 1677–1977* (London, Routledge and Kegan Paul, 1978), pp. 368–86.

34 R. Filmer, *Patriarcha and Other Writings*, edited by J.P. Sommerville (Cambridge, Cambridge University Press) 1991, III, 6, p. 42.

35 J. Locke, *Two Treatises of Government*, edited by P. Laslett (Cambridge, Cambridge University Press, 1988 [1960]), II, 2, §7, p. 271.

36 *Cf.* J. Dunn, *The Political Thought of John Locke: An Historical Account of the Argument of The Two Treatises of Government* (Cambridge, Cambridge University Press, 1969), and J. Dunn, *Locke* (Oxford, Oxford University Press, 1984), pp. 29–36.

37 *Cf.* L. Strauss, *Natural Law and History*, p. 194.

38 *Cf.* in particular, *Two Treatises* II, 16, §192, p. 394.

39 *Cf.* A.J. Simmons, *The Lockean Theory of Rights* (Princeton, Princeton University Press, 1992), particularly pp. 68–101.

40 *Cf.* in particular *Two Treatises*, II, 19, §222, p. 412.

41 *Cf.* B. Kriegel, *Les droits de l'homme et le droit naturel* (Paris, PUF, 1991).

42 *Cf.* S. Goyard-Fabre, 'Souveraineté et citoyenneté dans le libéralisme politique de John Locke' in *Cahiers de philosophie politique et juridique*, Caen, Université de Caen, 1984, no. 4, pp. 137–52.

43 P. Hazard, *La crise de la conscience européenne* (Paris, Boivin and Co, 1961 [1935]), p. 7.

44 *Cf.* P. Hazard, *La pensée européenne au XVIIIe siècle, de Montesquieu à Lessing* (Paris, Boivin and Co, 1946).

45 *Encyclopédia*, edited by Denis Diderot and Jean d'Alembert, was a famous – and controversial – attempt to make a summary of all contemporary knowledge. Many of its articles reflected the rationalist 'enlightenment' attitudes of contributors such as Voltaire and Rousseau. It was seen as a manifesto for a new way of looking at the world.

46 R. Derathé, *Jean-Jacques Rousseau et la science politique de son temps* (Paris, PUF, 1950), p. 52.

47 *Cf.* E. Weil, 'Jean-Jacques Rousseau and his policy' in *Criticism*, 1952, IX/56 pp. 3–28.

48 J-J. Rousseau, 'Discourse on the Origin and the Foundations of Inequality Among Men' (1754), in *The Discourses and Other Early Political Writings*, edited and translated by V. Gourevitch (Cambridge, Cambridge University Press, 1997), p. 126–7.

49 J.-J. Rousseau, *The Social Contract and Other Late Political Writings*, edited and translated by V. Gourevitch (Cambridge, Cambridge University Press, 1997), p. 41.

50 Derathé, *Jean-Jacques Rousseau et la science politique*, p. 223.

51 *Cf.* J. Shklar, *Men and Citizens: A study of Rousseau's Social Theory* (Cambridge, Cambridge University Press, 1969).

52 J.-J. Rousseau, 'Considerations on the Government of Poland', in Gourevitch, *The Social Contract and Other Later Political Writings*, p. 178.

53 J.-J. Rousseau, *Emile, Or, On Education*, Book I, translated by A. Bloom, (Harmondsworth, Penguin Books, 1991).

54 J.-J. Rousseau, *Lettres écrites de la montagne, in Oeuvres completes* (Paris, La Pléïade, 1958), lettre 6, p. 806.

55 *The Social Contract*, II, IV, p. 61.

56 *Cf.* R. Derathé, *Jean-Jacques Rousseau et la science politique*, pp. 165 and 34.

57 *The Social Contract*, II, IV, p. 63.

58 *Projet de Déclaration des droits de l'homme en société du Comité des Cinq* (1789) in L. Jaume (ed.), *Les déclarations des droits de l'homme de 1789 à 1946* (Paris, Garnier-Flammarion, 1989), p. 178.

59 *L'Encyclopédie, ou Dictionnaire raisonné des sciences, des arts et des métiers*, articles chosen by A. Pons, (Paris, Garnier-Flammarion, 1986), 2 vols., v° *Droit naturel*, by Diderot, vol.

1, pp. 333–39.

60 'As soon as men are in society, they lose their feeling of weakness; the equality that was among them ceases, and the state of war begins' this in turn brings about 'the Establishment of laws among men'. Montesquieu, *The Spirit of the Laws*, ed. and transl. by A.M. Cohler, B.C. Miller and H.S. Stone (Cambridge, Cambridge University Press, 1989), Book I, chapter III, p. 7.

61 *Cf.* L. Althusser, *Montesquieu: La politique et l'histoire* (Paris, PUF, 1992 [1959]), p. 9.

62 *Cf.* C. Eisenmann, 'L'esprit des lois et la séparation des pouvoirs' in *Mélanges Carré de Malberg* (Paris, 1933, pp. 190–227).

63 *Cf.* Althusser, *Montesquieu, La politique et l'histoire*, chapter V, pp. 98–108.

64 Ibid., p. 103.

65 *Cf.* J.G.A. Pocock, 'Cambridge paradigms and Scotch philosophers: a study of the relations between the civic humanist and the jurisprudential civilian interpretation of eighteenth-century social thought', in I. Hont and M. Ignatieff (eds.), *Wealth and Virtue: The Shaping of Political Economy in the Scottish Enlightenment* (Cambridge, Cambridge University Press, 1983), pp. 235–52.

66 B. Mandeville, *The Fable of the Bees; or, Private Vices, Public Benefits* (London, J. Tolson, 1728–9).

67 A. Smith, *An Inquiry into the Nature and Causes of the Wealth of Nations* (London, Methuen and Co, 1925) Vol. 1, I, II.

68 A. Smith, *Theory of Moral Sentiments* (Oxford, Oxford University Press) 1976, p. 97.

69 *Cf.* E. Halévy, *La formation du radicalisme philosophique*, vol. 1: *La jeunesse de Bentham*, (Paris, Alcan) 1901, pp. 160 sqq.

chapter four | from theory to politics: citizenship and modern revolutions

For a long time natural law was a critical discourse: to state that the people was the source of all legitimate authority when divine-right monarchies were still the rule; that men have rights by nature, when arbitrary royal power prevailed; and that men are born equal and free, when their submission was assured by the feudal organisation of society; all this was to undermine the established order. The democratic revolutions that took place at the end of the eighteenth century, in America and in France, were felt by their actors to be the beginning of a new era, the overturning of the old order and the start of an unprecedented project of building a new political order from concepts.

The men who made these revolutions understood politics in terms of natural law. They endeavoured to give a more tangible reality and constitutional expression to the concepts of republic, freedom and citizenship, which had been up to then confined to theoretical developments or to a mythical historical past. They felt all the difficulty of instituting the simple idea of freedom by obedience to the law one has given oneself. This supposed major institutional inventiveness: a public power had to be built in such a way that any decision could always be referred to the people as its author. This brought about long and chaotic constitutional debates, which gave citizenship its modern, representative form.

Generally, the concept of 'representative democracy' is everywhere the same and acknowledges, against Rousseau, that citizenship materialises in the choice, the election, of legislators. But this common matrix has major variations: when it comes to describing the way in which the rights of man are articulated with those of the citizen; to institutionalising the links between the citizen and the state; and to organising the various authorities born from sovereign power.

Since 1835, when the young Tocqueville showed his portrait of democracy in America to the French public, it has been traditional to oppose two versions – born from the same doctrinal matrix – of liberal democracy: the American version and the European version (primarily French in fact). It is commonly said that, on the European side of the Atlantic, the state is the unexceedable horizon of politics, the concept under which is subsumed all its grammar. Citizenship is understood as title for the individual's participation in the institutionalised creation of the general will. Freedom is not defined as opposed to the obstacles of public power but in its very movements, which give form to popular sovereignty:

> The respect of the written law, the refusal of the power of judges (like that of the recourse to the legislative power to decide a judicial issue), in short the sovereignty of the law, regulate, much more deeply and durably than political constitutions, the relations of Frenchmen among themselves and determine the experienced contents of their citizenship.[1]

On the other side of the Atlantic, 'government' was still held in suspicion. In the United States, democracy would take the path of 'civil society' and would deploy in the civilised confrontation of interests expected to harmonise themselves naturally, so that the state would be reduced to the supervision of the good development of this autonomous mechanism. Thomas Paine (1737–1809), who was involved in both revolutions, gave the clearest expression of the civil conception of the Americans: 'Society in every state is a blessing, but government even in its best state is but a necessary evil; in its worst state an intolerable one.'[2] An historically self-constituted society, which had to suffer the vexations imposed by the British Crown before declaring its independence and giving itself its own constitution, the American *civil society* was to keep an instinctive mistrust towards any form of governmental authority perceived as a disturbing factor for the natural harmony of interests.

These differences are important, because they will give citizenship very different forms on each side of the Atlantic. But they should not make us forget that the matrix of revolutionary citizenship was identical in both cases: the language of natural law, which had been slowly spreading for over a century and a half, was at that time the natural political vocabulary of the honest man. And on both sides of the Atlantic, the thinkers of the Enlightenment were seeking to reconcile the liberal rights of the individual and the republican freedom of the citizen.

CITIZENSHIP IN AMERICA

The first words of the 1776 Declaration of Independence, which seem directly borrowed from Locke's second treatise, perfectly illustrate the importance of this language in America:

> We hold these truths to be self-evident, that all men are created equal, that they are endowed by their Creator with certain unalienable rights, that among these are Life, Liberty, and the pursuit of Happiness. That to secure these rights, Governments are instituted among Men, deriving their just powers from the consent of the governed. That whenever any Form of Government becomes destructive of these ends, it is the Right of the People to alter or to abolish it, and to institute new Government'.

The institutions that the settlers gave themselves, after the Declaration of Independence, aimed to test in real life the natural-law ideas which were floating around at the time: all the constitutions of the autonomous states reflected, in one manner or another, the related beliefs that all power had to come from the people and not be concentrated in the same hands.

When, a decade later, they became aware of the gaps in the confederation which linked them, the leaders of the thirteen states adopted the opposite attitude to English-style reformists. It was not a matter of correcting outdated institutions while respecting the historical heritage but of creating a new order. The attitude is resolutely republican, as are the references of the authors of the Constitution, who have in mind the exhortations of Machiavelli or Rousseau for *modernisation* or *refoundation* of 'civil society' threatened by *corruption*.[3] In his foreword to his defence of the Constitution, Alexander Hamilton[4] (1757–1804) says that it is about deciding 'the important question, whether societies of men are really capable or not, of establishing good government from reflection and choice, or whether they are forever destined to depend, for their political constitutions, on accident and force' (*Federalist Papers* I). This constituent moment crystallises the fears and aspirations of the American people, guided by its elite: like the civic humanists of the Italian Renaissance, they intend to politically formalise the freedom present in the social order, in order to secure themselves against the dangers brought upon them by the never-ending risks of external wars and internal dissensions.

The republican orientation of American political thought also appears in the choice to write into the Constitution a principle which had never really penetrated English thought, and which was having trouble triumphing over European resistance: popular sovereignty. The refusal of the British model, and the experience of assemblies elected by a broad electorate in most of the states since independence, supported this idea. The Founding Fathers were clear that this was the essence of their government, corresponding to the national temperament: this 'pure and primitive source of all legitimate authority' was the only one which was 'reconcilable with the genius of the people of America' (XXIII, XXXIX).

However this doctrine does not simply repeat the ideas of Machiavelli and Rousseau, according to whom civic 'virtue' must triumph over the private passions of individuals for the common good to take shape. Americans no longer reasoned only in terms of passions. They knew, like Montesquieu and Adam Smith, that modern societies were dominated by the activity of trade, which creates between men feelings other than those that were formerly known as 'passions' and 'ambitions'. The American society, built on trade relations, could not neglect this new sociology.[5] And it was precisely from the confrontation of these two languages, of these two representations of social life[6] – the semantic confrontation of which the French revolution will be another theatre – that American republicanism was born.

The Founding Fathers did not intend to make do with giving a political form to the 'natural' solidarity of interests that Smith described in Europe, but neither did they claim to replace it with mechanisms of 'artificial harmonisation of the wills' as traditional republicans had hoped for. They wished to reconcile both demands, convinced that one could only supply 'by opposite and rival interests, the defect of better motives' (*Federalist* LI). Filled with the ambition of disciplining the dissimilarity of interests seen in daily life, but aware that these were impossible to eradicate, they resigned themselves to making the 'principle of interest rightly understood'[7] the base of their policy.

This difficult synthesis could have been carried out in theory – as Hegel would attempt a few years later – if the concern of the Founding Fathers had not been primarily, if not exclusively, political. Immersed in the concrete difficulties of their time, harnessing themselves to the construction of a constitution, they gave their 'political science' a pragmatic turn. All their inventions were not turned towards principles but towards the material forms principles could take on. Political experience forced them to slip from political philosophy to political science, as would French liberals a few decades later.[8]

To simultaneously lay down the *observation* of the division of society in antagonistic groups and the *requirement* of popular sovereignty entails stressing a major risk: how to prevent citizens dividing into two camps and refusing to agree on a common good, how to prevent factions from ruining the unity of the republic? Eager for past experiences and showing regard for the classics, the authors of the Constitution dug through the darkest corners of history and used the teachings of past masters to find lessons that could be transposed to their own situation. In vain: America was a new political entity to which no past experiment could apply *mutatis-mutandis*; invention was necessary. The Founding Fathers would invent with unquestionable delight.

Firstly they laid down an essential axiom: following Montesquieu, they stated that the democratic form of popular sovereignty was impossible in a vast and complex country because it opened the door to the tyranny of the majority. The republic, on the other hand, had institutions which helped to prevent this threat:

> The two great points of difference between a democracy and a republic are: first, the delegation of the government, in the latter, to a small number of citizens elected by the rest; secondly, the greater number of citizens, and greater sphere of country, over which the latter may be extended.(X)

Representation and geographical extent introduced between the people and the 'government' a mediation which made it possible to modernise the republic: thanks to these two instruments the submission of power to the people could be retained while avoiding the instability of popular moods. The effect of representation was universally known, Cicero had already described it and Montesquieu had reiterated his arguments:

> To refine and enlarge the public views, by passing them through the medium of a chosen body of citizens, whose wisdom may best discern the true interest

of their country, and whose patriotism and love of justice will be least likely to sacrifice it to temporary or partial considerations.(X)

The whole political science of the Founding Fathers aimed to put the people's representatives 'under circumstances favorable to deliberation, and to a judicious combination of all the reasons and inducements which were proper to govern their choice', (LXVIII) so that divergent passions and conflicts of interests were sublimated. The extent of the country, its social complexity, the great dispersion of conflicts contributed to this: if the Republic included 'a greater variety of parties and interests; you make it less probable that a majority of the whole will have a common motive to invade the rights of other citizens' (X).

This swept away the traditional objection according to which a republic was not viable in a big state: the multiplication of disagreements reduced their harmfulness; it made the forming of coalitions likely to impose their will on minorities impossible. The fragmentation of civil society along many lines, the multiple loyalties of citizens to their religious faiths, their regions, their professions, their social groups, far from being threats to concord, guaranteed social harmony: a 'pluralist' society without a single a dominant cleavage pitting one half of the people against the other needed consensus, since it was in the interest of each 'minority' to respect the others in order to be respected by them. Where the French would try to forget social memberships and promote the formal equality of citizens, Americans valued diverse identities, seen as so many guarantees against the permanent danger of factionalism.

A second problem arises however: if the constitution ensured power was relatively independent of changeable factional enthusiasms, it must not be emancipated to the point where the people no longer had a hold on it. It was necessary to prevent power from acquiring autonomous strength once it was invested by the people in their representatives and disencumbered of the pressures of sectoral interests. The solution to this essential question found by the authors of the Constitution consisted in, as Tocqueville would say, 'dividing power' (*Democracy in America*, I, I, V, p. 52). This involved, first of all, in accordance with the precepts of Montesquieu, distributing powers between various bodies; authorities that were independent from one another and which counterbalanced each other so that 'power stops power'. Moreover, the Americans extended this principle well beyond what European doctrines had conceived. Classical theorists assigned no proper role for the power to judge, the 'judicial power': for Locke and Rousseau it was a part of the executive power and Montesquieu, although he stated its organic autonomy, considered that it was 'in some fashion, null'.[9] The French tradition, obsessed by the pre-eminence of the legislative power, or pushed around by the excesses of its executive power, would accept the independence of the judiciary only with strong reservations. Generally in Europe, guarantees were granted to *magistrates* (irrevocability) without the *judicial power* being fully considered as a 'power' on the same level as the two others.[10] The Americans, on the other hand, tried to guarantee its autonomy. They stated that, by giving the judges the task of applying, and therefore of interpreting, the law, one did not encroach on the people's sovereignty for three reasons: firstly because this was not really a power since it was subjected to respect for the law; secondly because judges were indirectly chosen by the people; finally because judges' autonomy lasts only 'during good behavior' (*Federalist*, LXXVIII). Besides, the Americans did not give judges and courts the simple power of applying the law to cases in point but awarded them the right of checking the constitutional conformity of laws. The Constitution being the act of the people, the supreme manifestation of its sovereignty, it had to prevail against the will of the people's representatives, whose authority existed only *by virtue* of this Constitution.

> It is not otherwise to be supposed, that the Constitution could intend to enable the representatives of the people to substitute their WILL to that of their constituents. It is far more rational to suppose, that the courts were designed to be an intermediate body between the people and the legislature, in order, among other things, to keep the latter within the limits assigned to their authority (*Federalist*, LXXVIII).

The idea of controlling the legislative power, in the name of higher values and in particular in the name of those found in the Bill of Rights, was thus laid down, even if it would take practically a whole century for this to be actualised. This would result in increasing the pluralism of American citizenship, by regarding the judicial process as one of its normal paths: if judges emanated from the people, and if they could oppose the other representatives of the people, the legislators, the judicial path was one of the forms of popular sovereignty, one way for the governed to check their governors, a method of citizenship.

The authors of the American Constitution were not satisfied with dividing the *functions* of power between competing bodies; they also added a *geographical* division of public power. This was incongruous for a European spirit formed with the idea of the indivisibility of sovereignty; but in America it answered a material requirement: since the construction of a federal government could not abolish the pre-existing states, a division of sovereignty had to be conceived. Moreover, as Hamilton would eventually say to refute *a priori* any theoretical objection,

> To argue upon abstract principles that this co-ordinate authority cannot exist, is to set up supposition and theory against fact and reality. However proper such reasoning might be to show that a thing OUGHT NOT TO EXIST, they are wholly to be rejected when they are made use of to prove that it does not exist contrary to the evidence of the fact itself. (*Federalist*, XXXIV)[11]

The constitution combined features of federations and states, mixing federal techniques for the distribution of competences and the nomination of members of Parliament and the attributes of unitary states in the means of exercise of the powers and the hierarchy of norms. Thus, the Constitution of the United States escapes traditional classifications and to understand it one must 'bend the rules of logic' (*Democracy in America*, I, I, VIII, p. 122), according to Tocqueville's expression. The Americans did not bother with terminological issues and were satisfied with calling the republic they made 'compound'. The fact that two degrees of public power could share the same attributes of sovereignty did not appear illogical to them, since the situation had existed, in practice, even before independence, when the powers of the metropolis and those of the colonies superimposed themselves,[12] and since in any event one could not maintain the confederal structure nor centralise to the point of depriving the states of any legal existence. The people was the exclusive holder of sovereignty and the various degrees of power were only the various agents and representatives of the people. According to the Founding Fathers, this innovation strengthens the guarantees recommended by political science to submit the government to the people:

> Power being almost always the rival of power, the general government will at all times stand ready to check the usurpations of the state governments, and these will have the same disposition towards the general government. The people, by throwing themselves into either scale, will infallibly make it preponderate (*Federalist*, XXVIII).

This dualisation of public power contributes to the mediating of the relation between the people and power. In the American Republic, 'popular sovereignty manifests itself everywhere and nowhere':[13] all authorities emanate, in one manner or another, from an election – whether executive, legislative or judiciary, whether national or federal. To some extent, sovereignty is 'delocalised'; it is assigned no proper place. Thus, the Americans claimed to have abolished 'authority within the body politic of the Republic' by diffusing it in the social body, by disembodying it, in order to banish the tyranny whose spectre they always saw in sovereignty.[14] The defenders of the Constitution were convinced they had found the only formula that would make it possible to reconcile republican requirements with the conditions of their country:

> In the compound republic of America, the power surrendered by the people is first divided between two distinct governments, and then the portion allotted to each subdivided among distinct and separate departments. Hence a double security arises to the rights of the people. The different governments will control each other, at the same time that each will be controlled by itself (*Federalist*, LI).

In the same way that these doctrines were variants of the republican paradigm, the American conception of citizenship was another version of the concept formed in Europe. The word 'citizenship' was no more widespread in America at that time than it was in Europe: when Madison spoke of *citizenship*, he meant above all nationality in the legal sense of the term. It was only incidentally that he mentioned the political rights covered by this status (*cf. Federalist*, LI). The American specialists of public law knew the word, as did the British at the time (see Bentham), and its meaning remained very general: Thomas Paine called the 'right of citizenship' the 'civil' rights, i.e., those that the republic confers on individuals in addition to their 'natural rights',[15] in full accordance with the meaning given to the word in the republican tradition. Coming straight from European political theory, the American concept of citizenship takes with it all the classical republican vocabulary. This is evident in the famous decision of the Supreme Court, in the middle of the nineteenth century, *Dred Scott v. Sandford* (1857):

> The words 'people of the United States' and 'citizens' are synonymous terms, and mean the same thing. They both describe the political body, who, according to our republican institutions, form the sovereignty, and who hold the power and conduct the government through their representatives. They are what we familiarly call the 'sovereign people', and every citizen is one of this people, and a constituent member of this sovereignty.[16]

In these abstract terms, American citizenship was no different from its European cousin – except that it evoked the 'government' rather than the state, federal conflicts having resulted in keeping the substantive 'state' for the federate entities. As in France, citizenship in America evoked all at the same time the republican ideal, civic participation, membership of the nation and aspiration to equality – while maintaining in fact deep inequalities and racial exclusion.[17]

The principal difference between the two versions lay in the way in which the idea of popular sovereignty was institutionalised. In France, it would be necessary to create an abstract body, the 'Nation', to portray the form of popular sovereignty: composed *in fact* of members of Parliament, it would *in right* be considered consubstantial to the people which elected it. It was stated that citizens were free because the law was, through this artifice, their doing. The Americans elaborated a citizenship which fulfilled the same function: powers were functionally and spatially divided but they all stemmed from a single source, the people. Whether he elected the president or members of parliament, governors or senators, whether he demanded from a court compensation for his rights, the individual acted out his citizenship. The American Republic formalised freedom in a resolutely pluralist way.

Its greatest particularity by the standards of the European tradition probably lies in its spatial duality: in the composite republic, citizenship is double, the citizen simultaneously depends on his State and on the Union, he is the subject and the author of their respective laws. Tocqueville elegantly described the political and cultural characteristics of this double citizenship, such as it was registered in the everyday political life of the United States:

> The sovereignty of the Union only touches men through a few great interests; it represents an immense, distant native country, a vague and indefinite sentiment. The sovereignty of the states in a way envelops each citizen, and takes

him over daily in detail. It takes charge of guaranteeing his property, his freedom, his life; at every moment it influences his well-being or his misery. The sovereignty of the states depends on memories, on habits, on local prejudices, on the selfishness of province and family, in a word, on all the things that render the instinct for one's native country so powerful in the heart of man (*Democracy in America*, I, I, VIII, p. 158).

In other words, the citizenship of the state was a daily political practice which brought an emotional attachment, while the citizenship of the Union was a formal state, and covered abstract questions which were likely to arouse only a rational attachment. But one completed the other: 'Each citizen of the United States so to speak carries over the interest that his little republic inspires in him into love of the common native country' because he knew that by defending the Union 'he defends the common prosperity of his district' (*ibid.*, p. 153). Both statuses were not only compatible, they were complementary: the citizenship of the Union allowed the prosperity and the safety without which the citizenship of the State would not be possible. Here also, the difference from the conceptions carried by the French revolution are obvious: whereas the French put all their efforts into stating the unity of the republic and organizing the hierarchy of authorities, so that, in the last resort they all referred back to the legislative centre, the Americans developed the spatial division of power as a guarantee of the freedom of citizens and as a vector of the patriotism essential to republican freedom. Federalism was more than a technique of public law, it wanted itself to be a political theory closely connected with the republican aspiration.

American citizenship was daily reflected in the 'anxious activity' that Tocqueville perceived in American civic life; it was deployed through all the aspects of social life, from the local to the federal level, and used all the paths which were open to it: electoral, judicial or simple informal pressures, through clubs, the press and soon the lobbies which were the substance of this pluralist civil society. And whenever anyone wonders about the way to revitalise the American Republic, inspiration seems to be sought in this original dispersion. This was the case in 1927, when John Dewey claimed that

In its deepest and richest sense a community must always remain a matter of face-to-face intercourse...The Great Community, in the sense of free and full intercommunication, is conceivable. But it can never possess all the qualities which mark a local community. It will do its final work in ordering the relations and enriching the experience of local associations.[18]

This was still the case in the 1990s, when most political theorists considered that 'self-government works best when sovereignty is dispersed and citizenship formed across multiple sites of civic engagement'.[19]

CITIZENSHIP IN THE FRENCH REVOLUTION

The essence of the concept of citizenship, freedom by obedience to the law that one has given oneself, membership in a sovereign people, would be stated in identical terms by the French Revolution. And, like in the United States, the major problem of the French theorists of the revolution would be to make compatible the statement of 'popular sovereignty' and the preservation of certain social hierarchies.

On the eve of the revolution, the concept of citizenship did not contain the idea of civic participation. In his article '*Citizen*' in the *Encyclopédia*, Diderot (1713–84) stressed only the protective dimension covered by the title of citizen. He was opposed to Hobbes, who had used citizen as a synonym of subject, indicating that if both 'are equally governed', the first is 'by a moral being and the other by a material person'.[20] Citizenship, before the French Revolution, was understood in Montesquieu's terms: it was the benefit of the law, the contrary of 'tyranny'. The idea that citizenship also entailed participation in popular sovereignty had not yet penetrated the ordinary meaning. The *Cahiers de Doléances*, written on the eve of the revolution, revealed the same connotations: one finds references to the 'different classes of citizens', to the relations between the 'orders of citizens', mixing a term that evoked equality of status with the organicist and corporatist representations of the old order.[21]

However, the modern concept of citizenship, resolutely egalitarian and inseparable from the idea of popular sovereignty, spread on the eve of the revolution. Condorcet (1743–94) gave, in 1788, a rigorous expression of it, which is one of its rare systematic definitions:

By citizenship, one means the right bestowed by nature on every man who lives in a country to contribute to the formation of the rules which all the inhabitants of this country will obey in order to maintain the rights of all, and of those to which their common actions are submitted to ensure the first set of rules and thus uphold general security and peace.[22]

The perfect syllogism which is at the centre of the concept of citizenship, as it was formulated by Rousseau, is reiterated in constitutional language: men have rights by nature; common rules must be stated and enacted by a public power, to guarantee them; these rules can be enacted only by the holders of these rights themselves.

Condorcet specified, in his draft declaration of rights published in February 1789, the egalitarian scope of this concept: it was not enough that all citizens had the same right to vote, their votes must also have the same weight.

All citizens must equally enjoy the rights of citizenship; consequently all must have equal influence in the part of the establishing of a public power and in the making of the laws that each citizen immediately takes part in; and each must equally contribute to the election of the representatives in charge of exercising the other part of these functions, and be equally eligible to the office of representative.[23]

This meant, during the pre-Revolutionary period, contesting the doctrine of the 'state of orders', which organised the political representation not of citizens themselves but of the 'orders' to which they belonged – nobility, clergy or third estate (the bourgeoisie). This practice had a double consequence: first it left aside the great mass of those who belonged to no order; then it gave the privileged orders of the nobility and the clergy a predominant weight over the influence of the third estate. Few would oppose the first form of exclusion by calling for the granting of citizenship to the universality of male subjects.[24] The third estate, by abolishing the society of orders, would register the equality of citizens in positive law; but it would cross-breed this principle with hierarchies which preserved its own political supremacy.

The Abbé Sieyès (1748–1836), whose political role and intellectual influence were decisive in the 'legal revolution'[25] that overthrew the *ancien régime*, embodied this ambivalent posture. In his pamphlet 'What is the third estate?' the abbot gave a particular definition of citizenship: he first adopted the republican idea according to which the citizen was defined by his rights and not by his prerogatives: 'Freedom does not derive from privileges. It derives from the rights of citizens – and these rights belong to all'.[26] He then deduced from this, in very rigorous logic and in pure political provocation, that all those who were privileged were excluded from the common order, and on the basis of the active rights of citizenship, 'since social unity is attainable only through common characteristics, a right to legislate inheres only in the common capacity'.[27]

Sieyès intended to entrust the task of representing the nation to 'available classes'; 'and like everyone else I call 'available' those classes where some sort of affluence enables men to receive a liberal education, to train their minds and to take an interest in public affairs. Such classes have no interest other than that of the rest of the People'.[28] The abbot thus reformulated the traditional arguments of political exclusion and forged a doubly representative concept of citizenship: the identity of interest between the people and the *petit bourgeois* destined the latter to represent the masses *socially*, as voters chose those who would represent them *politically*. The genius of Sieyès was to reconcile the two contradictory requirements of the century: the statement of the equality of citizens and the safeguarding of the social hierarchy.

This skilful balance was moulded in the terms of a concept that was subject to dense semantic investments at the time: the 'Nation'. Up until the middle of the century, the term had only had a specialised meaning, the one it was still given by Montesquieu, designating the active and thinking fraction of the people, what we would now call the elite.[29] Since 1750, its meaning had widened; the Nation had become the name that the third estate gave itself, assimilating itself to the people.[30] Sieyès formulates most of his social theory under this category and the meaning he gives to the word spreads in the political vocabulary of his time.

He first says that the nation is none other than the fatherland, 'generality of citizens'[31] and it is known that he sets aside those who, because of their exceptional status and privileges, do not belong to the 'generality'. However, the observation of the reality of a country as large as France shows the illusory character of the myth of the general will.[32] Practical reason forces one to recognise that the general will can only be expressed through the artifice of representation. Sieyès indissolubly connects, as did the authors of the American Constitution, the idea of sovereignty and the idea of representation: laws could have no other origin than the nation, but the nation could give itself laws only through its representatives. The meaning of the word was divided in half, the Nation was simultaneously, in its general and abstract meaning, all the citizens, and in its specialised and actual meaning, the body of representatives; French constitutional law would borrow this artifice from Sieyès to identify the actual will of the national assembly with the rightful will of the nation.

The concept of citizen was affected by this specialisation of the term: in theory it still meant all who were subject to the law. But it also meant, *de facto*, the holder of political rights, the citizen who was 'representable'. The similarity of interests of certain citizens (the 'available classes') was the basis for the legitimacy of their call for 'political rights' and gave the citizen 'the capacity to be represented'.[33]

In his draft declaration, drawn up in July 1789, after the third estate had done away with the old order but before it had replaced it by a representative constitution, Sieyès used this idea and gave it, by means of a 'reasoned presentation of the rights of man and of the citizen', a univocal expression by the opposition between active and passive citizens:

> All the inhabitants of a country must enjoy the rights of passive citizenship: all have the right to the protection of their person, their property, their freedom, etc., but all do not have the right to take an active part in the forming of public authorities, all are not active citizens… All can enjoy the privileges of society; but only those who take part in the public enterprise are the true stockholders of the social company'.[34]

This modern commercial metaphor brought back into the light a conviction as old as politics itself. For a long time, the argument had hidden only a mistrust of the intellectual abilities and moral moderation of the lower classes. For Sieyès, as in the whole of the liberal tradition, it acquired a second pretext: the conviction that politics organises interests and that only those who, precisely, have an interest can take part. This belief led him to create a distinction in the very concept of citizenship: as a title it is universal, but as a right it is limited to those who have the capacity necessary to its exercise. The dissociation of the active and of the passive citizen marks this shifting of the socio-political border. The myth of the representative nation, introduced as a mediation between the physical mass of the people and the state, would be at the centre of the constitutional tribulations of France, and would long continue to make the statement of the equal dignity of citizens compatible with the preservation of forms of democracy based on capacity or census (the amount of tax paid that was required in order to get voting rights).[35]

In fact, the rupture with the old order happened first by the overturn of its constitutional order. Faced with the thundering revolt, the king turned to tradition to find a political answer: he decided to assemble the Estates-General, to let the representatives of the three orders expose their complaints. This was still the framework of absolute monarchy, where subjects were heard only if they presented themselves separately, according to the role their order gave them. But the third estate, which, according to the famous expression of Sieyès, had hitherto counted for nothing while it was all, intended to become something. It focused its dissent on a question whose technicality hardly dissimulates its fundamental political scope: the method of voting within the Estates-General. If they were forced to vote by order, the third estate, which represented the large number of the bourgeoisie, would be minimised compared to the nobility and the clergy; therefore this feudal method must be got rid of and the weight of each representative should be made equivalent by using the vote *per capita*. This meant that instead of making the orders sit separately, they were assembled. The third estate decided to materialise this change by checking the powers of the delegates in common. Some representatives of the lower clergy and of the liberal aristocracy joined forces with them and the delegates could legitimately consider that they accounted for, according to the expression of Sieyès, 'the ninety-six hundredths of the Nation' and declared themselves a 'National Assembly'. The legal revolution was achieved: the state based on orders gave way to the representative state; an atomist conception of society made up of equal citizens replaced the organicist conception of hierarchical orders. A political revolution completed the overthrow: King Louis recognised this National Assembly, its right to agree to taxation and to guarantee the protection of public freedoms. The absolute monarchy became constitutional, and the Assembly marked this change by immediately declaring itself constituent, and committing itself to translating the change in the balance of power into a fundamental text. As from this moment the assembly had become the major political player and held the king in check. It assumed the major mark of sovereignty, the power to make laws, within which all other powers, in the legicentrist tradition inaugurated by Bodin, were subsumed. And it used this power, making a number of laws that deeply transformed the old order and gave birth to the modern French Republic.

The work of destruction of the old order had to be finished first. It was not enough to have abolished the Estates-General, the remaining power of the orders in the social organisation still had to be eradicated. Sanctioning the popular revolts, the Parliament abolished, during the famous night of August 4th, all the privileges that subjected certain individuals to the patrimonial sovereignty of others: tithe, forced labour, and other personal constraints were destroyed; hunting rights and private hunting grounds, seigneurial justice and venalities disappeared; the same went for the privileges and immunities of the provinces, the cities or the corporations, and soon those of the Church. All private individual powers, feudal residues that the king had never been able to abolish and which limited the extent of his power, yielded to the determination of the National Assembly, leaving in their place the vacuum of a broad territory with no internal borders, a society with no formal hierarchies. A new administrative organisation would take its place, which would replace the partial, interlaced and competing authorities with a majestic pyramidal construction: the territory divided into departments, districts, cantons and towns, which, after an unfruitful phase of decentralisation, would be brought back to the central authority; justice would be reformed according to the same rules of uniformity and hierarchy. All the intermediate bodies that the old order set up between the subjects and the state vanished, to leave face to face only the citizen and the state, connected by an administrative structure that diffused the central authority into the furthest recesses of the territory. The French revolution 'achieves the individualist principle in the area of actual institutions'.[36] It expressed this with the greatest clarity by a solemn declaration, which appeared on the front of the constitution: 'Men are born and remain free and equal in rights'.

The Declaration of the Rights of Man and of the Citizen, adopted on August 26th 1789, registered in positive law the principles of natural law, and the individualism that was the basis of it. The members of the National Assembly were convinced, like the political and intellectual elite which had brought into being the Bill of Rights of the American colonies ten years previously, that natural rights had to be declared to be guaranteed. The rights inherent to nature, written in man, had to be reflected in a text of positive law to be constraining for men and power. They did not claim to invent these rights, to constitute them, but, more modestly, as the preamble to the Declaration says, 'to recognise and declare them'. These civil rights did not *replace* natural rights, they *expressed* them; man did not cease being man when he became citizen, as Rousseau thought, and the title of the Declaration intended to underline this by giving these rights to man and citizen simultaneously.[37]

This duality reflects the logic of contractualist thought: man has to be made citizen, without ceasing to be a man, in order to protect his natural rights. The legal fiction of citizenship was essential to the protection of human rights. Without it, men were condemned to the war of all against all which governed the state of nature; in a contract that would civilise them entirely and do away with their quality of man, they would trade their natural dependencies for subordination to the state. The tension between man and citizen was necessary: the citizen was protected from his fellow men by the state, man was protected from the state by his natural rights. This tension is not without difficulties: republicans would continuously fear that the part of man which escaped the law allowed the reintroduction of the natural inequality that citizenship claimed to abolish; while liberals would be wary of a law which, while claiming to free man from private domination, placed him under a public constraint.

The authors of the Declaration claimed to establish a virtuous circle between these two identities. 'The aim of all political association is the preservation of the natural and imprescriptible rights of man' says Article 2. This radically consecrates individualism: whereas the American Bill of Rights evoked among the aims of the republic the 'common good', the French Declaration ruled out this collective purpose to focus only on the individual and his rights.[38] The tool that synthesised the law and the state, which guaranteed that the state had no other purpose than to protect the law, was the law, the 'expression of the general will' according to the Rousseauian terms of Article 6. Since 'The principle of all sovereignty resides essentially in the nation' (Article 3) or, what is the same, in the legicentric conception, since 'Every citizen has a right to participate personally, or through his representative, in its foundation' (Article 6), the law would inevitably guarantee the rights of man. The citizen who gave himself his own law could not reasonably encroach on the rights of the man he was as well. The authors of the Declaration were convinced, as was Rousseau, that the principle of national sovereignty ensured in itself that the law would respect rights; in return, human rights being protected, 'the acts of the legislative power as well as those of the executive power', says the preamble, will be 'more respected'. The rights of man strengthened the effectiveness of the law, which in turn protected rights, in a perfect virtuous circle.[39]

Their great confidence in this mechanism – which was also, on the part of the members of the National Assembly whose role it is to legislate trust in their own moderation – prevented the authors of the Declaration from perceiving the risks concealed behind this tension. They had clearly seen, as Mirabeau stated during the preparatory debates, that the law and rights could be rivals: 'a pitfall that all the declarations of rights will come up against, is the quasi-impossibility of avoiding encroaching on the legislation, be it by maxims'.[40] Moreover, it is significant that he feared that it was rights that would curb legislative power and not that legislative power would transgress rights. This shows that members of the assembly did not for one moment doubt the temperance of the law, to the point of entrusting legislators the responsibility for determining the scope of rights: Article 4 allowed them to fix the boundaries of freedom in general; Article 10 declared freedom of opinion and of confession but subordinated them to respect for the public order defined by the law; in the same way, Article 11 allows the law to limit freedom of expression.

The authors of the Declaration did not think that the law itself could violate rights. Article 5 of the Declaration, stating that 'The law can only prohibit such actions as are hurtful to society', seemed moreover to trace around the individual the contours of a private sphere in which the law would not be involved – although the interpretation of 'actions hurtful to society' remained open. Having given themselves legislative power, in a constant battle against the king, the authors of the Declaration feared executive power and its subordinates but were not wary of themselves. This is why they stipulated that 'Society has the right to require of every public agent an account of his administration' (Article 15) and decreed that 'A society in which the observance of the law is not assured, nor the separation of powers defined, has no constitution at all' (Article 16). All that was needed was to ensure that all authority be subjected to the law to prevent it from violating rights; the law itself could only, almost by definition, guarantee these rights. The constitutional organisation, which would divide power and make the National Assembly predominate, would be enough, they thought. Their conviction was so strong that

Article 16 was adopted practically without discussion.[41] And as to the Constitution of 1791, it would only state in its fundamental provisions: 'The legislative power will not pass laws that undermine and hinder the exercise of civil and natural rights'. But no institutional guarantee would be established to give form to this principle, the provision being consequently ineffective; since the same legislative power was also invested with the power to regulate the use and the modalities 'and consequently, in fact, the very consistence of these rights'.[42]

Condorcet was one of the rare men of his time to perceive the danger of this assertion. In his draft Declaration of Rights of 1793, he reaffirmed that the 'social guarantee', i.e. the respect of rights for which society was established, rested first on 'national sovereignty' (Article 25).[43] He added, still mainly aiming at the executive power, that 'A social guarantee can not exist where the limits of political functions are not clearly defined by the law, and where the responsibility of every public agent is not assured' (Article 29). By this, he laid down the principle of what would later be called the 'legal state', in which all authority was subjected to respect for the law: if the law did not transgress the rights of man, all holders of power, subjected to the law, were prevented from attempting to do so. But Condorcet also seems to have perceived the insufficiency of these guarantees. He indeed required that citizens be given a 'legal means of resisting oppression' (Article 31) and listed among forms of oppression: violation of the law by public servants; arbitrary acts that violated rights against the expression of the law; and also – and this testifies to his suspicion towards the legislator's infallibility – cases where 'a law violates the natural, civil and political rights it must guarantee' (Article 32). Doubt of the rectitude of the law was creeping in and opening the way to the idea that there should be institutional mechanisms for the control of the constitutionality of laws.

To solve this contradiction, it would be necessary to invent the concept of the 'rule of law'. This meant first that one acknowledged the boundaries of legislative sovereignty. Liberals such as Constant would work on this, stating the primacy of personal freedom over laws: 'At the point where independence and individual existence begins, the jurisdiction of sovereignty ends'.[44] But in particular a means of applying this principle would need to be invented because, as Constant clearly saw:

> All the constitutions which have been given to France guaranteed the liberty of the individual, and yet, under the rule of these constitutions, it has been constantly violated. The fact is that a simple declaration is not sufficient; you need positive safeguards.[45]

According to Constant, these safeguards were to be found in the freedom of the press, the responsibility of ministers and public officials, the formality of legal procedures and the existence of broad political representation. But even these were preventive guarantees that, once again, would not prove sufficient. Only empirically, after painful political experiments, would it be understood that the rule of law was complete only if 'the Constitution determines in last resort and guarantees the individual rights of the citizens that must remain out of the legislator's reach'.[46] And it would still be necessary to understand that citizens must be given the means to have checked and sanctioned *a posteriori* violations of human rights by the legislator that could always occur, despite everything. It was only when the control of the constitutionality of laws by autonomous and supreme judicial bodies, guardians of the constitution and in particular of declarations of individual rights, was accepted, at the end of a long and difficult path for legicentric political cultures,[47] that the rule of law would finally be institutionalised, reconciling man and citizen.

The switch from a state based on orders symbolised by the Estates-General to a representative state centred on the National Assembly; the elimination of all hierarchies and feudal privileges, which placed men under the direct control of the law; the Declaration of the Rights of Man and of the Citizen, which subordinated the law and the state to natural laws, all signed the 'death certificate of the *ancien régime*'. Modern citizenship, understood as submission to the rule of a law stemming from the Nation, was translated into real institutions, even if Revolutionary France had some hesitation in granting these civil rights to religious and ethnic minorities.

The other aspect of the modern idea of citizenship, participation in the exercise of popular sovereignty, was only institutionalised after further objections. If it claimed to balance man and citizen, the Declaration appears all the same to be more anxious to protect the first than to promote the second. By giving political association the sole purpose of protecting natural laws, did it not reduce citizenship, understood as political participation, to an instrument of protection, depriving participation of any value in itself? Civic participation was not, contrary to what Robespierre would say, one of the natural rights, but a civil means of defending them; it appeared to be of secondary importance in the Declaration. It is significant that electoral rights are not mentioned. Admittedly 'The principle of all sovereignty resides essentially in the nation'; but the Nation was an abstract entity and not the sum of all citizens; as Sieyès said, one could be a member of the Nation without taking part in elections. Admittedly still 'the law is the expression of the general will', but the general will was not the will of all; it is the collective reason, which a small number of carefully chosen men could elucidate as well as, or even better than, the masses. Admittedly at last, 'Every citizen has a right to participate in its foundation', but the Declaration did not say who was a citizen. While natural rights belonged to man and no one could deprive him of them, political rights belonged to the civic body, from which certain men were excluded.

The law of December 22nd 1789 confirmed this ambivalence by using the distinction between active and passive citizens established by Sieyès. Those who paid a contribution at least equivalent to the local value of three days' work were alone granted the right to vote. These active citizens only designated electors, who, in turn, elected on the second level the representatives. To be an elector, one must pay the equivalent of ten working days and to be eligible for election one must own land and pay a contribution of one silver marc.[8] These conditions long led historians to state that 'this system replaced the aristocracy of birth by the aristocracy of money' while 'the people was shut out of political life'.[49] But more recent interpretations moderated this judgement. It has been stressed that the conditions established for the right to vote at the first degree (nationality, age, residence, tax and non-domesticity) led to a situation close to what would be later called universal suffrage. The large number of active citizens (two-thirds of men of age to vote[50]) indicates the will of the Assembly to extend the civic body greatly. The right to vote henceforth defined a social status, that of the individual as a member of the people which collectively replaced the king.[51] The fact that this right really determined the expression of the general seems secondary, provided that one was part of the citizen-body that constituted the nation. The exclusion from political rights, from active citizenship, could have only one justification in this framework: the absence of autonomy. All those who remained in a state of private dependence, who did not appear directly in the public sphere, were not called upon to constitute the nation: women, children and servants, confined in the *domus*, had no autonomous public existence; they were not members of civil society.

The two-level electoral system, which was not challenged by the Thermidorians when they widened the civic body in 1792 and suppressed the distinction between active and passive citizens in 1794, reflects the ambivalence of the concept of nation. The mass of active citizens was, as Machiavelli and Montesquieu had said, apt to choose those who will represent them; they are the Nation in the broad sense, the civic body. But the representatives themselves have to be found among reasonable men; they are the Nation in the strict sense, the legislative assembly. They will be chosen on the basis of their fortune, or, when this criterion will be deemed illegitimate, by an assembly of voters who were, in practice, from the well-to-do classes.[52] As says Leon Duguit at the beginning of the twentieth century, the necessarily representative idea of national sovereignty did not mean inevitably that all have

> an unspecified right to participate in the public power. Indeed, in the real doctrine of national sovereignty, the embodied nation is a person separate from the individuals who compose it; it is it which is the titular of sovereignty and not the individuals; consequently individuals as such have no share of sovereignty.[53]

If the Nation alone was sovereign, and if the will it expressed was considered to be that of all, it was, in fact, not necessary for all to take part in the expression of the general will. A double fiction justified this exclusion: the Nation was by law consubstantial to the people, and representatives were by law consubstantial to the Nation. The representatives were the Nation which *was* the people: between elected representatives and citizens a common will occurred fictitiously. Political rights were not essential to the definition of citizenship understood in this way; the elector 'is only an official in charge of identifying the will of the nation'.[54] Strictly speaking, political rights were not rights, but a function in that taking part in elections was a charge, a task, for citizens. Citizenship was an abstract principle which was only very partially reflected in public law:

> It is not the right to vote; it is the right to be recognised as an element of the nation, only holder of public power; but the citizen can vote only if the legislator gave him this function. Finally the elector citizen is simultaneously titular of a right and in charge of a function.[55]

This is the meaning behind the distinction between active and passive citizens. Above all, citizenship was a general principle: it stated that everyone was free because they were members of the nation, they were co-holders of sovereignty, they were subjected only to laws supposed to be of their own making. This singular abstraction, highly juridical, is at the centre of all the French hesitations relating to the extension of the suffrage: the constitutions of 1789–91 consecrated the idea of suffrage as a function by adopting the distinction between active and passive citizens; the Convention (1793) abandoned it by declaring all men to be electors and citizens and by thus amalgamating the *right* of citizenship and the *function* of the elector;[56] the constitution of the year III (1795) returned to the system of 1791; the Consulate and the first Empire purely and simply abrogated the right of citizenship, in its principle as well as in its actuality; in 1848, finally, the attitude of the Convention triumphed, political rights were set once more at the heart of citizenship. Beyond these developments, one sees the permanence of the universality of the status of citizen, and the hesitation between the extension of the suffrage to all – which made it a right – or its limitation to a few – which reduced it to a function.

It was against the background of this legal fiction that universalist republicanism revolted. It claimed to destroy all social categories and to make prevail against them the abstract man, the individual. Robespierre (1758–94) showed the unfinished aspect of the Revolution when he recalled that the universalist design of citizenship, denied in practice, had been at the heart of the Declaration of great principles:

> Can the law be the expression of the general will when the majority of those for whom it is made cannot participate, in any way, to its foundation? ... Can men be equal in rights when some enjoy exclusively the capacity of being elected members of the legislative body, or of other public bodies, others having only the right to choose them, and others still having none of these rights?...Finally, can the nation be sovereign when the majority of its members are deprived of the political rights that make sovereignty?[57]

The word 'citizen' would continue to carry these ambiguities and embody the oscillation of French political culture between the universality of political status and the privileges which mark its institution. Lanjuinais testified to this when he noted in 1793:

> The general idea that the word citizen evokes is that of member of the city, of the civil society, of the nation. In a rigorous meaning, it means only those which are admitted to exert political rights... in a word the members of the sovereign. But in practice, this expression is used to point out all those who are part of the social body, this means those who are neither foreigners nor civilly dead, whether or not they have political rights; finally all those which enjoy the plenitude of the civil rights.... These are the citizens in the most ordinary language. Specialists of public law and even legislators often confuse these two very different meanings.[58]

It is all as if, despite the revolution, despite the solemn character of its Declarations, the citizen had remained the same, defined primarily by the passive benefit of the law and only accidentally by participation in its formation. Nevertheless, the revolution had ensured that what it had achieved politically was translated into language; Chalier's suggestion to the Convention had been followed: 'Citizens, when the revolution is completed in facts, it must also be done in words. The title of citizen must alone be found in all the acts emanated from you'.[59] 'No more Sir, nor Madam, neither Sire nor so-called, all are citizens, all are "citizened"'[60] according to a pretty neologism. And by a cruel irony of history, which says more than all the semantic analyses and all the lexicological studies, this law became the subject of mockery: the only people addressed as 'citizen' were servants who bore the brunt of their employers' sarcasm: 'it will soon be stylish to say: Citizen Jean, clean my shoes, Citizen Angot, open oysters for me'.[61]

A few decades later, Immanuel Kant (1724–1804), would still find it difficult to reconcile the statement of men's equal dignity in the concept of citizenship and the social prejudice he doesn't manage to get rid of. When he gave an abstract definition of citizenship, Kant rather revealed Rousseau, as Eric Weil says, than invented a new concept. Like Rousseau, he refused to see order and freedom as two exclusive terms and reconciled them in the idea of autonomy. For the rights of all to be protected, a law was necessary; and for the law to be unable to transgress the rights of individuals, it must be 'the act of a public will', the act of the will 'of the entire people' for 'only towards oneself can one never act unjustly'.[62] Kant thought in the same terms as Rousseau that 'The basic law, which can only come from the general, united will of the people, is called the original contract' (*ibid.*) and made law the synthesis of order and freedom: by subjecting oneself to the law that one has enacted as a member of the people, by obeying all, one obeys only oneself and remains as free as before. Autonomy is the form of the citizen's freedom and the right to legislate is the essential manifestation of citizenship.

However, Kant acknowledged the mystifying character of this concept when he tried, with difficulty, to establish the requirements necessary to the achievement of autonomy: 'In the question of actual legislation, all who are free and equal under existing public laws may be considered equal, but not as regards the right to make these laws' (*ibid.*). All can enjoy the rights conferred by the law, but only those who have, in addition to 'natural' qualities (to be neither woman nor child), the quality of *sibisufficientia*, which consists in being 'his own master' (*ibid.*, p. 78), can take part in the decision-process. Pulled between his egalitarian principles and his oligarchical prejudices, Kant inextricably engulfed himself in contradiction. He did not acknowledge it explicitly but the idea that underpins his reasoning is that the exercise of citizenship supposes a high degree of rationality for individual wills to be united in a general will. The problem, then, is to fix the boundaries of the civic body and Kant loses himself in biased syllogism on the independence granted by the fact of having an independent profession, before recognising, 'but I do admit that it is somewhat difficult to define the qualifications which entitle anyone to claim the status of being his own master' (*ibid.*, p. 71, n.).

He came back to this question a few years later, in his *Metaphysics of Morals*, without solving the contradiction. The citizen, he recalled, was characterised by three essential attributes: 'lawful freedom to obey no law other than that to which he has given his consent'; civil equality, which consists in having to obey no one that one could not also legally bind; and 'civil independence, which allows him to owe his existence and sustenance ... purely to his own rights and powers as a member of the commonwealth'.[63] But he immediately underlined that 'Fitness to vote is the necessary qualification which every citizen must possess', which supposed independence' (*Metaphysics of Morals*, p. 139). He must then distinguish those who are only 'part' of the republic and those who are 'members', i.e. those who by their own 'free will actively participate in a community of other people' (*ibid.*). This meant, he continued, that there were active citizens and passive citizens, before conceding that 'the latter concept seems to contradict the definition of the concept of a citizen altogether' (*ibid.*). The dividing line remains difficult to trace, and Kant resorted to examples as the only proof. By this he admits defeat because, whatever appearance he tried to give them, his justifications were purely pragmatic and not of a legal or deontological nature.[64]

The consequences of this are considerable. Kant did not manage to maintain the consistency of the idea of autonomy: those who do not have civil independence – because their professional status forces them to obey others – are not free as citizens; strictly speaking, they are not even citizens. Kant tried to argue that their dependence and their inequality 'does not however, in any way, conflict with the freedom and equality of all men *as human beings*' (*Metaphysics of Morals*, p. 140). Consequently for these 'subjects among other subjects', the guarantee of freedom did not rest in the nature of the general will, which could not do itself wrong, but in the benevolence of the 'members of the state':

the positive votes to which the voters agree, of whatever sort they may be, must not be at variance with the natural laws of freedom and with the corresponding equality of all members of the people whereby they are allowed to work their way up from their passive condition to an active one (*ibid.*).

Therefore, for Kant, there are two ways of being free: by law, i.e., in a reasonable prospect, one is freed by obedience to the law that one gave oneself; but in fact this condition is only accessible to a minority, the citizens, while others owe their freedom to the moral duty that citizens have to protect them, while they must nourish the hope of someday reaching this prestigious status themselves.[65] Contrary to what he claimed, Kant never forgot his mistrust of the plebs. The anthropology on which he bases the idea of the social contract is more Hobbesian than Rousseauian: man was fundamentally evil; it was thus necessary to build the republic to find out:

> how the mechanism of nature can be applied to men in such a manner that the antagonism of their hostile attitudes will make them compel one another to submit to coercive laws, thereby producing a condition of peace within which the laws can be enforced (*Perpetual Peace*, p. 113).

The republican idea and, consequently, that of citizenship is, with Kant, closer to being a regulatory idea than a real constitution; he recommends encouraging 'public use of one's reason in all matters',[66] in the hope that 'a few who think for themselves ..., once they have themselves thrown off the yoke of immaturity, will disseminate the spirit of rational respect for personal value and for the duty of all men to think for themselves'.[67] When humanity becomes enlightened, and only then, will the republic become possible and one will be able to hope to finally reach it by successive reforms.

CRITICS OF REVOLUTIONARY CITIZENSHIP: HISTORY AND UTILITY *VS*. NATURAL LAW

The concept of sovereignty contained in the French Declarations spread throughout Western Europe. Two centuries later, the political freedom of the citizen was still understood as obedience to the law that one had given oneself; this idea is still wedded to the representative mechanism. European states have certainly given different interpretations of this idea but all acknowledge, or at least give away, their debt towards it.

The expansion of the French Revolution in the decade following the Declaration shows that it owed less to French genius than its name leads one to think, and that, in many of its aspects it was a European revolution. Jacques Godechot showed how much the revolutionary blaze that seemed to spread like wildfire actually owed to similar social, economical, demographic and institutional structures; the French Revolution had rather confirmed and encouraged than caused this conflagration of *anciens régimes*.[68]

The Declaration of Rights, at the heart of events, was the object of the most contradictory passions. The prestige of France – a big state, centralised for centuries, whose language was the language of diplomacy, philosophy and the arts, the language of most European courts – meant that its revolution would be simultaneously glorified and demonised. In the revolutionary effervescence, 'patriots' from all over Europe flocked to France; others came together in their countries; however far they were from Paris, for scientists or philosophers, indifference was impossible without seeming to be in bad faith. The revolution travelled on its own, before Revolutionary France exported it via weapons, pens and conspirators. All the nuances of modern ideologies were determined in relation to the French Revolution: from the pure and simple reaction with the Paulian idea of original sin (Maistre, Bonald), to the socialist critics, finding fault with the formal equality which would not become real; through Romanticism, intuitionism and all kinds of irrationalisms... All these reactions share a certain number of elements. They all strongly battle against the rationalism of Enlightenment, aiming particularly at the 'metaphysical' idea according to which man has rights by nature; all or almost all find fault with the constructivist character of a revolution that had aimed at realising in practice what it thought to be true in theory; finally they all try to demonstrate the internal contradictions of the Declaration of Rights.

In fact, the rehabilitation of history and empiricism against the abstraction of natural law did not wait for the revolution. As early as the year 1770, Herder (1744–1803) prefigured a refutation of the Enlightenment which would have many followers, in Germany and beyond. In his attempt to define 'yet another philosophy of history', he used treasures of irony to disprove the belief in an ineluctable march of humanity towards its fulfilment, which was, according to him, the main misconception of French thinkers. Against these wanderings he recalled the coincidental character of history, which is only the 'result of thousands of competing causes'[69] and opposed to the idea of 'universal values' his doubts about the pretension according to which 'all the inhabitants of earth must be Europeans to live happily'.[70] According to his understanding, history was a long and capricious succession of infinitely different events, linked by logic that the human mind cannot grasp, and the philosophy of history could not be reduced to the idea of the spontaneous and imperturbable development of the virtualities found in humanity. 'Indeed none of us becomes man on his own. The entire structure of man's humanity is linked by a spiritual genesis – education – to his parents, teachers and friends, to all the circumstances of his life, and through that, to his fellow countrymen and ancestors'.[71] The central category of the philosophy of history is no longer progress, but 'tradition and organic forces'.[72] However, Herder did not oppose the march of history with the return to an unchanging history. His criticism was modern, he was still working within a perspective of the earthly development of humanity.[73] It is more epistemological than it is political: natural law was a misconception of humanity because it abolished the historical dimension and, by its abstraction, neglected the real process of the formation of societies.

This fundamental criticism had many followers after the French Revolution pushed to its culmination the 'flaw' of Enlightenment by claiming to rebuild history on theoretical bases. At the end of the eighteenth century, amid the clamour of protests from every quarter, Edmund Burke (1729–97) waxed indignant at the enthusiasm generated by the French Revolution in his country, even in his own party (the Whigs), and he decided to use his pen to prove that the revolution of

1789 was the negation of its 'Glorious' ancestor of 1688.

Hiding behind solid good sense, he simply admits: 'I have nothing to say to the clumsy subtlety of their political metaphysics'.[74] Burke shared more than this contempt of 'cold reason' with Herder: like him, he was a modern who revolted against what he saw as the excesses of modernity. 'In denying their false claims of right, I do not mean to injure those which are real, and are such as their pretended rights would totally destroy'. Burke expressed his famous real rights, in a curious combination, mixing the right to live under the benefit of the law, the right to justice, to property, to inheritance and the rights 'to instruction in life, and to consolation in death' (*Reflections*, p. 59).

Like all the men of his time, Burke believed that public authority proceeded from conventions by which 'each person has at once divested himself of the first fundamental right of unconvenanted man, that is, to judge for himself' (p. 59). And in the purest Hobbesian tradition, he deduces from this that the only rights that exist are those that the positive texts express: 'Men cannot enjoy the rights of an uncivil and of a civil state together' (p. 60). Burke wrote that acknowledging that all rights were positive was a simple question of coherence. A natural right that positive law did not consecrate was only a philosopher's fantasy.

In fact, through this distinction, Burke denounced the pretension of French revolutionaries to build a political order based on abstract concepts. The French Declaration was an arbitrary translation of concepts forged by philosophers. The British Bill of Rights, on the other hand, was the product of centuries of history; it was the formalisation of the experience of generations, the result of an empirical rather than theoretical knowledge. 'The Revolution was made to preserve our *antient* indisputable laws and liberties, and that *antient* constitution of government which is our only security for law and liberty'. The revolution of 1688 aimed to legitimise a historically built social order, whilst the one of 1789 aspired to establish a legitimate order *against* history. The English Declaration of Rights expressed privileges patiently established by 'great lawyers and great statesmen, and not by warm and inexperienced enthusiasts' (p. 16). For that matter, Burke was not surprised, after having read the list of those who were elected to the third estate, by their results: 'Among them, indeed, I saw some of known rank; some of shining talents; but of any practical experience in the state, not one man was to be found. The best were only men of theory' (p. 40).

If there was one matter above all in which they went astray, blinded by their principles and ignorant of their history, it was on the so-called right of the people to chose its own government. Burke used here an argument that mixes contractualism and traditionalism in a curious synthesis: he said that only a people with a 'collective capacity' artificially created by contract[75] could give itself a government. This could not be done by a shapeless multitude devoid of a common will. And

> To enable men to act with the weight and character of a people, and to answer the ends for which they are incorporated into that capacity, we must suppose them (by means immediate or consequential) to be in that state of habitual

social discipline, in which the wiser, the more expert, and the more opulent conduct, and by conducting enlighten and protect the weaker, the less knowing, and the less provided with the goods of fortune. (Ibid., p, 216)

In other words, only a historically constituted society, characterised by slowly elaborated hierarchies, and not a mythical egalitarian and abstract people, could give itself its own government.[76] Burke developed, against the republican idea of freedom as autonomy, a definition of freedom based on the common law, the rule of law and the efficiency of justice. Freedom, according to Burke, was the peaceful benefit of the rights granted by the authority and protected by the law. The *liberties*, in fact, slowly settled since the Middle Ages, and not *freedom*, brutally proclaimed by men with no history.

The argument will often reappear under various forms, to the point of being at the centre of two great conceptions of political life. The first, 'liberal' in the widest meaning of the word, is based on an a-historic conception of humanity: man is thought to be of an immutable nature, which can be expressed as subjective rights, and from this axiom stems the statement that the abstract people is the source of authority. The other, which could be called 'traditionalist',[77] is based on an historicist conception of humanity: human nature can not be deduced *in abstracto* but is described from the empirical examination of history; society is not defined in legal terms as the object of a pact but is understood as the result of a long history. Hence, its representation is no longer atomist but organicist: constituted bodies are an integral part of the social nature, it is only through a false abstraction that society can be seen as the sum of interchangeable individuals. Nor is the state the result of a hypothetical pact but of slow evolutions that consecrated the domination of some and the subjection of others; if men can be free, it is not because they are the source of authority, but because they have gradually won, in real power struggles, freedoms that protect them from power. The opposition between these two visions of the world, from which Burke borrows in turn, is analytical and normative: those who state that the truth of things lies in their history generally consider that what is historically built cannot be swept away and thus protect social orders, political hierarchies and, at times, the freedoms within these; on the contrary, to reason in the abstract terms of an immutable human nature allows one to delegitimise all the historical advantages contrary to natural law and to call for the upheaval of the world.

In England, at the end of the eighteenth century, this rationalist conception was only enthusiastically received in the framework of a minority of scattered schools, while the great majority of public opinion was acerbic in its criticism. As early as the middle of the eighteenth century, David Hume (1711–76) had attacked the idea of the social contract and denied its historical value:

Almost all the governments, which exist at present, or of which there remains any record in history, have been founded originally, either on usurpation or conquest, or both, without any pretence of a fair consent, or voluntary subjection of the people.[78]

The natural-law fiction has no basis; it conceals the true logic of power, the fact that submission is based on the servile opinion and the habits of men. Hume shared the political scepticism of Adam Smith, which forced him to be satisfied with the present state of domination: he valued efficiency and said of the established government that it has 'an infinite advantage, by that very circumstance of its being established; the bulk of mankind being governed by authority, not reason, and never attributing authority to any thing that has not the recommendation of antiquity'.[79] The legitimacy of politics depended on its capacity of meeting its aims.

The charge of Jeremy Bentham (1748–1842) against the political work of the French Revolution and of its Declaration in particular – the most violent of its kind – stemmed from this ideological matrix, which spread widely during the last decades of the eighteenth century in England. From his first writings, the young jurist admitted his intellectual debt to the 'liberal' movement. He pursued the criticism of the contractualist representation, which he had hoped, had been 'effectually demolished by Mr. Hume'.[80] The idea of a social contract did not permit one to determine *in practice* the legitimacy of authority; it did not dictate the clauses of the contract 'and these would of course be, on each occasion, what the interest of the occasion required that they should be'.[81] The social contract was an ideological excuse, a fable, aiming to justify the political supremacy of those who used it. The French Declaration, which Bentham criticised after its proclamation, could be subjected to the same criticism, which reveals how his epistemology was radically opposed to that of the defenders of the French Republic. According to Bentham there were three different types of objections to the idea of the rights of man: first of all it has no utility; it was also in blatant contradiction with empirical reality; finally, it was theoretically incoherent.

The first remark was not novel. It was common to all criticisms of the revolutionary definition of citizenship: Bentham pointed out, as does Burke, that the Declaration was, because of its abstractness, less useful to the limitation of public power than the British Constitution and *habeas corpus*.[82] Using the same empirical reasoning, he observed how much general principles issued against history were weakened by their disdain for experience: while, in the field of chemistry, the French were able to capitalise on the teachings of their predecessors, they 'have sunk below the profoundest ignorance' ('Anarchical Fallacies', p. 522) in the sphere of legislation. The fundamental error of the writers of the Declaration is to have mistaken a state of fact for an ideal: 'the man who penned it knew no difference between a declaration of what he supposed was or is the state of things with regard to this or that subject, and a declaration of what he conceived ought to have been or ought to be that state of things' (p. 517). Bentham pretended to believe that the writers mistook their beliefs for reality; also it was easy for him to criticise what he thought to be misinterpretations of reality: *'All men are born free? All men remain free?* No, not a single man: not a single man that ever was, or is or will be. All men, on the contrary, are born in subjection...*All men are born equal in rights.* The rights of the heir of the most indigent family equal to the rights of the heir of the most wealthy' (p. 498). Bentham thus expressed the revolt of a utilitarian way of thinking against the revolutionary intent of natural law. He uses as his own the argument which Burke had opposed to the idea of pre-civil rights:

> There are no such things as natural rights – no such things as rights anterior to the establishment of government – no such things as natural rights opposed to, in contradiction to legal…Natural rights is simple nonsense: natural and imprescriptible rights, rhetorical nonsense – nonsense upon stilts (pp. 500–1).

Bentham recalled, like Burke, that rights cannot simultaneously be those of the pre-civil man and of the citizen; and he added that logic taught that, by its very definition, the word rights could only mean the rights of the citizen. There was only positive law; the rest is fiction. Hence, the internal contradictions of the Declaration were to be compared to those that existed between the practice and the text. If this doctrine is condemned to be incoherent, it is because the project itself is absurd: 'it is not that they have failed in their execution of the design by using the same word promiscuously in two or three senses – contradictory and incompatible senses – but in undertaking to execute a design which could not be executed at all without this abuse of words' (p. 522). Entirely coherently with his 'realist' analysis of power, Bentham invalidated any political legitimising that used arguments other than public interest and common sense. The sole outcome of this project was anarchy: 'in justifying past insurrection, they plant and cultivate a propensity to perpetual insurrection in time future (p. 496).

Bentham uses different premises from Burke's but reached similar conclusions: only tradition and the habits it produces could be the basis for a viable political order. In both cases, the categorical refusal of modern political law, of the abstract theorisation of the status of citizenship, prevailed. Against the philosophical idea that freedom lies in the obedience to the law one has given oneself, they state the historical concept of the protection of the individual by the balance of the constitution.

However, Bentham's thought contains more than negative criticisms. By invalidating the way of thinking of natural law, he did not fall into pure scepticism but replaced it by a very different paradigm, which did not 'depend on any higher reason but is, in itself a sufficient reason for any practical question whatever' (p. 59). This new mode of political thinking would have a considerable influence on political conceptions of citizenship in the nineteenth century. Once more, the phrasing was borrowed from Hume: it was the 'utility principle' that was meant to decide all issues according to the criterion of the 'greatest good of the greatest number', to be a 'standard of good and evil in general morality and in Government particularly' (p. 116). This principle, to the contrary of those stemming from the contract, has the advantage of 'being known of all men' in its clarity and the immediate intellectual satisfaction it gives, all being able to assess whether their interests are acknowledged. It is relevant because it is based on common sense, accessible to all, and not on theoretical truths jealously guarded by philosophers. Man was a being whose moral sense was shaped in contact with reality, in the experience of good and bad, of pleasure and suffering. Hence, the sole aim of humanity could only be the abolition of pain. And legislation was the way to do it: by prescribing penalties and rewards, it induced good human behaviour and prevented harm; legislation was 'the science of intimidation'.[83] Bentham believed, as did Smith, that men's interests naturally tended towards harmony but he acknowledged the need to lay down norms to prevent the degeneration of this natural order; he admitted the fact that legislation was indispensable.

This utilitarian way of thinking cares little about political forms; a government was good if it created good legislation. Thus, a rudimentary people needed an enlightened despotic government, but a 'democracy' could be granted to a people of reasonable individuals. The reason for this was simple: if the government aimed to harmonise different interests, its actions must be guided by those who have the best knowledge of these interests: citizens themselves. Moreover, its decisions will then be stronger, since they will have the approval of the 'greatest number'. Bentham added that this method was the only one that could prevent the corruption of the state:

> Every other species of government has necessarily, for its characteristic and primary object and effect, the keeping the people or non-functionaries in a perfectly defenceless state, against the functionaries their rulers, who being, in respect of their power and the use they are disposed and enabled to make of it, the natural adversaries of the people, have for their object the giving facility, certainty, unbounded extent and impunity, to the depredation and oppression exercised on the governed by the governors'.[84]

By basing himself on the pessimistic analysis of power developed by Hume, Bentham gave a utilitarian value to the extension of the suffrage. He considered it to be the political translation of the harmony of interests: all being the best judges and best defenders of their interests, the system that gave each a say guaranteed the greatest efficiency of power and prevented it from serving its own interests and not those of the greatest number.

The shift from a contractualist paradigm to a utilitarian paradigm offered the strongest argument in favour of universal suffrage: when the state was thought of as the agency whose purpose was the artificial harmonisation of wills, a certain degree of rationality and social homogeneity could (implicitly) be required of those who were called upon to take part in the formation of the general will; at first, Bentham shared this belief. But, like Smith, he was led to distance himself from it: all having an interest and being able to acknowledge it immediately, the political decision no longer required particular wealth or knowledge.[85]

This conception of suffrage would have a strong influence in Great Britain. Nineteenth-century liberalism, John Stuart Mill's in particular, would repeat this argument and it would underlie the political debates that accompanied the step-by-step extensions of suffrage in that country in 1832, 1867 and 1884. While the change from subjection happened brutally in France in the overturning of the traditional conception of power by the axiom of popular sovereignty – and restorations and *coups d'état* regularly brought back the citizenship of subjection – in Great Britain utilitarian reasoning lead to progressive joining of individuals to the nation as they became property owners.[86]

In other nations, the French Revolution also led theorists to try to put right the 'mistakes' of natural law by rehabilitating the historical perspective and an awareness of power struggles. This would in particular become the basis of socialist criticism, which, even if it led to totally opposed conclusions, largely shared the premises of historic criticisms. This was also the case, before the tangible existence of industrial society, for Hegel (1770–1831), who, with a prescience that is still fascinating, gave one of the clearest conceptions of the reality of modern citizenship as it exists in the states of the nineteenth and twentieth centuries.

Like all his contemporaries, the major event that hardened his political thought was the French Revolution. He was nineteen years old in 1789 and was one of the young German liberal intellectuals who were enthusiastic about this revolution that heralded the end of the *ancien régime* and the birth of political modernity. But over the years his enthusiasm weakened: the Robespierrist Terror, as heads began to roll at an increasing rate, and the rise of Napoleon Bonaparte and of imperialism, of which Germany was a victim, forced him to wonder about the causes of the revolutionary lurch. Why did a movement that had begun by a declaration of the rights of man and of the citizen degenerate into terror, war and tyranny?

According to him, the reason lay in the methodological error of the revolutionaries: by abolishing the *ancien régime* and replacing it brutally with the Republic, they went against history too quickly and too radically. Trusting in 'enlightenment' to the point of blindness, they believed that a whole political system could be built from theoretical speculations and reality ignored:

> Consequently, when these abstractions were invested with power, they afforded the tremendous spectacle, for the first time we know of in human history, of the overthrow of all existing and given conditions within an actual major state and the revision of its constitution from first principles and purely in terms of thought; the intention behind this was to give it what was supposed to be a purely rational basis. On the other hand, since these were only abstractions divorced from the Idea, they turned the attempt into the most terrible and drastic event.[87]

In other words, the French were impudent enough to think they could make history. But, Hegel writes, the state is formed progressively and is not decreed: as soon as rules appear in a society, as soon as institutions are set up (such as courts of law), the germ of a state emerges. In truth, the state is no more than the sum of the institutions born spontaneously within society, the sum of the laws and rights that men acknowledge themselves in a customary manner, the organisation of authorities they have created to solve their conflicts. The constitution 'should *not* be regarded as *something made*, even if it does have an origin in time'.[88]

The description Hegel gave of the Constitution of Germany[89] in his youth, around 1800, describes *a contrario* what he meant by state and citizenship. If he stated bitterly that 'Germany is no longer a state', it was because all the rules and institutions that ruled Germany in his time were not a rational and conscious system. The multiplication of partial, and at times competing authorities, had reduced the state to 'anarchy':

> Political powers and rights are not offices of state designed in accordance with an organisation of the whole, and the services and duties of individuals are not determined by the needs of the whole. On the contrary, every individual member of the political hierarchy, every princely house, every estate, every city, guild, etc., everything which has rights or duties in relation to the state – has acquired them for itself; and in view of this reduction of its power, the state has no other function but to confirm that it has been deprived of its power. Consequently, if the state loses all authority, and individual ownership rests on the power of the state, the ownership of those who have no other support but the power of the state, which is virtually nil, must necessarily be very precarious. ...German constitutional law is not a science based on principles but a register of the most varied constitutional rights acquired in the manner of civil law. Legislative, judicial, spiritual and military powers are intermingled, divided, and combined in the most irregular manner and in the most disparate proportions, just as diverse as the property of private individuals ('German Constitution, pp. 29–30).

Citizenship as such did not exist in this non-state since, as in feudal Europe, the political identity of the individual was defined by multiple allegiances to partial and private communities, without being subsumed under a common law. While, in the modern state, citizenship was defined by the constitution and the law, the status of the individual was stated *against* them in pre-state Germany 'and everyday he attempts to withdraw himself from the influence of the community' (p. 32).

In the absence of the state, there is no citizenship; sticking to the medieval corporatist conception of politics, 'the Germans have not wished to transform this free personal share, which is dependent on the arbitrary will, into a free share independent of the arbitrary will and consisting in the universality and force of laws' (p. 10). In his negative description of the German state, Hegel stated, on the contrary, what he meant by citizenship: it was membership in a public order ruled by a law that dominated private privileges; it was, as Bodin, and then Hobbes, had said, the freedom that results from obedience to the law. It was not submission but liberation, because, by realising the sovereignty of the state, it was possible to put an end to corporatist authorities and patrimonial domination. Citizenship was the status of the individual in the modern state, as opposed to the subjection of pre-state societies. The rest is accessory: for Hegel, the ways in which the individual took part in the exercise of sovereignty were secondary. It did not matter much 'which particular mode is responsible for legislation, and what relative share the various estates or citizens in general have in this process' (p. 18); 'the uniformity or lack of uniformity of civil rights among the individuals who are subject to the universal political authority' was also irrelevant (p. 17).

Hegel ignored the idea of popular sovereignty to concentrate on clarifying the sovereignty of the state in a country in which its authority was rivalled by the remnants of private powers. Citizenship ensured the liberty of its holders, even if they did not take part in the practice of power, because it made them members of the sovereign state. The citizen needed to be capable of acknowledging that his obligations towards the state were 'in the same time the existence of my particular freedom' (*Elements* § 261, p. 284) of understanding that, when he accomplished his duties as a citizen, he found 'his own interest and satisfaction or settled his own account':

> The individual, whose duties give him the status of a subject, finds that, in fulfilling his duties as a citizen, he gains protection for his person and property, consideration for his particular welfare, satisfaction of his substantial essence, and the consciousness and self-awareness of being a member of a whole (§ 261, p. 284).

Faithful to his model, Hegel looked for the confirmation of the value of his model in history: according to him, the most rational state was the one with the strongest historical base, which has been patiently constructed through the adventures of men, tested by reality and, for this reason, more solid than states whose principles were simply born from intellectual speculations.

In the finest liberal tradition and according to the reality of the time, he stated that 'the political authority and government, must leave to the freedom of the citizens whatever is not essential to its own role of organising and maintaining authority' ('German Constitution', p. 23). The Hegelian state was 'minimal', cut down to the kingly functions of police and justice domestically and of defence against exterior dangers. Any other economic, social and cultural functions could be entrusted to society, without interference from the public authority. As to the forms of the state, they could be summarised in three essential elements:

> a) the power to determine and establish the universal – the legislative power;
> b) the subsumption of particular spheres and individual cases under the universal – the executive power;
> c) subjectivity as the ultimate decision of the will – the power of the sovereign, in which the different powers are united in an individual unity which is thus the apex and beginning of the whole, i.e. of constitutional monarchy
> (*Elements*, § 261, p. 284).

The main element of the Hegelian state was the monarch. It is he who gave the state its substance: as supreme power he represented the unity of institutions, which all depended upon him. In this, Hegel, once more, did no more than translate conceptually the reality of nineteenth-century Europe: the state was personified by its leader. He represented it to foreign powers and embodied public authority for his subjects. With no monarch, there was no state, because powers would be spread out instead of being organised under the central figure of the king, and subjects would be unable to understand that they belonged to a state.

> Without its monarch and that articulation of the whole which is necessarily and immediately associated with monarchy, the people is a formless mass. The latter is no longer a state, and none of those determinations which are encountered only in an internally organized whole (such as sovereignty, government, courts of law, public authorities, estates, etc., is applicable to it (§ 279, p. 319).

Hegel was far from medieval doctrines of absolute monarchy. Indeed, his monarchy was constitutional. This implied in the first place that, according to liberal doctrine, there should be limits to the actions of authorities; the state must abide by the rule of law, all its powers: parliament, government, courts, administrations, must respect the law so that citizens' rights would be protected. This implied that the function of the king was essentially symbolic: he represented authority but did not use it.

The two other primordial political functions defined by Hegel are the legislative function, which consisted in legally translating the general will, and the governmental function, which applied these necessarily general laws to particular cases. Hegel's historicism dictated every detail of his organisation of power. In as much as he considered that laws were created slowly in the course of social life, he understood the legislative function not as a pure creation of law but as a task that consisted of detecting the pre-existing will and of expressing it clearly in a legislative text. The parliament did not have the power to decide what the law would be but must try to understand and put into words the pre-existing will of the people. Its mission was to 'bring the universal interest into existence...i.e., to bring into existence the moment of subjective *formal freedom*, the public consciousness as the *empirical universality* of the views and thoughts of the *many*' (§301, p. 339). This modest conception of the legislative function accounts for the fact that Hegel suggested a corporatist organisation of parliament: it would have two chambers which contributed to the formation of the law, the first representing landowners and the other representing trades. The first chamber would bring to light the general interest and, like most of his contemporaries, Hegel limited political rights to landowners for two main reasons: first, because landowners were the only citizens capable of freely expressing their will, others who depended on masters being deprived of freedom of thought; secondly, because landowners alone have an 'interest' to defend, while the 'plebs' having nothing, was animated by passions. Next to this assembly of the bourgeois, the corporative chamber, made up of representatives of all trades, would express the sectoral interests of all of them. The general will of all would be deduced from the conjugation of these two types of wills, the general interests of landowners and the particular interests of trades.

This parliament must only edict general laws and never be concerned with particular issues. These were the task of government. But, to mirror social reality, the government must be strongly anchored in it. This is why Hegel gave such weight to the administration, to the development of a large bureaucracy made up of qualified public servants who were deeply involved in the social web. This was how the benefits of oligarchic government could be safeguarded: the extensive tasks entrusted to the administration would be taken on by 'scientists', those who, from their training, knew society and were best able to solve its problems. Once more, this conception was less conservative than it seems: traditionally bureaucrats were aristocrats privileged by their birth and often incompetent. Hegel replaced this traditional legitimacy by a technical legitimacy based on personal worth.

One can only be impressed by the prophetic character of his definition of the state. His analysis is very close to the European state we know today. A head of state who embodies the sovereignty of the state but who does not govern; a parliament that tries to join together individual wishes and that hardly legislates; a corporatist representation of trades that reminds us of the role of trade unions; a government which, by using an extensive bureaucracy spread throughout the social body, takes on most political issues; a technocratic administration which prepares and implements all decisions: Hegel conceived the modern state as it is, the contemporary state.[90] In the same way, he forethought what citizenship would be in the real state. Its material form was not in the autonomy of the citizen by obedience to the law he had given himself, with no mediation between the individual and the state, but in the idea of his immediate membership in the state, of the sublimation of his social being into a political identity. To be a citizen according to Hegel is to acknowledge the state as the place were freedom is possible, it is not to be free as an active member of the sovereign. A few years after its heyday, the republican ethos had lost much of its sparkle.

NOTES

1   C. Nicolet, *La République en France: état des lieux* (Paris, Seuil, 1992), p. 141.
2   T. Paine, *Common Sense* (London, Everyman's Library, 1994), p. 251.
3   On the penetration of 'republican language' into the political culture of the American political elite on the eve of the drafting of the constitution, see G.S. Wood, *The Creation of the American Republic, 1776–1787* (Chapel Hill, University of North Carolina Press, 1969) and J.G.A. Pocock, *The Machiavellian Moment* (Princeton, Princeton University Press, 1975), pp. 506–52.
4   A. Hamilton, J. Jay and G. Madison, *The Federalist Papers* (New York, Bantam Books, 1982).
5   *Cf.* B. Bailyn, *To Begin the World Anew: The Genius and Ambiguities of the American Founders* (New York, Vintage Books, 2004).
6   *Cf.* the classic work of A.O. Hirschman, *The Passions and the Interests: Political Arguments for Capitalism Before its Triumph* (Princeton, Princeton University Press, 1977).

7   A. de Tocqueville, *Democracy in America*, translated by Henry Reeve (London, Longman, Green, Longman and Roberts, 1862), II, II,VIII, p.145.

8   In the swirl of the 'democratic revolutions' of the time, the American-specific character lies in these institutional innovations. See R.R. Palmer, *The Age of Democratic Revolution* (Princeton, Princeton University Press, 1959), pp. 213–35.

9   Montesquieu, The Spirit of Laws, edited and translated by A.M. Cohler, B.C. Miller and H.S. Stone (Cambridge, Cambridge University Press, 1989) VI, p. 160.

10 *Cf.* C. Soboul, *Le pouvoir judiciaire* (Paris, Sirey, 1911).

11 *The Federalist*, XXXIV.

12 See R. Palmer, *Age of the Democratic Revolution*, (PrincetonNJ, Princeton University Press 1959-64) p. 234.

13 D. Howard, *Naissance de la pensée politique américaine* (Paris, Ramsay, 1987), p. 311.

14 *Cf.* H. Arendt, *On Revolution* (New York, Viking, 1963), p. 224.

15 *Cf.* T. Paine, *Rights of Man*, [London, Everyman's Library, 1994] pp. 58 and 113.

16 US Supreme Court, *Dred Scott v. Sandford*, 1857.

17 *Cf.* J. Shklar, *American Citizenship: The Quest for Inclusion* (Cambridge, MA, Harvard University Press, 1991).

18 J. Dewey, *The Public and Its Problems* (1927), in *Dewey Later Works*, vol. 2 (Carbondale, Southern Illinois University Press, 1988), p. 367.

19 M.J. Sandel, *Democracy's Discontent, America in Search of a Public Philosophy* (Cambridge MA, The Belknap Press of Harvard University Press, 1996), p. 347. This axiom is a constant of contemporary northern-American political theory. It is found among republican or communitarian authors such as Benjamin Barber and Robert Putnam as well as liberals like Robert Dahl or among advocates of a deliberative conception of democracy like those assembled by S. Benhabib (ed.), *Democracy and Difference: Contesting the Boundaries of the Political* (Princeton, Princeton University Press, 1996).

20 *Encyclopedia, Citizen*, by Diderot.

21 'Remontrances, moyens et avis que le Tiers Etat du bailliage de Nemours charge ses députés de porter aux Etats Généraux (1789)' in L. Jaume, *Les Déclarations des droits de l'homme* (Paris, Garnier-Flammarion, 1989), pp. 80, 84.

22 Condorcet, 'Essai sur la constitution et les fonctions des assemblées provinciales' (1788), in *Sur les élections et autres textes* (Paris, Fayard, 1986), p. 283.

23 Condorcet, *Projet de déclaration des droits*, 1789, in L. Jaume, *Les Déclarations des droits de l'homme*, pp. 111–16; p. 115, Article I of the subparagraph relative to the 'right of natural equality'.

24 Condorcet was also one of the few who cautiously thought of granting active citizenship to women. *Cf.* his 'Essai sur la constitution', p. 293 and W.H. Sewell, 'Le citoyen/la citoyenne: activity, passivity, and the revolutionary concept of citizenship', in C. Lucas (ed.) *The French Revolution and the Creation of Modern Political Culture* (Oxford/New York, Pergamon Press, 1988), pp. 105–23.

25 A. Soboul, *La Révolution française* (Paris, Editions Sociales, 1984 [1982]), pp. 145–50.

26 E. Sieyès, *What is the Third Estate?*, translated by M. Blondel (London, Pall Mall Press, 1963), p. 58.

27 *Ibid.*, p. 163.

28 *Ibid.*, p. 78.
29 *Cf.* G. Zernatto, 'Nation, the history of the Word', in *The Review of Politics* 1944, VI/3, pp. 351–66.
30 *Cf.* J. Godechot, 'Nation, patrie, nationalisme et patriotisme en France au XVIIIe siècle', in *Annales historiques de la révolution française* 1971, 206, pp. 481–501.
31 E. Sieyès, *Essai sur les privileges.*
32 *Cf.* V. Wright, 'Les sources républicaines de la Déclaration des droits', in F. Furet and M. Ozouf, *Le siècle de l'avènement républicain* (Paris, Gallimard, 1993), pp. 127–64.
33 *What is the third estate?*, p. 25.
34 E. Sieyès, *Projet de déclaration*, in S. Rials, pp. 591–606, p. 600.
35 *Cf.* P. Rosanvallon, *Le peuple introuvable: Histoire de la représentation démocratique en France* (Paris, Gallimard, 1998).
36 R.R. Palmer, 'Man and citizen: applications of individualism in the French Revolution', in M.R. Konwit and E. Murphy (eds.) *Essays in Political Theory, Presented to G. H. Sabine* (New-York/London, Kennikat Press, 1972 [1948], pp. 130–52; p. 131.
37 *Cf.* S. Rials, 'Généalogie des droits de l'homme', *Droits* 1985, 2, pp. 3–12.
38 *Cf.* N. Bobbio, 'La révolution française et les droits de l'homme', in M. Telò (ed.), *Etat et démocratie internationale*, translated by N. Giovannini, P. Magnette and J. Vogel (Bruxelles, Complexe, 1998).
39 P. Raynaud, 'La Déclaration des droits de l'homme', in Lucas, *The French Revolution*, pp. 139–49.
40 *Annales parlementaires*, 18 August 1789, p. 463, quoted in Rials, p. 206.
41 *Cf.* S. Rials, *'Genealogie'*, pp. 252–255.
42 Carré de Malberg, *Contribution à la théorie générale de l'Etat* (Paris, Sirey, 1920, reissued CNRS, 1961), vol. 1, p. 236.
43 Condorcet, *Projet de Déclaration des droits naturels, civils et politiques des hommes*, 15 February 1793, in Jaume, *Les Déclarations des droits de l'homme*, pp. 240–3.
44 B. Constant, 'Principles of politics', in *Political Writings*, translated and edited by B. Fontana (Cambridge, Cambridge University Press, 1988), p. 177.
45 *Ibid.*, p. 289.
46 R. Carré de Malberg, *Contribution à la théorie*, vol. 1, p. 492.
47 On the limits of the conception of the rule of law in Carré de Malberg and his contemporaries, *cf.* P. Raynaud, 'Des droits de l'homme à l'Etat de droit. Les droits de l'homme et leurs garanties chez les théoriciens français classiques du droit public', *Droits* 1985, no. 2, pp. 61–73.
48 That is 52 pounds, five to ten times more than was needed to be an elector.
49 A. Soboul, *Le pouvoir judiciaire*, p. 188.
50 *Cf.* P. Guéniffey, *Le nombre et la raison, La révolution française et les élections* (Paris, Editions de l'Ecole des hautes études en sciences sociales, 1993), pp. 44–5. There were approximately 4,400,000 active citizens, that is 15.7 % of the overall population and 61.5% of the adult male population.
51 P. Rosanvallon, *Le sacre du citoyen* (Paris, Gallimard, 1992), p. 71.
52 *Cf.* P. Guéniffey, *Le nombre et la raison*, pp. 411–3.
53 L. Duguit, *Traité de droit constitutionnel, vol. 2, La théorie générale de l'Etat* (Paris,

Fontemoing, 2nd edition, 1923), p. 442.

54 *Ibid.*, p. 443.

55 *Ibid.*, p. 444.

56 Limits remained: one had to be over 25 years of age, resident for at least a year (so as to exclude vagrants, seasonal workers and travelling tradesmen) and living from the product of one's work. It appears, however, that former passive citizens little used these new rights. *Cf.* P. Guéniffy, 'Suffrage', in F. Furet and M. Ozouf (eds), *Dictionnaire critique de la révolution française, vol. III, Institutions et créations* (Paris, Flammarion, 1993 [1988]), pp. 329–48.

57 Robespierre, 'Discours sur le marc d'argent', in M. Bonloiseau, G. Lefebvre and A. Soboul (eds) *Œuvres*, vol. VII (Jan-Sept. 1791), (Paris, PUF, 1950), pp. 158–74, 161–2.

58 *Arch. parl.*, vol. LXIII, p. 962, quoted by A. Lefebvre-Teillard in 'Citoyen', *Droits* 1993, no. 17, pp. 32–42, p. 40.

59 Quoted by L. Brunot, *Histoire de la langue française*, vol. IX, *La Révolution* (Paris, publisher and year unknown), p. 683.

60 *Ibid.*, p. 688.

61 *Ibid.*, p. 686.

62 I. Kant, 'On the common saying: "this may be true in theory, but it does not apply in practice"', in *Political Writings*, translated by H.B. Nisbet, edited by H. Reiss (Cambridge, Cambridge University Press, 1971), p. 77.

63 I. Kant, 'The Metaphysics of Morals', in *Political Writings*, p. 139.

64 *Cf.* A. Philonenko, *Theory And Praxis in the Moral and Political Thought of Kant and of Fichte in 1793* (Paris, Vrin, 1976 [1968]), chapter VII, pp. 59–67.

65 The question of the form of sovereignty was, for Kant, relatively secondary: noting that, in practice, it is the king who represents the people, Kant accepted a very imperfect version of the republican government; while considering that if the monarch acts *as if* powers were separate, like 'Frederick II (who) at least *said* that he was merely the highest servant of the state' ('Towards Perpetual Peace', in *Political Writings*, p. 101), he draws close to the republican spirit but fails to embody the letter of it. *Cf.* G. Stedman-Jones, 'Kant, the French Revolution and the definition of the republic', in B. Fontana (ed.), *The Invention of the Modern Republic* (Cambridge, Cambridge University Press, 1994), pp. 154–72.

66 I. Kant, 'An answer to the question: "what is enlightenment?"', in *Political Writings*, p. 55.

67 *Ibid.*

68 J. Godechot, *La grande nation, l'expansion révolutionnaire de la France dans le monde de 1789 à 1799* (Paris, 1958, reissued Aubier Montaigne), 1983.

69 J.G. Herder, 'Yet another philosophy of history', in F.M. Bernard (ed.), *J.G. Herder on Social and Political Culture* (Cambridge, Cambridge University Press, 1969), p. 201.

70 *Ibid.*, p. 308.

71 *Ibid.*, pp. 312–3.

72 *Ibid.*

73 *Cf.* L. Dumont, 'Le peuple et la nation chez Herder et Fichte', in *Essais sur l'individualisme* (Paris, Le Seuil, 1983), pp. 115–31.

74 E. Burke, *Reflections on the Revolution in France*, edited by L.G. Mitchell (Oxford, Oxford University Press, 1993), p. 58.

75 E. Burke, 'Appeal from the new to the old Whigs', in *Works*, London, 1815–27, vol. 6, pp. 210–1.

76 *Cf.* C.B. Macpherson, *Burke* (Oxford, Oxford University Press, 1980).

77 Following K. Mannheim, *Essays on Sociology and Social Psychology* (London, Routledge, 1950).

78 D. Hume, *Political Essays*, edited by K. Haakonssen (Cambridge, Cambridge University Press, 1994), pp. 189–90.

79 *Ibid.*, p. 221.

80 J. Bentham, *A Fragment on Government*, edited by J.H. Burn & H.L.A. Hart (Cambridge, Cambridge University Press, 1988), p. 51.

81 *Ibid.*, p. 116.

82 *Cf.* J. Bentham, 'Anarchical Fallacies', in *Works*, edited by J. Bowring (New York, Russell & Russell, 1962), vol. II, pp. 491–92.

83 The expression belongs to E. Halévy, *La formation du radicalisme philosophique*, vol. III, *le radicalisme philosophique* (Paris, Félix Alcan, 1904), p. 334.

84 J. Bentham, 'Constitutional Code', in *Works*, vol. IX, p. 47.

85 C.B. Macpherson, *The Life and Times of Liberal Democracy* (Oxford, Oxford University Press, 1981).

86 *Cf.* P. Rosanvallon, *Le sacre du citoyen*, pp. 37–8.

87 G.W.F. Hegel, *Elements of the Philosophy of Right*, edited by A.W. Wood, translated by H.B. Nisbet (Cambridge, Cambridge University Press, 1991), § 258, p. 277.

88 *Ibid.*, § 274, p. 312.

89 G.W.F. Hegel, 'The German Constitution (1798–1802)', in *Political Writings*, edited by L. Dickey and H.B. Nisbet, translated by H.B. Nisbet (Cambridge, Cambridge University Press, 1999), p. 6.

90 *Cf.* E.Weil, *Hegel et l'Etat* (Paris, Vrin, 1950).

chapter five | citizenship and modern society

From the dawn of modern times, the concept of citizenship has referred to the rule of law: the condition of man in the modern state, his rights and his status, are defined by the law of the state, which is the same for all, and not by private authorities and communities which previously determined his identity according to his position in the social hierarchy. Since the democratic revolutions of the end of the eighteenth century, citizenship had also meant popular sovereignty, what we call today 'democracy' but then, with more etymological rigour, a 'republic'. The French and American revolutions put the people back in the position it had occupied in the Roman Republic: the source and the measure of power.

In any case this is the tale told by the declarations, constitutions and political theories that formalised revolutionary principles. In modern as in ancient republics, the invocation of popular sovereignty was associated with *de facto* popular infantilisation. The leading classes persisted in their mistrust of the masses and sought ways to neutralise them; at times, purely and simply pushing them away from power but often, more subtly, by strictly limiting their participation. The myth of the nation, in which all the citizens were supposed to be represented, whether they took part or not in the election of their representatives, enclosed popular participation, at best, in an electoral act – sometimes two-levelled, in order to reduce its impact even more – at worst in a status of passive citizenship. Exclusion from the civic body, or from the suffrage, remained widespread in Europe: women and children, represented by the *pater familias*, had no access to the political sphere; servants – that is workers – and the indigent, considered at times to have no interest and at others to not have sufficient ability to reason, often both, were also excluded; as to foreigners, they did not even belong to the nation, not even passively, and could not benefit from the civil rights of citizens.

The industrial revolution, which spread during the whole of the nineteenth century, and the deep social changes which were associated with it, undermined these implicit and explicit forms of exclusion. The industrial revolution wrote down in facts the upheavals that the political revolutions of the eighteenth century had proclaimed in law: aristocratic privileges had been abolished, a new bourgeois class had hoisted itself to the summit of the social ladder; the corporations that had limited the freedom of work had been banned, industrial capitalism benefited from this absence of rules to spread; the possessions of the church and of part of the nobility had been confiscated: they were in the hands of the new capitalist masters. The aristocracy lost its power, the bourgeoisie asserted its own, the rural classes were eradicated, the proletariat was growing, craftsmen saw their corporatist protections disappear, their social mobility was fabulous and swelled the middle-class of tradesmen, small employers and moneylenders, public servants and soldiers.

This double upheaval, of the economic order and of social hierarchies, entailed political disturbances. These were particularly notable in France, where the revolution, initiated in 1789, reverberated throughout the whole of the next century: the aristocracy did not give up the fight and attempted on multiple occasions to restore the old order. It came up against the new bourgeoisie, which wanted to add political power to its economic domination and was forever changing the constitution; the members of the middle classes tried to follow suit and recurrently demanded to be included with the active citizens; at times the proletarians rebelled against an unjust order which set them aside, kept them out of political life and strengthened their economic exploitation. France was a society in the midst of a permanent revolution, going from the *ancien régime* to constitutional monarchy and on to a republic; from the republic to monarchy, then back to the republic again, before going back to the empire and seeing monarchy restored once more. The cycle of regimes, which all the classical political theorists, from Aristotle to Montesquieu, had deemed unavoidable, revolved at a frantic pace, which of course worried the rest of Europe. Indeed, if Great Britain was a more consensual society, where aristocracy was able gently to accommodate itself to the burgeoning bourgeoisie, the British elite nevertheless feared that the French unbalance might spread to the whole of Europe. Not without reason in fact, since the French revolution expanded, engendering many rebellions, and was then exported by force of arms, as the Napoleonic empire spread over a large part of Europe. All the great nations knew that the economic and social changes that France was going through affected their own societies as well and risked bringing down in their wake old political regimes. Every era has its political cardinal point: the decline of feudalism in the sixteenth century, which had called for a theory of the state (Machiavelli); the civil and religious wars at the turn of the sixteenth and seventeenth centuries, which supposed a neutral and undisputed power (Bodin, Hobbes); royal absolutism at the turn of the seventeenth and eighteenth centuries, which made necessary a theory of moderate power (Locke, Montesquieu). In the nineteenth century, the main political problem, which obsessed political thinkers and gave birth to modern liberalism and subsequently socialism, was the issue of the social and industrial revolution, which lead to a deep redefinition of thought on state and citizenship.

THE LIBERAL SOCIOLOGY OF CITIZENSHIP

Like all political doctrines, liberalism is marked by a strong doctrinal heterogeneity: there is a great difference between the British economic liberals – who were not far from considering that the market could be a social order – and the French political liberals, who remained strongly attached to public power and political life. But beyond this diversity, liberal thinkers had a number of common beliefs.

First among these was a shared conception of man, totally different from that of their predecessors. From Machiavelli to Rousseau, European political theorists had perceived man as a passionate being, animated by desire, ambition, egotism, jealousy and fear. They had presented themselves as doctors of the social body: they studied society as if it were a patient, described its ailments (civil war, corruption) and tried to find remedies (centralisation of authority, separation of powers, neutralising opposite ambitions). It was the thought of an aristocratic age: the nobility, formed by centuries of its martial and knightly habits, tended towards passionate inclination rather than rational calculation. Now, in the nineteenth century, the dominant class was much milder and the bourgeoisie's attitude was dictated by more moderate feelings: it bought and sold, invested, calculated the risks it ran and the profits it could hope for. Liberal thought is part of a bourgeois age: man is no longer subjected to his passions, he is dominated by his *interests*.[1]

The liberal conception of society flowed naturally from this new psychology. When Hobbes and his contemporaries saw men as wolves, they could only imagine society as a battle of packs: the passions of the ones and the others were fatally opposed and brought about conflict and war. Liberals reasoned in totally different terms: since they believed that men essentially acted according to the benefits and losses they thought they could expect from their behaviour, it seemed normal to them that this rational attitude produced a harmonious society. This was a true revolution in perspective: for republicans, society was necessarily chaotic because men were passionate and their passions were unavoidably conflictual; for liberals, society was naturally harmonious because men were guided by their interests and these interests were complementary.

Political thought was totally challenged by this new social conception. When it was thought that society was naturally conflictual, the existence of the state was justified: a public power, superior to individual wills, was necessary to ensure concord and order. But if one thought that society was naturally harmonious, what could be the meaning of the state? A purely instrumental role, according to Adam Smith: the state must bring about a harmonious society and then disappear. In a well regulated society, the state was detrimental: its interventions in social life disrupted natural harmony and disturbed the subtle mechanism of interests interacting. The French and German liberals thought along similar lines: they all thought, following Smith's reasoning, that modern society was fundamentally harmonious and that the action of the state must only correct its rare faults and fill in its gaps. The state, which in classical thought had no explicit limit, was now subsidiary, exterior to society. This was the first axiom of liberal political thought, which still shapes contemporary ideologies.

There is a second axiom. The etymology of liberalism shows its founding ambiguity: the word appeared only in the middle of the nineteenth century, when its followers referred to doctrines centuries old. What came to be named liberalism was only the disparate combination of old elements. The 'liberals' of the nineteenth century made reference to Locke or Montesquieu, who had never considered themselves as liberals, in order to give their ideas illustrious forefathers. They valued these noble ancestors' defence of 'individual freedom' against the weight of public power. The originality of the nineteenth-century liberals was the way in which they tried to reconcile this demand – most often posed as an axiom – with the social representation built by other 'liberals', the British and French political economists. Society preserved the freedom of all but the action of the state, though at times necessary, could jeopardise it. The political question had moved on: it was no longer a matter of thinking out the founding principles of the state but rather of placing oneself in an existing state and thinking about the tensions within it. Political thought that had been philosophical slid towards sociology and political science. The question was no longer the foundations of the state but its concrete reality, its institutions. History, which had been neglected by the thinkers of natural law to the profit of abstract reasoning, became relevant again: the nineteenth-century thinkers had in common a critique of the abstract reasoning of classical thinkers, which they considered to be responsible for the ancients' blindness towards reality, which caused them to look for their arguments in law and metaphysics rather than history, materiality and experience.

This change of method led liberals to develop institutional doctrines which would become the skeleton of political liberalism, also retrospectively called constitutionalism. All agreed on the fact that power must be contained: it must be prevented from infringing on the sphere of individual liberty and must refrain from interfering in the autonomy of society. They agreed that, in order to be limited, power must be divided: following Montesquieu, they tried to subdue power by opposing it to itself; they divided it into competing functions and rival spatial levels. Finally, they all saw political representation as a means to preserve the influence of the superior classes, thought to be moderate, in a time when the demand for political equality became irrepressible. And when they understood that the popular majority could no longer be excluded from national sovereignty they thought of ways of spreading public enlightenment, of putting into the minds of the masses the meaning of moderation and the attachment to the liberal state that was needed for the exercise of citizenship. This was the origin of the semantic extension of the concept of citizenship. In natural-law theory, which thought along the lines of rights and principles, citizenship referred to a status of rights and remained an abstract concept; when the issue of institutions and morals came to the forefront, the word citizenship came to mean the idea of public spiritedness and civic participation; the conditions of the exercise of rights became part of the common meaning of the concept.

No one has better expressed than Benjamin Constant (1767–1830) the intellectual break that liberalism brought about. According to him, the main mistake of the revolutionaries, and of the great republican minds that inspired them, was not to have conceived modern society: to have believed that social life was still organised according to the principles that animated ancient cities and to have copied their institutions: 'Montesquieu, who had a less excitable and therefore more observant mind, did not fall into quite the same errors. He was struck by the differences…but he did not discover their true cause'.[2] This was a necessary task that Constant offered to accomplish. The major fact of his time, the principle of modern life, the great force that shaped it, was no longer war, civil or international, but trade. Henceforth, trade governed the world, it was in the lap of trade that slavery was abolished, that the virus of war weakened, that states were reinforced. Commercial society transformed the aspirations of men, diverted them from violence, dulled their gregarious instincts, concentrated their desires towards a focal point: individual independence.

Constant followed explicitly in the footsteps of Smith and of those authors who considered that the great transformation of modern life lay in the fact that men, from passionate, became more modestly interested. From then, their aspirations were different. Suffice to see what they mean by freedom to measure all that separates them from men of other eras. For the ancients, and for the republican thinkers who, like Rousseau, were inspired by ancient ideas, freedom meant inclusion in the political body, the active participation in the life of the republic, the primacy of civic values over particular interests. Freedom in the modern meaning was much more modest. It was inspired from a materialist psychology rather than political passions:

> The aim of the ancients was the sharing of social power among the citizens of the same fatherland: this is what they called liberty. The aim of the moderns is the enjoyment of security in private pleasures; and they call liberty the guarantees accorded by institutions to these pleasures ('Liberty of the Ancients', p. 317).

The consequences Constant draws from this have become the axioms of liberal orthodoxy. Since men aspired above all to live a peaceful private life, the public authority must be as discreet as possible: 'Let them confine themselves to being just. We shall assume the responsibility of being happy for ourselves' (p. 326). This could be the motto of liberalism: men find their own happiness in society; the state, being only a necessary evil, must interfere as little as possible. The whole political science of liberals stems from this belief. The state must be prevented from abusing its power, and to this end, a sphere of personal autonomy must be preserved and hidden from power: 'At the point where independence and individual existence begin, the jurisdiction of sovereignty ends'.[3] The aim is to guarantee the rights of man that revolutions had only proclaimed. The issue is not so much to consecrate them as to have them respected. The cardinal belief of political liberalism was that these safeguards lie above all in the organisation of powers. The state, which perpetually threatened to abuse its authority, must be curbed, by following the rules that Montesquieu, yet again, had formulated: division and limitation of powers. Like the men of the revolution, Constant still wished to believe in the moderation of the representatives of the nation and did not really imagine that the law could threaten rights, if the powers were well organised.

This trust was only possible because Constant kept the popular masses out of the 'exercise of the rights of citizenship'. Even though he recognised great civic virtues in the 'working class' which died for their country, he denied it political capacity:

> The patriotism which gives one the courage to die for one's country is quite different, I believe, from the patriotism which enables one to fully understand its interests. There must be a further condition in addition to those prescribed by the law of birth and age. This condition is the leisure indispensable for the acquisition of understanding and soundness of judgement. Property alone makes men capable of exercising political rights (p. 214).

Proletarians may have the civic virtues of the antique citizen but they lack the moderation of the modern bourgeois. Political rights in the hands of the masses 'will inevitably serve to encroach upon property. They will pursue it by this irregular course instead of following the natural one: labour' (p. 215). The freedom of the moderns was private enjoyment, and if the only function of political rights was to preserve private enjoyment, such rights must be exclusively given to those who benefit from it: owners. The working classes were not forever relegated to civic passivity: if they used their freedom to work and to own, they would in turn access the rights of citizenship. The social mobility inherent to capitalist dynamism theoretically permitted society to move towards universal suffrage. It theoretically reconciled over time universal principles and discriminatory practices.

However, this social distinction was not sufficient to guarantee the freedom of the moderns. Owners themselves tended to be immoderate. More guarantees were necessary: a mixed regime must be set up by mixing and opposing the various social forces. A hereditary chamber (aristocracy) and a chamber representative of public opinion (bourgeoisie) should share the legislative function and control the executive power; an independent judicial power submitted to formal procedures should apply the law to specific cases; and a monarch, as a neutral force, exterior to the power-game, should arbitrate their quarrels and re-establish the balance when it was threatened (Chapter 2). Having thus controlled the state on the outside and contained it on the inside, Constant hoped that it would stay within the realm of its meagre competence and leave men free to determine their lives as they wish.

Constant gave politics a position inferior to private life but he acknowledged its instrumental value. Individual freedom was his ultimate aim, but he admitted that 'Political liberty is its guarantee, consequently, political liberty is indispensable' (p. 323). If public opinion did not make sure constantly to remind its leaders that their ministry must be exercised in the interest of the people, if it did not prevent them from encroaching on its private spheres, it would be solely responsible for their violence and corruption. Constant recalls, in the purest republican tradition – from Machiavelli to Robespierre – that civil liberty could only be ensured by the exercise of political freedom; that the rights of man and of the citizen were not contradictory but united; that the so-called inalienable rights could always be violated if their holders, acting as scrupulous citizens, did not make sure that they were respected. He goes so far as to be worried, a whole generation before Tocqueville, by the disdain of the bourgeois class for political liberty. If the ancients 'exclusively concerned with securing their share of social power, might attach too little value to individual rights and enjoyments', the risk for the moderns is that 'absorbed in the enjoyment of our private independence, and in the pursuit of our particular interests, we should surrender our right to share in political power too easily' (p. 326). In a sense Constant devalued 'citizenship', stripping it of its value and bringing it down to the level of a means of private freedom. However, by doing so, he prepared for the advent of a more ambitious liberal conception of citizenship. Anxious to develop every bulwark against the corruption of the state, Constant rehabilitated a classic argument in favour of citizenship, which would become an axiom of the liberal sociology of citizenship for the next generation:

> Political liberty, by submitting to all the citizens, without exception, the care and assessment of their most sacred interests, enlarges their spirit, ennobles their thoughts, and establishes among them a kind of intellectual equality which forms the glory and power of a people (p. 327).

This plea for the educational virtues of citizenship can seem misplaced, at the heart of a eulogy to private enjoyment and political moderation. It shows the durability of a bias favourable to knowledge, to public enlightenment, which had already been advocated by Condorcet and Kant, at the heart of 'aristocratic liberalism'. Liberals' attachment to the idea of moral and intellectual progress explains the importance Constant gave to freedom of conscience and of expression, which were the conditions for the formation of a 'public opinion', solicitous of public welfare and attentive to the lurches of power. For Constant it was still only a digression, a passing defence of one of the benefits of citizenship, but for Toqueville and John Stuart Mill it would become one of the strongest arguments in favour of equality of condition. Over the decades, liberal thinkers would polish Constant's doctrine but they would not challenge his premises or his mode of reasoning. One could even say that liberal epistemology become hegemonic during the nineteenth century. Both Tocqueville in France and John Stuart Mill in Great Britain employed the analytical and prescriptive methods used by Constant: they posed as preliminaries a contradictory observation – the *demand* of liberal freedom and the *state* of social equalisation – and tried to make these two compatible.

Tocqueville (1805–1859) was convinced during his North American journey that the major tendency of the half-century that separated him from the French Revolution was that of social equalisation. 'Amongst the novel objects that attracted my attention during my stay in the United States, nothing struck me more forcibly than the general equality of conditions.'[4] His observation owed a lot to the image he had kept of a new civilisation built on a socially homogeneous population, but he also had the intuition – which he would repeatedly confirm – that a similar evolution existed latently in Europe. The abolition of privilege, the exclusion of aristocracy from political power, changes in economic life and their social consequences all heralded a radical alteration of the social state, of morals and of the political structure. Whatever the area of investigation, be it social, political, moral or even aesthetic, one could already see that the 'extremes are softened or blunted: all that was most prominent is superseded by some mean term, at once less lofty and less low, less brilliant and less obscure, than what before existed in the world' (*Democracy in America*, II, IV, VIII, pp. 397–8). With the serene nostalgia of an enlightened aristocrat, Tocqueville deplored the universal standardisation, the triumph of mediocrity, that he saw happening, without going so far as to hope for the return of the old order. He knew that the world would no longer be what it was, he noted with disdain that men tended to absorb themselves in the trivial activities of the commercial society, that their private and collective lives had lost much of their splendour, but he kept himself from reproaching them.

The same state of mind kept him from being touched by the growing extension of political rights. His observation of the United States convinced him of the intimate solidarity of the political order and the moral and social state: 'In Connecticut the electoral body consisted, from its origin, of the whole number of citizens; and this is readily understood, when we recollect that this people enjoyed an almost perfect equality of fortune, and a still greater uniformity of opinions' (I, II, p. 29). Political equality, generalisation of citizenship, was a corollary of social equalisation; and, if equality of condition was taking shape in Europe, democracy was on the horizon. This was a 'political issue' at the heart of his work. The aim was to save freedom against all odds. Tocqueville's theory was clearly expressed: 'The nations of our time cannot prevent the conditions of men from becoming equal; but it depends upon themselves whether the principle of equality is to lead them to servitude or freedom, to knowledge or barbarism, to prosperity or to wretchedness' (II, IV, VIII, p. 400). Tocqueville offered to show, by comparison with the American situation, the risks that democracy entailed for liberty.

Let us see first the dangers which, according to Tocqueville, awaited these virtual democracies[5] that were the standardising states. His verdict makes reference to the cycle of regimes that the ancients – and then the men of the Renaissance – considered to be unavoidable. He recalls that the government of all leads naturally to its own destruction when it is given free rein. Indeed, in egalitarian regimes, there is an inclination towards concentration and extension of power:

But this is as yet only one side of the picture. The authority of governments has not only spread ... throughout the sphere of all existing powers, till that sphere can no longer contain it, but it goes further, and invades the domain heretofore reserved to private independence (II, IV, V, p. 366).

Tocqueville expresses here a theme to which he would often come back, and which would become fundamental for liberal thought: criticism of the paternalist state. According to him, the growth of the state contained the seeds of its own destruction. Tocqueville reinterpreted the republican argument of corruption, characterising it as caused by the growth of the state: since the state 'protect(s) the tranquility of my pleasures, and constantly avert(s) all dangers from my path, without my care or my concern', it weakened morals by making citizens lose consciousness of the price of freedom; the state 'so monopolizes all the energy of existence, that when it languishes everything languishes around it, that when it sleeps everything must sleep, that when it dies the State itself must perish' (I, V, p. 94). Tocqueville's attachment to the tradition of civic republicanism shows in his vocabulary and particularly in the strong meaning he gives to the word 'citizen'. Contemplating the fate of these standardising nations, he echoes Montesquieu's theories on the decline of the Roman Empire:

> When a nation has arrived at this state, it must either change its customs and its laws, or perish: the source of public virtue is dry; and though it may contain subjects, the race of citizens is extinct.

Only an active society, whose members all keep personal watch over their own well-being, could live in a democracy. It was because they were animated by a 'worried activity' in the private sphere that Americans were also active citizens, conscious of the public good, in the public sphere. Fifteen years later, his sharp condemnation of socialism stemmed from this belief. According to him, socialism is characterised as:

> the idea that the state must not only be the director of society but must be, so to speak, the master of every man...his guide, his teacher; that from fear of letting him err it must be constantly at his side, under him, around him, to guide, assure, maintain and hold him up...that is how the realisation of socialism appears to me...it's a new form of slavery.[6]

Tocqueville's defence of the autonomy of civil society has a very different basis from Constant's. While the latter gave citizenship instrumental value for the defence of private enjoyment, on the contrary, Tocqueville valued private activism as an instrument of civic identity; the priorities were turned around. And, as it eroded individual responsibility in social life, by erecting the state as a paternalistic authority, socialism seemed, for Tocqueville, a threat to the foundations of civic life. Civil society must be protected against the actions of the state to keep its vitality intact, a condition of the republic's good health.

Like the ancients and like Machiavelli, Tocqueville admired the virtue of popular government, which generated its own forces for regeneration and improvement. This regime, because it involved citizens in the government of the republic, was the only one that could convince them that their own interest was the same as the general interest: 'A man comprehends the influence which the prosperity of his country has upon his own welfare; he is aware that the laws authorise him to contribute his assistance to that prosperity, and he labours to promote it as a portion of his interest in the first place, and as a portion of his right in the second' (*Democracy in America*, I, VI, p. 331). There is a virtuous circle between democratic society and political democracy: social activity prepares civic activity, which in turn encourages social activity.

For Locke, Spinoza, Rousseau and Kant, citizenship required a certain amount of rationality, and this justified the exclusion of poor people from the civic body. Tocqueville developed a central argument of political liberalism that overcame this pessimistic observation: the exercise of political rights was the best school of civic identity, the best guarantee of the preservation of the public spirit without which the republic could not live (*Cf.* I, VI, p. 330 onwards). Citizenship was perceived as the condition of its own possibility.

Tocqueville aimed to show Europeans that the forms of American democracy were a remedy for the faults that so badly affected European governments and would guard against the risks contained in a popular regime. It was a matter of, in the moderate tradition – from Guicciardini to Locke and Montesquieu – limiting the extent of power and of controlling its excesses by pitching it against itself. Tocqueville was amazed by the American system, as Montesquieu was by the British system, and he set out to do an inventory of its innovations. He recalled, in the purest liberal tradition, that the exercise of public power must be contained by various unbridgeable limits (*cf.*, in particular, I, V, p. 52 and II, VII, p. 396); in echo of Condorcet's idea of 'social guarantee', he called for the control of the administration, which must be distinguished from the state as such – 'The State governs but does not interfere with administration'(I, V, p. 80) – and stays under the control of the law; he also borrows from the liberal tool-box the idea of political representation as the only possible form of popular sovereignty (*Cf.* I, IX, p. 193).

All this was borrowed from an earlier doctrinal base: the originality of his method lies elsewhere. In America, Tocqueville became convinced that it was not enough to divide powers into *functions* but, following in the footsteps of the Founding Fathers of the American Republic, he also opposed various *spatial* levels of power to each other. According to him, American laws contributed to the preservation of the republic because they established a balance of powers on the functional as well as on the geographical level (*Cf.* I, XVII, p. 340). Above all, Tocqueville admired the federal character of the American constitution; he believed that in this lay the source of the efficiency of a public power, since each level governs what it knows of (*Cf.* I, VIII, p. 117). As well as the being the fountain of Americans' civic spirit and the main source of their political socialisation, township institutions have the tremendous merit of interesting every citizen in the administration of the township: they 'are to liberty what primary schools are to science; they bring it within the people's reach, they teach men how to use and how to enjoy it' (I, V, p. 55). 'Local citizenship', as the modern expression has it, participates in the education of the people and prepares them for the exercise of citizenship in the state. Federalism and decentralisation are the indispensable rectifiers of the modern state, the functional equivalents of the aristocracy of the *ancien régime*, which introduced various intermediate bodies between citizens and political power and allowed the political community to benefit from the advantages of a central power without bearing the inconveniences.

> It is both necessary and desirable that the government of a democratic people should be active and powerful: and our object should not be to render it weak or indolent, but solely to prevent from abusing its aptitude and its strength. The circumstance which most contributed to secure the independence of private persons in aristocratic ages, was, that the supreme power did not affect to take upon itself alone the government and administration of the community; those functions were necessarily partially left to the members of the aristocracy: so that as the supreme power was always divided, it never weighed with its whole weight and in the same manner on each individual...I readily admit that recourse cannot be had to the same means at the present time: but I discover certain democratic expedients which may be substituted for them. Instead of vesting in the government alone all the administrative powers of which corporations and nobles have been deprived, a portion of them may be entrusted to secondary public bodies, temporarily composed of private citizens: thus the liberty of private persons will be more secure, and their equality will not be diminished (II, IV, VII, pp. 386–7).

The diffusion of power in the social body, its fragmentation in autonomous organs, was a guarantee of the 'negative freedoms' because it prevented the state from misusing its power. It was also a medium of 'positive freedoms', because it implicated citizens directly in political life. The science of society was the most original part of Tocqueville's political science. Against republican centralism, which opposed the citizen and the republic, society and state, he called for the creation of an intermediate stratum, a group of collective actors, which had their roots in civil society and were the borders of the state.

Tocqueville's effort illustrates better than anything else the change in language which took place in the political theory of the nineteenth century under liberal influence. The predominant vocabulary and syntax on the eve of the French and American Revolutions were still, as we have seen, largely marked by natural-law accents. Political freedom was conceived through a concept of citizenship defined in quasi-legal terms: a hypothetical conception of the formation of the state (the state of nature and the social contract) was used to comprehend its actual principle; citizenship was defined as an abstract status that man donned in defence of his natural rights. In the face of the difficulties that resulted from the implementation of these principles and their authoritarian wanderings, the nineteenth century saw this question evolve. It was no longer a matter of legitimising the state but rather of reforming it. A corrective attitude comes after the founding action.

Liberalism answered this question by basing itself on a new understanding of society: rather than abstractly opposing naturality and civility, it distinguished, in practice, state from society. In this respect, British economists, French liberals and Hegel took parallel paths.[7] The very nature of politics – and incidentally the definition of citizenship – was reconsidered: in contractualist political law, citizenship was understood as a second social state, its transubstantiation accomplished in order to cover the defects of society. In the liberal language, social and political conditions are not thought of as consubstantial but separate and competing.

In this new political language, the concept of citizenship was doubly reconsidered. On the one hand, the valorisation of private life and the use of political rights as a means of defending it seems to devalue citizenship, to reduce it, as the socialist criticism will say, to the defence of the middle-class man. On the other hand, the liberal reinterpretation saw civic practice as a means of social activity and intellectual progress.

The 'moral' side of citizenship, bearing individual development, finds its most advanced expression in the work of John Stuart Mill (1806–73). Raised in the hard utilitarian teachings of his father, James Mill, the young John Stuart Mill brutally discovered during his youth the barrenness of what had been up until then his way of thinking: reducing man to a calculating being, seeking only to maximise his pleasures and minimise his pains, seemed to him to be unacceptable. Faithful to his masters, he continued to believe that 'the greatest possible happiness for the greatest number' was the ultimate measure of all social rules, but considering that 'this end was only to be attained by not making it the direct end'[8] and that 'the cultivation of the feelings' (*Autobiography*, p. 118) and of subjectivity should be considered as ends in themselves – and the only ends which were worth pursuing. The utilitarian vision of man could only survive if it was placed within in a more generous and ambitious conception of humanity, in which personal development was the ultimate aim.

As a consequence, Mill had to revise the liberal sociology of citizenship deeply. He sentenced himself to subordinate the whole of his doctrine of political organisation to this demand. On the one hand, this led him to push to the extreme the liberal theory of the autonomy of society and the independence of the individual: 'there is a sphere of action in which society, as distinguished from the individual, has, if any, only an indirect interest; comprehending all that portion of a person's life and conduct which affects only himself, or if it also affects others, only with their free, voluntary, and undeceived consent and participation'.[9] The state, the government, the power – Mill does not clearly differentiate these terms – are only legitimated in acting for the preservation of the individual and for the development of his feelings and his evolution. This aspect of Mill's thought is not very original: he uses most of the liberal dogmas and reaffirms their pragmatic basis. The people must be the origin of decisions in a way that reflects its interests, it must be represented in the political sphere, the representative can only keep watch over governmental actions, powers must be divided and subsidiarity encouraged.[10] All this contributed, as Bentham and James Mill had already pointed out, to preventing political power from encroaching on the pre-rogatives of individuals.

But Mill did not stop there. He also tried to prove that democracy was not only a means but also, in itself, an essential element of individual development. Basing his political science on a sensorial psychology (in which the progress of intellect was seen to be the result of practical experiments), Mill set out to discover all the possibilities inherent in citizenship and the difficulties it must face.

As to the effects of citizenship, echoing Tocqueville, he praised the 'education of the intelligence and of the sentiments, which is carried down to the very low-est ranks of the people when they are called to take parts in acts which directly affect the great interests of their country' (*Considerations*, VIII, p. 330). He was enthusiastic about the educational strength of this 'school of public spirit' and promised that all those who benefited from the 'full privileges of citizenship' (IV, p. 255, 253)[11] would reach political maturity. Democracy, in its liberal version, contributed to the development of the human conscience by making it release itself from the egotistical interests that human consciousness was otherwise instinctively drawn to. The argument was not new but it found a particular reso-nance in Mill: political practice not only produced a form of political socialisation that was necessary to its very object, it also broadened intelligence and sensibili-ty, and was thus a good as such, and not only as a political tool. According to Mill, being a citizen was one of the essential elements of individual development.

This progressive reasoning also contained a conservative element. If citizen-ship reflected the development of individual consciousness, it also supposed, *a priori*, a certain level of intelligence on the part of the citizen. While valuing the *effects* of citizenship, Mill defines the *conditions* for the granting of political rights: 'I regard it as wholly inadmissible that any person should participate in the suffrage, without being able to read, write, and, I will add, perform the common operations of arithmetic' (VIII, p. 330). As an intellectual, cognitive and reason-ing exercise, citizenship developed knowledge. But because political understand-ing cannot be entirely built in the practice of citizenship, it also required some prior knowledge.[12] Mill seemed to think that political participation developed intellectual capabilities but could not create them if at least a basic level was not present beforehand. From the moment he tried to define an objective threshold of political competency, Mill realised the frailty of his argument. His answer, marked by empirical caution, consisted of limiting 'exclusions' as much as possible. Against one of the strongest prejudices of his time, he rejected the exclusion of women; he was one of the rare men, along with Condorcet, to do so explicitly: 'I consider it (difference of sex) to be as entirely irrelevant to political rights, as dif-ference in height, or in the colour of the hair' (VIII, p. 341). This statement was revolutionary for the times. But it was perfectly logical in the psychology of Mill: since intellectual capacities, rather than moral qualities or independence of status, are the conditions of access to citizenship, there was no reason to keep intelligent women out of it.

Mill's contribution to the definition of citizenship is essentially found in this shift in psychology. Access to citizenship can be extended as society progresses intellectually and morally; the progressive widening of citizenship will initiate a virtuous circle, the practice of political rights being one of the most powerful tools for the development of public spirit. As to the rest, Mill's institutional considerations were no different from the solutions worked out empirically by European states and defended by their liberal theorists. But his empiricism caused him to set conditions of access and benefit – intellectual in both cases – to citizenship, and this would have considerable influence over British liberal ideology. The great reforms of the electoral laws in Great Britain at the end of the nineteenth century that progressively lead to universal male suffrage were nourished by these empiricist arguments. The great theorist of public law, Bagehot, stated in the last decades of the century that if the English system worked so well, it was because it was based on the rationality of those who governed it: 'No barbarous, no semi-civilised nation ever possessed this. The mass of uneducated men could not now in England be told "go to, choose your rulers"; they would go wild'.[13] In the period between the world wars, the advantages and inconveniences of universal suffrage were still being very seriously discussed. Jennings, one of the most renowned theorists of public law of the second half of the century, recalled in a treatise of constitutional law that the extension of suffrage was a perilous act:

If they (the people) are so ignorant of political problems that they can be stampeded by slogans or specious promises or allegations of unknown terrors ... a wide franchise is merely an invitation to corrupt demagogy.[14]

But he refused to give in to the objections of the opponents of universal suffrage, and his argument seems to come straight from Mill:

There is strength in the argument that an illiterate electorate is likely to be led astray by unscrupulous demagogues; but, in the first place, the British people is not illiterate and, in the second place, reason and experience show that the necessary educational facilities are made available very slowly, if at all, so long as they are deprived of the vote (p. 212).

Generally, liberalism greatly influenced the concept of citizenship, giving it inflections that long seemed inseparable from the new political language in which citizenship was discussed. The core of republican principles remained but they were de-sanctified. The discourse of politics lost its solemnity and became more empirical, opening the way for new forms of analysis which would come to dominate classical political science. From 1850 to 1950, political thought would dwell on the most efficient means to defend individual freedoms, on the best forms of balance between powers, on the extent of the power of the state and its concentration, on the way to grant political rights to the largest number without endangering the regime. And political sociology would continue, and still continues, to study the impact of associations, of federalism and decentralisation, of mandatory schooling, on civic participation.

On the other hand, these liberals were incapable of thinking out the full implications of the social issue. The process of equalisation of conditions and the material misery of the working classes marked Tocqueville as well as Mill. Both felt the imminence of this issue and tried to prevent the radical changes that it implied. For that matter, the French liberal acknowledged the limits of his answer, when he admitted that no sooner was it posed than it already seemed outdated:

> This state of dependence and wretchedness, in which a part of the manufacturing population of our time lives, forms an exception to the general rule, contrary to the state of all the rest of the community; but, for this very reason, no circumstance is more important or more deserving of the special consideration of the legislator; for when the whole of society is in motion, it is difficult to keep any one class stationary; and when the greater number of men are opening new paths to fortune, it is no less difficult to make the few support in peace their wants and their desires (*Democracy in America*, II, III, VII, p. 226).[15]

Nevertheless, liberals continued to state their confidence in the virtues of trade; they long feigned to believe, or sincerely believed, that the freedom to work and the right of property held the promise of a fairer society and grimly refused all state intervention in the 'private' sphere of work. Meanwhile socialists, and Marx in particular, were giving the 'social issue' a crucial importance, using it against Europeans tradition, both republican and liberal, in one of the most radical theoretical destructions in the history of western political thought.

THE SOCIAL ISSUE: FROM REFUSAL TO COMPROMISE

The contractualist tradition had always, in one way or another, set unbridgeable boundaries to the exercise of public power: whether what preceded the state was considered to be out of its realm (Hobbes), or natural law was invoked (Locke and Spinoza), or natural rights were proclaimed (Rousseau), it had always been acknowledged that the fundamental rights of man ought to be preserved, even if the means to do so were not always sufficient. The liberals went beyond this principle: they extended the sphere of the individual's autonomy, the catalogue of his rights, to all aspects that they sought to designate as private. With no reliable criteria for defining the private sphere, and with no obvious logic, they carved out from the political sphere, previously consubstantial to society, a new, unlimited sphere of what 'concerns the individual alone' – the principle was generous but totally inept so long as what was essentially individual had not been defined. Whatever its coherence, this principle legitimised the social and economic inequality that characterises the history of capitalist states, and the privatisation of various public functions that were considered to be less political and were now defined as 'economic'.

It was not by chance that, in the middle of the nineteenth century, the social issue jostled modern political theory. Rampant industrialisation and the pauperisation it brought blatantly exposed the hypocrisy of classical political law: when the law was supposed to establish and orientate society, one could still believe oneself free through it. When the general interest forwent the ambition of being above particular wills, the myth worked no longer. This was all the more true since it took so long for democratic principles to be given substance: in France particularly, the fiction of the representative nation was introduced to deprive the people of the effective right to take part in the formation of the general will, that is, when the republic was not simply abolished. The social issue appeared as the political and philosophical formulation of this deficiency in modern political theory, at a time when the social and political condition of the people made a strong impact on minds, in the middle of the nineteenth century.[16] The real political order was challenged not just for its blatant injustice but all the more strongly because it professed to base itself on principles that it denied in practice.

The political strength of democratic principles was illustrated from the start by the passionate reactions to the French Declaration of the Rights of Man and of the Citizen. For some this was the epitome of theoretical evil; for others, it merely drew a chaste veil over the flaws it professed to combat. Robespierre attacked its hypocrisy when he denounced the disdain in which it was held by those who had proclaimed it. Marat criticised the text whose solemnity only blinded gullible citizens. Babeuf regretted the fact that, having been expressed, equality remained a declaration of principle. Echoing the critics of the Declaration who derided its abstract character, a large republican movement criticised the gap that remained between theory and practice. The critique of the proclamation of inviolable rights put republicans closer to more conservative reactions, though the conclusions they drew from it were opposed: for revolutionary critics, the rights of man were not inoperable but needed to become reality.[17] The main fault of the Declaration was, for conservatives, inherent in its principle. For these radical revolutionaries, formal rights, whose natural and inalienable character had been proclaimed, did not consecrate the equality of men as they claimed, but, on the contrary, mocked it. The Declaration was only, according to Babeuf, a 'perfidious Declaration of the Rights, not of Man but of gamblers, usurers, grabbers, of insatiable and murderous leeches, of all sorts of greedy speculators'.[18] It was a sham, a diversionary move.

The double socialist criticism of the rights of man is in this line of thought: refusal of their internal contradictions and of their formal status, which make them irremediably mystifying. In the years immediately following the French Revolution, this criticism remained within the republican tradition; rather than rebelling against it, critics took republicanism as being as good as its word and begged it to keep its promises. The criticism of Marx, however, even if it shared these premises, adopted a totally different attitude: it targeted the republican idea itself, the idea of the social contract and the legal language in which it was formulated. Marx undermined all the pillars that supported contractualism and the legal discourse of rights: statism, legalism and normative individualism.

As a young man, Marx had been very enthusiastic towards this tradition. He was part of the generation which kept from Hegel's work only what could be put to use in the framework of the Prussian state, what was most liberal. His articles in the *Rhenan Gazette* borrowed from the rationalism and humanism of Kant and Fichte in order to fight censorship, despotism and feudal residues. Marx was first a young German polemecist for whom the republican tradition, based on a vision of man as a sensible and reasonable being, was the antithesis to be opposed to the archaisms of a state ignorant of the rule of law and right. He was a son of the *Aufklärung* and, action following words, he broadcast the seeds of public enlightenment in his ardent editorials.

Then came the deception. The state, as Marx saw it act, did not seem capable of honouring its promises, of embodying, as Hegel had wanted it to, universal reason in the form of law. Marx came to think that the faults of the state were congenital, essential, incurable. The problem was not the so-called contradiction between the essence of the state and its existence, it was inherent in the idea of the state itself. Marx had this intuition at the time when he realised, with the help of Feueurbach, the particularity of German philosophy, of which Hegel was the symbol: it had criticised religious representations and tried to replace them by a secular conception of politics but had remained prisoner of the idealism that initially drove it.[19] To go beyond this, it was necessary to ask a new question: 'It is above all the *task of philosophy*, which is in the service of history, to unmask human self-estrangement in its *secular forms*, once its sacred form has been unmasked'.[20] Following the work of philosophical modernity, Hegel had replaced the immutable dogmas of religion by a legal representation of the political; this meant exchanging one alienation for another, Marx thought. He continued the demystification: 'Thus, the critique of heaven is transformed into the critique of the earth, the *critique of religion* into the *critique of law*, the *critique of theology* into the *critique of politics*' (*ibid.*).

Through Hegel, Marx was not only aiming his criticism at German idealism but at the whole of the republican tradition that, since Grotius and Hobbes, had used the state as the cornerstone of the freedom of man. Their ambition had been to emancipate men from the natural and divine constraints in which they had been stuck for centuries, and the idea of a social contract, of a state stemming from the will of the assembled people, had been their tool. Or, said Marx, 'in freeing himself *politically* he frees himself in a round-about way, through a *medium*' ('The Jewish question', *ibid.*, p. 34). And it is precisely this that makes emancipation illusory. The state, in Marx's conception, did not replace men's previous unfree condition but only partially neutralised it when it 'calls on every member of the nation to be an *equal* participant in the national sovereignty' (p. 35) . The state understands men in universal categories, but the equal status it grants them does not erase their primary condition: 'Far from superseding these factual distinctions, the state's existence presupposes them: it feels itself to be *political state* and can affirm its *universality* only in opposition to these factors' (*ibid.*).

Marx understood the state in the exact terms that Hegel laid down: as the sub-limated form of civil society, completing it without overturning it. But he refused to see the state as the *achieved* form of universality, the place where men developed fully by being conscious of the effectiveness of their freedom through the community. He refused this because the Hegelian state did not totally absorb man but only his political dimension, neglecting his social condition: 'All presuppositions of this *egoistic* life are retained *outside* the sphere of the state in *civil society*' (p. 36). Political emancipation was an illusion because the real place of alienation was civil society, which politics withdraws from: 'this civil society is the true crucible and theatre of all history' and one then sees how 'absurd the traditional concept of history is which neglected real relationships and limited itself to high-sounding activities of princes and states' ('The German Ideology', p. 134).

Marx showed the influence of the conceptions of society given by the first political economists, such as Adam Smith, in the formation of his thought. Like them, he considered the sphere of production and trade as the main place of men's life and the state as a 'superstructure', which could have only, by its essential nature, a limited influence on civil society.[21] It is a true reversal of the Hegelian conception: while the philosopher from Jena rehabilitated the state as the finished form of the incomplete human community (civil society), Marx criticised the failure of the state and opposed to it the primacy of civil society. Hegel had refuted Smith with the tools of the republican tradition; Marx dismantled the idea of a republic with the weapons of the first liberals.[22]

His reading of the republican tradition is, by the way, a brilliant interpretation of his fundamental operation, which shows the crucial part that the concept of citizenship played in it. Political emancipation, he wrote, is based on a 'decoupling of man into a public man and a private man'.

> The disintegration of man into Jew and citizen of a state, into Protestant and citizen of a state, into religious person and citizen of a state, this disintegration is no lie *about* citizenship, it is not a circumvention of political emancipation, it is *political emancipation itself*, the *political* manner of emancipating oneself from religion' ('The Jewish question', p. 38).

In its very expression, the Declaration of the Rights of Man and of the Citizen revealed the particular nature of citizenship. Citizenship was only a legal status, a 'political lion's skin' said Marx, that man must wear to defend his integrity as a man: 'the so-called *human rights*, the *droits de l'homme*, in contrast to the *droits du citoyen*, are nothing but the rights of the *member of civil society*, i.e. of egoistic man, of the man who is separated from other men and from the community' (p. 44). Marx undeniably understood the ambition of the modern concept of citizenship but he refused to acknowledge that it had achieved its aim. On the contrary, he stated that the artifice, far from permitting the development of man as its promoters wished, impoverished him:

> Citizenship in the state, ...the *political community*, is even reduced by the political emancipators to the status of a mere *means* for the preservation of these so-called human rights, in other words...the citizen is declared to be the servant of the egoistic man and the sphere in which man functions as a communal being is degraded and subordinated to the sphere in which he functions as a partial being; finally...it is not man as citizen but man as bourgeois who is taken to be the *real* and *true* human being (p. 46).

The abstraction of citizenship is a failure because it divided man into a community being on the one hand (citizens) and an isolated being on the other (man); and it subordinated the first to the second. Marx was still in the humanist tradition, insofar as human emancipation was the perspective of his system, but his humanism was communal, that is, concerned with the individual *in his community*, and not individualistic. For him, true emancipation could only come through the *collective* accession to freedom, and he saw individual, liberal freedom as an obstacle to this goal. This explains his disdain for modern political law, based entirely on the natural rights of man. From here stemmed his project of 'real' emancipation, by opposition to the formal freedom of statism:

> Only when the actual individual man absorbs the abstract citizen of the state into himself and has become in his empirical life, in his individual labour, in his individual relationships a *species-being*; only when he has recognised and organised his 'own forces' as *social* forces and therefore no longer separates the social force from himself in the form of *political* force; only then is human emancipation completed (p. 50).

Marx, having the whole statist tradition in mind, aimed his criticism at Rousseau, whom he held responsible for the abstraction of sovereignty and considered guilty of the perpetuation of alienation. We cannot avoid thinking that this accusation is based on a misunderstanding. Benjamin Constant reproached Rousseau and his predecessors for ignoring the nature of modern society, its dissociation from the state. On the contrary, Marx criticised in the project of Rousseau this very same separation that Constant did not see. This was because Marx read Rousseau, and all the republican tradition, with a liberal bias. He understood the artificiality of citizenship but refused the republican argument, in the Declaration, according to which a virtuous circle existed between man and citizen – citizenship allowing the protection of the rights of man and these favouring the efficiency of political activity. Marx shared the liberals' scepticism towards the strength of the law and the state, which he believed incapable of efficiently governing the course of things. For political economists, the state must be contained because its action affects spontaneous social harmony. For Marx, the perspective is reversed: the state was condemned because it was limited, because it was incapable of inflecting social life, in fact because it was liberal. The observations of Marx echoed those of the liberals but his conclusions were reversed: he condemned the unfairness of civil society and the incapacity of the state to put an end to it. Animated by the same *goals* as the republicans (collective autonomy), he criticises their *means* (state and citizenship), with the help of the liberals' *analyses* (the independence of society from politics)

The young Marx laid down the choices that would guide his work: he philosophically broke with modern political law, he forced himself to consider all representation as an illusion and to look elsewhere, in what he believed to be the immediate reality, for the answer to the political problem of alienation: 'we will begin with real, active men, and from their real life process we will expose the development of the ideological reflections and echoes of this life process'. Philosophy no longer revealed reality; analysis of reality would reveal the shams of philosophy. The task was no longer a matter of ideally elaborating a legitimate policy but of building the *science* of real politics. Marx believed he could demonstrate from history that the state, which claimed to be 'an independent shape, separate from the genuine individual and collective interests', was only the place where were reflected the struggles that the division of labour created between social classes: 'all struggles within the state, the struggle between democracy, aristocracy and monarchy, the struggle for the right to vote, etc. are nothing but illusory forms…in which the genuine struggles of the various classes among themselves are carried out' ('The German Ideology', p. 131). The state was not just an impartial arena in which the general interest was constructed but the tool of the dominant class, which used the state to defend its interests. The state did not solve the contradictions of civil society, it reinforced them. This was how Marx parted ways with the liberals: all his mature work aimed to 'scientifically' prove the wrongness of the ideology of the harmony of interests. The criticism of political law was extended to the criticism of political economy. The market society separated man from himself, insofar as he could not freely use his labour power. To free men, the blind game of production relations must be replaced by an association of individuals 'that puts the conditions of free development and movement of the individuals under their control'. This form of free association, which he called communism, and which 'consciously treats all the presuppositions previously considered natural as being in fact creations of earlier generations of men, thus stripping them of their naturality and subordinating them to the power of united individuals' (p. 174), must be reached. Only then would personal development and material life be brought together, 'the development of individuals into total individuals': 'At this time the transformation of labour into self-activity corresponded to the transformation of previously restrained interaction into an interaction of individuals as such' (pp. 179–80). When the people became conscious of their alienation (political and economic) they would be able to decide to free themselves and to create an autonomous community in which man would be reconciled with himself. 'In place of the old bourgeois society, with its classes and class antagonisms, we shall have an association in which the free development of each is the condition for the free development of all'.[23]

Marx pushed to the farthest point this ideal of an immediate and transparent community. He rejected all the mediations that political modernity had set up as conditions of freedom, and that are understood under the sign of citizenship. He redefined a collective practice that was, in some ways, close to that of the ancient cities, but which kept the political institution, the administration of collective issues in a specialised framework. For Marx, politics are diluted in the wholeness of society. In his circumstantial writings, like those on the Paris Commune (1871), one finds a sketchy political formalisation of his ideal complete and unitary community. It could be said that he defended a citizenship without a state. The 'government of producers by themselves' replaced the statist organisation. The nation governed itself after being freed of 'the State power which claimed to be the embodiment of that unity independent of, and superior to, the nation itself, from which it was but a parasitic excrescence'. The functions of power were no longer divided or delegated – the officials elected by universal suffrage being accountable and dismissible workers. 'The Communal Constitution would have restored to the social body all the forces hitherto absorbed by the State parasite feeding upon, and clogging the free movement of society'.[24] The political activity of citizens, in the sense of autonomous and collective administration of common issues, is highly valued by Marx, but it is, according to him, resolutely exterior to the state.

His interpretation of the Commune tried to show that it embodied the fleeting hope of a communist policy, immersed in society, unspecialised, delocalised – having no fixed place. He knew what errors he risks: 'It is generally the fate of completely new historical creations to be mistaken for the counterpart of older and even defunct forms of social life, to which they may bear a certain likeness' ('Civil War in France' p. 515), he regretted, alluding to the feudal cities with which he was afraid his communism would be confused. In any case it is undeniable that the politics of Marx borrowed some features of the pre-modern forms of politics. It was an intellectual return, albeit after a conscious repudiation of historical organisations, to a holist, immediate and social conception of the city, while the whole effort of the moderns had been to acknowledge the individual as the basic unit of analysis and to translate into law the organisation of a society thus conceptualised. This voluntary regression, brought about by his refusal of the individualistic perspective, is imbued with the republican ethos. Marx respected its oratorical power; his political texts had its inflections. In the revolutionary excitement of 1848, he borrowed a language that would not have been disowned by the most eloquent republicans:

> Citizens, the democratic association aimed towards union and fraternity amongst all people (...) has come to offer you the homage of its congratulations for the great task that the French nation has accomplished as well as its gratitude for the immense favour this nation has done to the cause of humanity.[25]

The phrasing will always have republican features and the citizen will remain a highly esteemed word. But these are only words, only appearances; in his concepts, Marx denied all that was the essence of the republic, and particularly its idea of citizenship.

After Marx, those concerned with the social issue did not follow this theoretical destruction of the republican tradition. While keeping the Marxist critique of capitalism and revolutionary rhetoric, democratic socialists again tried to frame the social issue in the terms of the republican conception of citizenship. Aware of the dangers posed by emancipatory social movements, conservatives tried to cool revolutionary ardour by undermining its material basis. In Germany, popular demands were dealt with by using the power of royal authority: Bismarck pulled out the rug from under the feet of protesters by instituting the first elements of what later will be called social security. Everything happened as if the idea of protection, the *raison d'être* of the state, was spread to economic safety, and as if the state was consequently only assuming its traditional tasks in the face of new preoccupations. In the United Kingdom, conservatives used the same logic. The Poor Laws and the support system set up in the nineteenth century were, as the British sociologist Thomas Marshall rightly observed, a negative of citizenship: 'The Poor Law treated the claims of the poor, not as an integral part of the rights of the citizen, but as an alternative to them – as claims which could be met only if the claimants ceased to be citizens in any true sense of the word'.[26] Only those who were unable to use their civil and civic rights – freedom of work and right of property – were entitled to the help of the state.

Part of the socialist movement also perceived the social issue as exterior to citizenship in the state. The answer theorised by Proudhon in France and the Fabians in Great Britain was mutualist or co-operative: it was a matter of encouraging workers to take their destiny into their own hands and to organise autonomous forms of mutual help, even of production. This meant that citizenship was considered to be powerless to solve the social issue, and displacing the issue out of its sphere – or constituting a new citizenship, more autonomous and independent from the authority of the state.

Other parts of the socialist movement adopted, on the contrary, republican tradition: far from banishing the social issue to civil society, they tried to solve it politically. Jean Jaurès gave the most eloquent formulation of this project. He reproached, in words that recall Robespierre or the young Marx, the powerlessness of the state in the thought of orthodox republicans, who were strongly influenced by liberal culture:

You have made the republic, but in doing so you have set up a true contradiction between the economic and political orders of our country. In the political order, the nation is sovereign. You have made all citizens, workers included, into an assembly of kings...but while the worker is sovereign in the political order, he is reduced to serfdom in the economic order. And at any given time, this king in the political order, can be thrown into the street.[27]

Now, Jaurès, and with him a large number of European socialists,[28] declined to accept this separation. But he also refused the abolition of the state that Marx had called for. In his meaning, socialism is the complete form of the republic, where the contradiction is solved because the parliamentary political game (which he accepts and honours) must aim to orientate things in the direction of the general interest, and close the gap between principles and practices: 'The triumph of socialism will not be a break from the French revolution, but the accomplishment of the French Revolution in new economic conditions'.[29] Jaurès was indeed a figure of republican tradition when he thought of freedom in the words of the Declaration: citizenship was participation in the formation of the law, one is submitted to. He simply extended the spectrum; he criticises liberals' separation of state and civil society, which allowed, as Marx had understood, the perpetuation of social inequality while declaring political equality.

In Germany, Eduard Bernstein took a parallel path. He tried to deduce socialism from the democratic idea, rather than opposing the two ideas: 'Socialism is nothing else than the application of democracy to all social life.... Democracy is both means and end. It is a weapon in the struggle for socialism, and it is the form in which socialism will be realised'.[30] He even went so far as to put socialism in the lap of liberalism, by calling it 'organised liberalism', opposing it to 'expectant liberalism' that only acts to free the individual from political constraints while neglecting his state of economic and social subjection.

In practice, the social issue influenced the liberal-republican conception. Its very nature presumed that the traditional representation of law and the individualistic premises it is based upon, be questioned. In Europe, the modes of opposition and resolution varied from one country to the next, but everywhere similar elements were joined. The 'working classes' organised forms of mutual help by themselves, which the state sometimes afterwards organised and made mandatory; socialist parties worked in parliaments on the drafting of work regulations or norms of social security; conservative or liberal governments, under pressure from protests and organised workers' movements, took the initiative in legislating for those types of mechanisms, or of consecrating, extending and rationalising those already in use. Trade unions obtained from the state the right to exist and to declare norms governing these matters. As a result, social law was built by the state but also largely outside of it, and was sometimes against it.

Political citizenship, in the meaning it had up to this point, was replaced by other forms of organisation of freedom. As Thomas Marshall says, the collective use of their civil rights by workers united in trade unions was an 'anomaly, because hitherto it was political rights that were used for collective action...whereas civil rights were intensely individual'.[31] From the moment when the liberal state acknowledged the legitimacy of trade union negotiations, it admitted the incompleteness of the model of citizenship it had promoted and to which it had had the pretence of reducing politics. Marshall deduces from this that the social normative system, accessory to traditional legislation, should be seen as a 'secondary system of industrial citizenship parallel with and supplementary to the system of political citizenship'.[32]

But the conceptual reconciliation is maybe not as easy as Marshall hoped. Social law not only completed civil and political law, it questioned the whole legal logic upon which citizenship had been based until then. The doctrine of the state as sole origin of the law disappeared: acknowledging the autonomy of civil society, social law gave it the right to draw up its own norms. The individual character of rights was also altered: rather than looking for *responsibilities*, social law pointed out *risks,* and instead of inflicting *punishments* it established *insurances* and handed out compensations.[33] Finally, social law broke the universality of classical law: each citizen was no longer treated equally but instead the social circumstances in which he evolved were taken into consideration – the compensation or allowance was not universal but conditioned by an accident, a particular situation. A *sociological* logic replaced *philosophical* reasoning.

The invention of social law created an intermediate sphere between the citizen and the state: conflicts appear between social groups and not among individual men, and that is where they must be solved. The procedural social law – labour law – organises the permanent negotiations of the stakes in this space that the state withdraws from, that it only marks out. A substantial social right results from this – labour law and social security – which is marked by collective logic, acknowledging groups that civil law ignored. Is this a break from or the extension of the classical conceptions of citizenship? The procedural social rights, insofar as they formalise a normative system based on the participation of workers, can be understood, as Marshall did, as a parallel form of citizenship, a side-lane for bridging the gaps in the traditional normative process. Social rights have a more ambiguous status and, for this reason, some tend to refuse to consider them a part of the rights of man and of citizen. Marshall already noted that they are not, at the difference of civil and political rights, really subjective, and that the citizen cannot obtain their application from a jurisdiction, their aim being essentially collective; these rights must then be understood as 'the declaration of a policy that one hopes to see applied one day'.[34] They are a 'regulatory horizon' expressing, like natural rights, an ideal towards which political society tends. But this distinction is not always easy to implement: the right to healthcare, to justice, to education and so on, are ideals if they refer to an outcome; but they are also authentic subjective rights, in the sense that the citizen of a welfare-state has a right to access healthcare, justice, education. The state does not promise the same welfare to all, but he gives everyone the same access, free or proportional to revenues, to the collective tools of wellbeing. In this meaning, social rights are more than an ideal, when they correspond to effective public services.

There is no other explanation of the fact that the concept of citizenship has gone through a new semantic extension over the last few years, by integrating this dimension of participation in a society of social justice: 'One should not lose sight', writes Pierre Rosanvallon, for example, 'of the fact that social benefits also have a dimension of citizenship. They are one of the expressions of the social bond and testify to a form of equality. This symbolic dimension is essential.'[35]

In the liberal language of the nineteenth century, citizenship was not only a number of rights, it was also the civic identity which came with it. In today's language, marked by the welfare state's ambitions of social equality, the concept of citizenship incorporates social rights and integrates the feeling of membership in a social community. The state is no longer only the place where the general will is formed, it is also a common heritage to which all citizens are both indebted and creditors. The distinction between state and civil society is blurred since social goods are the object of political negotiations. The historical compromise of the welfare state was bringing the social issue back into the lap of the law, to make it a matter of popular sovereignty, rather than excluding it, as liberals required. Political equality was not translated into social equality but it allowed workers to act on social inequality as citizens: 'those who do not own instruments of production consent to the institution of the private ownership of capital stock while those who own productive instruments consent to political institutions that permit other groups to effectively press their claim to the allocation of resources and the distribution of outputs'.[36]

The rights-claims are a development of the idea of citizenship because they result from and reinforce the community of citizens. Citizens have a right to livelihood only because they all, identically, form a political community that they give themselves to and that gives itself to them. They are entitled to the holdings of the state because they contribute to them. One could say, in natural-law language, that as they renounced their natural freedom to enjoy equal freedom, they renounced their natural holdings in order to benefit from collective wealth. Social contributions and taxes are to social security what obedience to law is to the rule of law: it is only when all the citizens follow the rules, that the (material) security of all is ensured. Rights-claims are part of the same logic as political rights: they all result from the same anthropological axioms – the rights of man – they have the same universal character and they contribute in the same way to the constitution of a community. They do not change the essence of the republican concept but extend its reach: they extend sovereignty to the processes of social negotiations and community to social holdings. When laws can influence social and economic life, when it is submitted to the deliberations of citizens, through the state or at its side, one can once more be free by obeying the self-imposed law.

NOTES

1   Cf. A.O. Hirschmann, *The Passions and the Interests: Political Arguments for Capitalism before its Triumph*, (Princeton, Princeton University Press) 1977.
2   B. Constant, 'The liberty of the Ancients compared with that of the Moderns'(1819) in *Political Writings*, edited by B. Fontana (Cambridge, Cambridge University Press, 1988), p. 319.
3   B. Constant, 'Principles of politics' (1815) in Fontana (ed.), *Political Writings*, p. 177.
4   A. de Tocqueville, *Democracy in America*, translated by Henry Reeve (London, Longman, Green, Longman, and Roberts, 1862), Introductory Chapter, p. xlvii.
5   Cf. J.-C. Lamberti, *Tocqueville et les deux démocraties* (Paris, PUF, 1983).

6   A. de Tocqueville, 'Discours sur le droit au travail' (1848), in *Egalité sociale et liberté politique*, edited by P. Gibert (Paris, Aubier, 1977), pp. 197-198.

7   *Cf.* A. Renaut, 'Genèse du couple Etat-société' *Projet* 1993, 233, pp. 7–16.

8   J.S. Mill, *Autobiography*, edited by J.M. Robson (London, Penguin, 1989), p. 117.

9   J.S. Mill, *On Liberty*, edited by S. Collini (Cambridge, Cambridge University Press, 1989), p. 15.

10 *Cf.* J. S. Mill, *Considerations on Representative Government*, edited by J. Gray (Oxford, Oxford University Press, 1991), respectively chapters III, V, XV, and XVII.

11 The semantic extension of the *word* citizenship happened in English and not in French. For Mill, citizenship meant the modern *concept* in its full meaning.

12 Concerned with social justice, Mill added that 'the means of attaining these elementary acquirements should be within the reach of every person, either gratuitously, or at an expense not exceeding what the poorest, who earn their own living, can afford', (Considerations. VIII, p. 330).

13 W. Bagehot, 'The prerequisites of Cabinet Government, and the peculiar form which they have assumed in England, in *Collected Works*, edited by N. Saint John-Stevas (London, The Economist, 1974), vol. V, *Political Essays*, I, pp. 367–71, p. 369.

14 W.I. Jennings, *The British Constitution* (Cambridge, Cambridge University Press, 1941), p. 2.

15 For J.S. Mill, see *Autobiography*, particularly VII, pp. 216–29.

16 *Cf.* J. Donzelot, *L'invention du social* (Paris, Fayard, 1984).

17 *Cf.* B. Binoche, *Critiques des droits de l'homme* (Paris, PUF, 1989), chapter V, pp. 97–101.

18 Quoted in Binoche, *Critiques*, p. 101.

19 We follow here the intellectual chronology established notably by L. Althusser, 'Marxisme et humanisme' in *Pour Marx* (Paris, Maspero, 1967), pp. 225–49; and F. Châtelet, 'Marx, encore', in *Questions, objections* (Paris, Denoël/Gonthier, 1979), pp. 145–241.

20 K. Marx, 'Critique of Hegel's philosophy of right: introduction', 'The Jewish question' and 'The German ideology' in *Early Political Writings*, edited by J. O'Malley and R. A. Davis (Cambridge, Cambridge University Press, 1994), p. 58.

21 *Cf.* Renaut, 'Genèse du couple Etat-société'.

22 *Cf.* Rosanvallon, *Le libéralisme économique*, pp. 179–207.

23 K. Marx and F. Engels, 'Manifesto of the Communist Party', in *Marx*, edited by M. Adler (Chicago, University of Chicago, 1990), p. 429.

24 K. Marx, 'The Civil War in France', in *The Portable Karl Marx*, edited by E. Kamenka (Penguin, 1983), pp. 514–5.

25 K. Marx, 'Appel aux citoyens membres du gouvernement provisoire de la République française' (1848), in *Le mouvement ouvrier français*, vol. I (Paris, Maspero, 1974) p. 119.

26 T.H. Marshall, *Citizenship and Social Class, and Other Essays* (Cambridge, Cambridge University Press, 1950).

27 J. Jaurès, Chambre des députés, 11 novembre 1893, quoted in Donzelot, *L'invention du social*, p. 68.

28 *Cf.* A. Bergougnioux and B. Manin, *La social-démocratie ou le compromis* (Paris, PUF, 1979); A. Przeworski, 'Social Democracy as a Historical Phenomenon' in *Capitalism and Social Democracy* (Cambridge, Cambridge University Press), 1985, pp. 7–46.

29 J. Jaurès, 'Discours de Toulouse', in *L'esprit du socialisme* (Paris, Denoël, 1971), p. 71.

30 E. Bernstein, *The Preconditions of Socialism* (Cambridge, Cambridge University Press, 1993), p. 142.

31 Marshall, *Citizenship and Social Class*, p. 40

32 *Ibid.*, p. 26.

33 *Cf.* F. Ewald, *L'Etat-Providence* (Paris, Fayard, 1985).

34 Marshall, *Citizenship and Social Class*, p. 29.

35 P. Rosanvallon, *La nouvelle question sociale* (Paris, Seuil, 1995), p. 98.

36 Przeworski, *Capitalism and Social Democracy*, p. 207.

chapter six | citizenship and diversity

Political concepts never cease to evolve. Reflections of the preoccupations and ways of reasoning of their time, they change with the time. As much as any keyword of our political language, and certainly more than some, citizenship remains at the centre of passionate debate. If one observes the contemporary use of the concept of citizenship, in scientific writings as well as in political discourse, the main issue seems to be the link between citizenship and the nation-state. Until recently, this link seemed unbreakable. Citizenship had been invented by the ancients to define the link between the citizen and the political community; the concept reappeared for the same reasons during the Renaissance and modern times. After the democratic revolutions of the eighteenth century, the link between citizenship, state and nationality became increasingly strong. Modern states required of their citizens that they pay taxes and defend their country at the cost of their lives. In order to ensure their loyalty, states created national histories, invented traditions and did not stop short of rewriting history and giving themselves origins that were more often imagined than real.[1]

The loyalty of citizens was strengthened still by the praxis of mass democracies during the twentieth century: the social and democratic states built around both world wars gave their citizens political rights and social benefits. Simultaneously, in the western world, the borders of citizenship, of gender and of race were starting to fade away. After the gradual disappearance of social distinctions at the beginning of the century, women were being granted the right to vote and racial discrimination was slowly being abolished. All this contributed to the reinforcement of the civic link. The citizen is ever more attached to the state if he thinks he is a member of an historic community, if he perceives himself as a holder of a portion of sovereignty and if he knows himself to be supported by his fellow-citizens united in solidarity. The contemporary state, simultaneously a liberal democracy and a welfare state, could have seemed to represent, over a few decades, a complete community of citizens.

Historical irony has it, that barely had this 'complete' citizenship been established, than it seemed to enter a crisis. The western world went into a long phase of economic recession at the end of the 1970s, which led to the cutback of the new social benefits. Now, a few years later, awareness of economic and financial 'globalisation' and the emergence of supra-governmental authorities, foster the feeling that the state is losing control of its destiny. A citizenship confined to the nation-state seems insufficient, or, to be more precise, out of focus with the real places of power. This observation is the dominant feature of contemporary politics and leads to the re-evaluation of the conceptual link between citizenship, the state and the nation.

This is all the more true since groups on the inside are again calling into question the 'national' character of the state. Ethnic and religious minorities that modern states had oppressed or relegated to the private sphere have initiated a struggle for recognition. They are challenging the universal claim of the modern idea of citizenship as a decoy used by the main ethnic or religious group to legitimise its domination, and are demanding that their differences be taken into consideration. The political science of the end of the twentieth and beginning of the twenty-first century focuses on the meaning of citizenship in multi-national states and in a world where states are no longer as sovereign as they claim to be.

The coincidence between the two phenomena is striking. National citizenship is challenged from the bottom in the name of 'multiculturalism', at the very same time as it is accused of being drained of its substance from the top through globalisation.[2] And despite the very dissimilar historical origins of the two phenomena, the challenges posed by multiculturalism on the one hand and the surpassing of the state on the other hand, are largely the same, conceptually speaking. In the last resort, they all come down to the same fundamental question: what are the conditions of a viable citizenship? What is the minimal threshold of rights and duties that must be imposed on all citizens to preserve the coherence of the political community?

RETHINKING CIVIC INCLUSION

The issue was evaded for a long time. Before democracies appeared, states imposed their laws upon their subjects without asking for agreement or tolerating opposition. The issue was also avoided during the time when modern democracies were being formed: the nationalist myth was so strong that, except for very rare exceptions, no one challenged the forced assimilation of small minority groups. The creation of a homogenous people, with a common language and history, relegating other traits of personal identity to the private sphere, seemed to be the price to be paid for a common citizenship. The optimistic philosophy of history which marked nineteenth century liberalism and which lasted long into the twentieth century legitimised the voluntary eradication of differences: everything that was an obstacle to the reign of modern citizenship was seen to be 'archaic', 'barbaric', or 'obscure'. Liberal citizenship embodied the ideals of liberty and equality, as opposed to the domination, obscurantism and intolerance of the old forms of collective life. John Stuart Mill, an icon of the liberalism of that time, perfectly sums up this feeling shared by the highest social classes:

Nobody can suppose that it is not more beneficial to a Breton, or a Basque of French Navarre, to be brought into the current of the ideas and feelings of a highly civilized and cultivated people – to be a member of the French nationality, admitted on equal terms to all the privileges of French citizenship, sharing the advantages of French protection, and the dignity and prestige of French power – than to sulk on his own rocks, the half-savage relic of past times, revolving in his own little mental orbit, without participation or interest in the general movement of the world. The same remark applies to the Welshman or the Scottish Highlander, as members of the British nation.[3]

Even if, still today, many political leaders privately think this way, rare are those who would publicly acknowledge it. Contemporary liberalism is more concerned with the situation of individuals than with collective destiny and no longer dares to impose such an uncompromisingly teleological view of the ends of social development. Because of the predominance of the philosophy of rights and of personal development, today's political science is forced to acknowledge these demands and to rethink the bases of citizenship in more accommodating terms. The challenges that liberalism poses to the concept of citizenship are not all of the same order. Some are real conceptual problems, as we will see, but most of them are easily solved.

Among the demands of ethnic and religious minorities that challenge the so-called neutrality of contemporary citizenship are claims for autonomy. It sometimes happens that an ethnic group (or a political movement that claims to represent an ethnic group) believes itself so different from the other elements of the state that coexistence is impossible. The nationalist movements that have flourished in Europe over the last twenty years, in Corsica, Flanders, the Basque country, Scotland and Northern Ireland, illustrate this feeling. When faced with this type of demand, a liberal democracy finds itself confronted with a true dilemma. Experience shows indeed that, when the state grants these groups a certain autonomy, 'this may simply fuel the ambitions of nationalist leaders who will be satisfied with nothing short of their own nation-state'. But on the other hand, the state which resists these 'demands for self-government rights will simply aggravate alienation among national minorities, and increase the desire for secession.[4]

Politically, this tension seems practically insoluble. Conceptually however, these demands are not a threat to the classical conception of citizenship. Far from challenging the modern definition of the citizen, separatist movements rely on it: it is in the name of the very same ideology of autonomy and rights that they claim independence. And the citizenship they aspire to build has all the features of the one they are fleeing. It is only a question of falling back on smaller homelands, thought to be more united.

The other demands made in the name of ethnic diversity are also most often within the framework of the philosophy of citizenship. As Will Kymlicka very rightly showed, groups who put forward their identity and their difference generally do so in order to reach the ideal of equality inherent to citizenship. They argue that, in contemporary societies, civic inequalities remain strong. Even if formal discrimination has mostly disappeared, citizens of foreign origin, and even women, are still less advantaged than the average, be it on the social-economic and political level, or as regards their fundamental rights. According to them, the explanation lies in the hypocrisy of liberal citizenship. By denying the objective differences between ethnic and religious groups, between genders and social groups, the state allows inequalities of opportunity to be reproduced, and to hinder a true civic equality.[5] According to this argument, to acknowledge different rights for citizens belonging to disadvantaged groups would not violate the civic ideal but, on the contrary, take us closer to it. Groups claiming their own rights of representation – through quotas for political representation, or funding, for example – with those who ask the state to recognise multiple ethnicity, are inspired by the idea of citizenship. 'The philosophy underlying multi ethnicity is an integrationist one, which is what most immigrant groups want. It is a mistake, therefore, to describe multiethnic rights as promoting "ghettoisation" or "balkanisation"'.[6] Moreover, these demands can draw on historical precedents. Even if the means are different, they are only reproducing the ambitions of the working class who, a century earlier, also demanded inclusion in the political community. Furthermore, federalism, which appeared in North American history at the same time as the invention of modern citizenship, acknowledged outright specific representations, and different, at times competing, levels of loyalty. Multicultural citizenship only extends these mechanisms to new, geographically dispersed, groups.

Acknowledging multiculturalism necessitates the rethinking of the structure of the state and of the forms of representation but, as long as it aims at political inclusion, it does not contest the concept of citizenship. To the contrary, it is the ideology of citizenship itself, brandished by public powers and ethnic groups, which generates these aspirations for recognition. Hence, today, the political theory most attached to the ideal of civic participation tends to value these differences. In the United States in particular, where class identities have always been weaker than in Europe and where the coexistence of different ethnic groups is more ancient, diversity is seen by liberal theorists to be a means of civic equalisation: it allows citizens to become aware of their individual rights, to unite their strengths, to develop their social sense and through that to 'play a critical role in combating civic inequalities and unequal freedoms and opportunities'.[7]

For that matter, those who defend the traditional conception of national citizenship find it quite difficult to establish that acknowledging diversity is a real menace to the concept and the ideal it covers. Firstly, one practically never comes across supporters of the ethnic conception of national citizenship in the political or intellectual field – except racist approaches based on prejudice rather than arguments. On this level, without always being aware of it, contemporary political thought is rediscovering the heart of the civic philosophy of Ancient Rome. But, contrary to Roman political science, our contemporary one, fashioned by the notions of state and sovereignty handed down by the moderns, is not yet able to imagine political multiplicity.

The French 'republicans' and the Anglo-American 'civic-nationalists', who are attached to the unity of citizenship and are unwilling to or even flat-out refuse to accept differentiated rights, have risen up against multiculturalist theories. Some, like the French sociologist Dominique Schnapper, simply try to deny the novelty of this issue by recalling that the '"multi-ethnic" or "multicultural" society is not an invention of American democracy ... nor is it a recent characteristic of Western European nations, as the theorists of new citizenship so willingly state, it is engraved in the very definition of the nation'.[8] By saying this she agrees with multiculturalist theories in their aspirations for inclusion. But, regarding the means to reach inclusion, she is satisfied with repeating the aspiration of citizenship to universality: 'It is the effort to break from identities and memberships that are felt to be natural through the abstraction of citizenship which characterises the national project'. She persists in confining differences to the 'private sphere' by allowing foreign residents 'the right to cultivate their differences in their personal life and in social life', while considering that 'these particularities should not be the basis of a specific political identity, acknowledged as such within the public space'.[9] In these paraphrases of classical republican theories, one searches in vain for the shadow of an argument. More prudently, defenders of the civic nation and of the 'republican view of citizenship, according to which the citizen should be actively engaged at some level in political debate and decision-making'[10] concede that 'in multicultural societies group and national identities should co-exist, the challenge being to develop forms of each that are consonant with one another'.[11] What then differentiates this 'republican view of citizenship' from multiculturalism? Both approaches agree on the objective – civic inclusion – and acknowledge that differences in fact must be taken into consideration to fight inequalities.

E PLURIBUS UNUM: CONCEPTUALISING MULTIPLE CITIZENSHIP

The situations that are most complex and problematic on the conceptual level are those which are half-way between the two examples presented so far; those who aspire neither to separation nor to inclusion but to a relative autonomy. Some minority groups ask that their differences be acknowledged within states and wish for a certain amount of independence without going so far as separatism. In this case, differentiated rights no longer aim at inclusion but, on the contrary, serve partially to withdraw their bearers from the common citizenship.[12] This raises the issue of the coexistence of two forms of civic identity that are, at least potentially, in competition with one another.

On a theoretical level, these same issues are addressed in a wholly different political context, in international organisations that, like the European Union, want to create a common citizenship while preserving national identities. The states that have engaged in the process of European political integration put their citizens in the same dilemma that is posed by the coexistence of communities within a common citizenship: since citizens are now directly subjects of European law, how can they reconcile their national loyalty with their membership in a larger union? Can a European citizenship develop without hindering the diversity of national civic identities?

These questionings are not entirely new. We saw in Chapter four that they had already been debated during the drafting of the American constitution. The Republic's Founding Fathers, ever anxious not to impair citizens' attachment to their states, strove to create a dual citizenship: every citizen would depend simultaneously on his state and the federation, both of these memberships having their own rights and obligations. But they did not go beyond this assertion of principle. They did not really ask themselves how citizens could reconcile these two levels of citizenship, or how the tensions that would arise from this could be dealt with. The issue of diversity in unity remained untouched.

Looking into this problem half a century later, Tocqueville sized up its difficulty. In the many passages of his *Democracy in America*[13] in which he wondered at the viability of the federation, he was very careful not to draw definitive conclusions, and confined himself to identifying the conditions favourable and unfavourable to the conservation of unity amidst diversity. According to him there are three factors that make the federal link possible. The first is accidental: it pertains to the geographical situation of the United States, which protects them from the threat of wars and thus allows them to survive despite their frailty. 'The great advantage of the United States does not, then, consist in a Federal Constitution which allows them to carry on great wars, but in a geographical position which renders such enterprises extremely improbable' (*Democracy in America*, I, VIII, p. 192). The second element that preserves the federal pact is sociological: the states remain united despite their differences because their citizens share a conception of social life that avoids divisions over essentials. Tocqueville insisted that the material advantages which citizens found in the Union were not sufficient: 'A certain uniformity of civilisation is not less necessary to the durability of a confederation, than a uniformity of interests in the States which compose it' (p. 188). He added that this level of homogeneity was more easily found when the assembled states were young, as was the case for the thirteen founding states after independence: 'they had not contracted the habit of governing themselves, and their national prejudices had not taken deep root in their minds' (p. 175). Without defining it clearly, Tocqueville attempted to explain what he means by 'uniformity of civilisation': it was, according to him, not based on ethnic characteristics but on common beliefs and values, on the fact that 'a great number of men consider a great number of things in the same point of view' (I, XVIII, p. 469). Amongst these elements of a common culture he mentions religious beliefs as much as political opinions, the conception of human nature, knowledge and history, in short all the 'moral and philosophical principles which regulate the daily actions of life, and govern their conduct' (p. 470). Moreover, Tocqueville emphasised the fact that this moral base tends to be strengthened over time, and this is the third favourable factor for the preservation of the Union: 'The Union has now existed for forty-five years, and in the course of that time a vast number of provincial prejudices, which were at first hostile to its power, have died away. The patriotic feeling which attached each of the Americans to his own native State is become less exclusive; and the different parts of the Union have become more intimately connected the better they have become acquainted with each other.' This is also favoured by technological progress 'The Post, that great instrument of intellectual intercourse, now reaches into the back-woods; and steamboats have established daily means of communication between the different points of the coast. An inland navigation of unexampled rapidity conveys commodities up and down the rivers of the country' (p. 484).

Tocqueville warned, however, that one would be wrong to think that this movement was in one direction (towards strengthening the Union) and irreversible. On the contrary, other evolutions tended constantly to weaken the links on which the Union rested. Three parallel tendencies threatened the cohesion of the Union. Firstly, its increasing population and territory reintroduced heterogeneity into the social body; he worried that 'until human nature is altered, and men wholly transformed, I shall refuse to believe in the duration of a government which is called upon to hold together forty different peoples, disseminated over a territory equal to one-half of Europe in extent' (p. 474). This was all the more true since the increasing territory exacerbated tensions due to the difference of wealth between regions. This was the second seed of disunion: 'It is difficult to imagine a durable union of a people which is rich and strong, with one which is poor and weak, even if it were proved that the strength and wealth of the one are not the causes of the weakness and poverty of the other' (p. 486). Finally, paradoxically, habit worked against the union. There was a true federal paradox: as it created order and peace and brought prosperity, the federal government was less and less criticised; but, at the same time, the successes of the central authority made people 'forget the cause to which it was attributable' (p. 486). Citizens were less critical of the federation but less interested in it, thus depriving it of the attachment that had allowed federation to be built.

The American experiment does not make it possible to draw definitive conclusions about the forces that make the persistence of 'unity in diversity' possible. More than a general principle, it is the improbable balance of elements of homogenisation and of factors of tension that maintain this hybrid state. The threat of secession is always present, as much as the possibility of standardisation.

The history of the United States illustrates this dynamic very well: the issue of the compatibility of state and federal citizenship was acutely posed when a federal decision – the abolition of slavery – collided with the interests and the prejudices of the states. Anticipating such a conflict, Tocqueville thought that 'If the sovereignty of the Union were to engage in a struggle with that of the States, at the present day, its defeat may be confidently predicted' (p. 462); state citizenship would prevail, thus emptying the federal law of its substance. It is known that the reverse came to be. The Fourteenth Constitutional Amendment (1865), adopted after the Civil War, and aiming to avoid such conflicts between both levels of citizenship stated that 'No state shall make or enforce any law which shall abridge the privileges or immunities of citizens of the United States; nor shall any state deprive any person of life, liberty, or property, without due process of law'. This text laid down the principle that would gradually make the states respect the rights contained in the federal Bill of Rights, and thus avoid contradictions. But in doing so, the very idea of dual citizenship was abandoned, the Fourteenth Amendment nationalises 'the Bill of Rights by nationalising the definition of citizenship'.[14] The compatibility issue between state and federal rights was resolved by imposing the supremacy of the centre over the parts. Unity prevailed over diversity: rights were standardised and political life became 'nationalised'. The tensions inherent to dual citizenship finally led to its disappearance and its replacement by a homogeneous citizenship, comparable to that of a unitary state. Thus, the American experiment seemed to confirm a commonplace idea of the time: federal entities are fundamentally unstable and condemned either to disintegration or to centralisation. Unity in diversity can only be a transitional state.[15]

These judgements show that the concept of citizenship, as it was redefined by the moderns, holds a strong aspiration towards unity. If it remains so difficult for us to create the concept of a 'multiple citizenship', it is because modern historical experience was dominated by the figure of the nation-state, and the rare federal exceptions all tended towards centralisation.

This undoubtedly explains why a hybrid entity such as the European Union remains so difficult to conceptualise. One certainly often reads that in our pluralist world, citizenship can only be multiple, that it must simultaneously deploy on several levels: local, regional, national, continental and global.[16] But this solves nothing: it does not say how these levels of citizenship are to be articulated, how the conflicts that can always arise between our different levels of loyalty are to be dealt with, nor how diversity can be compatible with the participation in a common entity.

The authors who attempt to answer this question do not always avoid the 'unitarian tropism' inherent to modern citizenship. This appears clearly in the critics of 'European citizenship' or cosmopolitanism, which come from authors who attach great importance to the republican conception of citizenship. The French 'republicans' and the Anglo-American 'civic-nationalists' consider a citizenship detached from the nation[17] as a 'contradiction in terms'.[18] According to this opinion, the link between citizenship and the nation is not simply historical and contingent, but conceptual. It cannot be undone without abolishing the concept of citizenship itself. The mode of reasoning is the same as the one used to fight multiculturalism.[19] The nation is a 'tangible universality': larger and more abstract than the local, domestic, religious or confessional identities handed down by history; it is also more concrete and perceptible than supranational communities or the whole of mankind. The nation, as a 'half-way house' between the global and the local, would thus be the basis for a feeling of identity that was sufficiently universal to avoid the forms of domination inherent to imposed social communities (race, religion, family, class), but also strong enough to establish relations of trust and solidarity between individuals. Thus, it is not by chance but by necessity that citizenship blossomed in the framework of the nation-state. Nationality alone 'helps to foster the mutual understanding and trust that makes democratic citizenship possible'.[20] It alone fosters the feeling of solidarity that permits the reduction of inequalities within the civic body: 'The Welfare state[s] ... have always been national projects, justified on the basis that members of a community must protect one another and guarantee one another equal respect'.[21]

Based on these convictions, 'republicans' believe that a community larger and more abstract than the nation is unable to create the two conditions essential to active citizenship: trust and solidarity. This means that this entity deprives itself of its very bases. Their argumentation is more pragmatic than ethical: they doubt the possibility for entities larger than states to 'inspire the identification and allegiance – the moral and civic culture – on which democratic authority ultimately depends', by observing that states themselves find it difficult to maintain these civic foundations: 'Except in extraordinary moments, such as war, even nation-states find it difficult to inspire the sense of community and civic engagement self-government requires. Political associations more expansive than nations, and with fewer cultural traditions and historical memories to draw upon, may find the task of cultivating commonality more difficult still'.[22]

These approaches have the virtue of contributing some important points to current thinking on the moral and sociological bases of citizenship. Underlining the conceptual link between the civic bond and nationhood reminds us that citizenship is not natural. It asks sacrifices from the citizen: obedience to law, tax-paying, political participation, dying for the country; none of the above are inherent to human psychology. Collective life is what socialises the individual and turns him into a citizen. It is the exercise of citizenship itself that creates feelings of trust and solidarity, which, in turn, found the community. And in this continuous practice, the memories of a shared – and largely mythical – history, a common language and cultural affinities that unite us and distinguish us from other groups play an essential role.[23] If these conditions are missing, citizenship might not disappear but it would be reduced to its liberal dimension, like the *civitas romana* of the declining Empire; it would only be *libertas*, the protection against wrongful use of power and abuse by society. But it would lose what has been its core value since Athens: autonomy through civic participation. Without this essential element it would be greatly weakened: for the civic-nationalists, when citizenship is 'detached from the exercise of self-government and conceived instead as the capacity of persons to choose their own ends', the danger that 'individually and collectively, we will find ourselves slipping into a fragmented, storyless condition' increases.[24]

Faced with these warnings, other contemporary theorists argue that the nation-state is not the end of history, and that, if citizenship was able to go from the small ancient city to the large modern state, nothing prevents us from thinking that the multinational communities that are forming today, of which the European Union is the most advanced example, will also create their own civic representations. The theory developed by these authors, for whom Jürgen Habermas is the spokesman, is that the European Union can produce a new kind of patriotism, which is not the simple reproduction at the continental level of historical nationalism. Habermas calls this 'constitutional patriotism'.[25] His argument consists of firstly recalling that republican citizenship is artificial or constructivist by definition, as opposed to the ethnic conception of romantic nationalism. The first mistake of those who think that multinational citizenship is impossible, would be forgetting 'the voluntaristic character of a civic nation, the collective identity of which exists neither independent of nor prior to the democratic process from which it springs'.[26] The practice of the job of citizen requires symbols, representations and narratives but these are not offered by race or history; they are built by the political community. Habermas draws two conclusions from this. He considers, firstly, that the link between nationality and citizenship is not conceptual but historical and that nothing prevents the forming of a larger civic bond: 'why should this generation of a highly artificial kind of civic solidarity – a "solidarity among strangers" – be doomed to come to a final halt just at the borders of our classical nation-states?'. He then states that, far from being a constraint, the history of national citizenship is a resource for this larger civic bond: 'the artificial conditions in which national consciousness came into existence recall the empirical circumstances necessary for an extension of that process of identity-formation beyond national boundaries. These are: the emergence of a European civil society; the construction of a European-wide public sphere; and the shaping of a political culture that can be shared by all European citizens'.[27] Still following this constructivist model while denying projecting 'a familiar design from the national onto the European level',[28] Habermas then gives a very conventional version of constitutional patriotism. He thinks that the adoption of a European constitution could be the 'symbolic crystallization' of a 'political act of foundation'; that a charter of fundamental rights would help to emphasise 'the common core of a European identity' by recalling 'the character of the painful learning process it has gone through' and the 'lasting memories of nationalist excess and moral abyss'; that federal-type institutions would help to politicise the stakes and to lead real economic and social policies so as to embed 'economic arguments for an ever-closer union into a much broader union'; and even that, while preserving multilingualism as a symbol of the mutual recognition of national cultures, the Union should use English 'as a working language at face-to-face level, wherever the parties lack another common idiom'.[29]

This outline, which is essentially a projection of the West German experiment on to the European model, shows that Habermas takes the criticism of civic-nationalists seriously. They claim that constitutional patriotism 'does not provide the kind of political identity that nationality provides'[30] because 'the intellectual adherence to abstract principles – human rights, respect for the state of law – must not replace, at least in the foreseeable future, the sentimental and political mobilisation that is aroused by the internalisation of the national tradition'.[31] By recalling that civic identity is built through the democratic experience, and by thinking of the institutions and policies that could arouse a transnational political mobilisation in Europe, Habermas is intent on proving that 'constitutional patriotism' is not a perspective as disembodied as is often said.

But Habermas tries so hard to convince the most traditionalist republicans, that he slips towards political imitation and eclipses another essential feature of post-national citizenship. Far from being only a new level of citizenship that simply completes the national civic bond, transnational citizenship is also, and above all, a principle that deeply modifies the citizenship anchored in nationhood. By setting up a community of rights, the member states of the European Union voluntarily place themselves in the power of legal principles that force them to revise their national norms and practices when they contradict European principles. The creation of a European citizenship does not replace national citizenship, but it nevertheless challenges national statuses and rights. In Weiler's powerful and elegant metaphor, paraphrasing Marcuse, European citizenship confronts Eros and civilisation: the aspiration of 'supranationalism' is not to replace national identity and rights, but to 'keep the values of the nation-state pure and uncorrupted by the abuses'[32] amply demonstrated by recent history.

This was the ambition of Kant's 'right of hospitality': when citizens of a state visited another state and came into contact with its citizens and its public authorities, this forced them to think about themselves.[33] The principle of 'equal treatment' enforced by the European Court of Justice at the request of migrant workers has progressively deprived national laws and administrative practices of their most obvious discriminatory features. The 'vertical dimension' of European citizenship, which connects citizens directly to EU institutions, is very limited, but the 'horizontal dimension' of EU citizenship is extensively developed.[34] The principle of free movement of persons, limited as it is, has generated increased relations between citizens and public authorities of other member states. The principle of non-discrimination (or equal treatment) has granted these moving citizens a legal instrument to challenge discriminatory national laws and administrative practices. The fact that the authors of the treaty have developed this horizontal dimension of citizenship, rather than the vertical bonds between the citizens and the Union, confirms that they intended to build a 'federation of states' rather than a 'European state'. In contemporary Europe, as in the ancient leagues of Greek cities, the *isopoliteia* is more developed than the *sympoliteia*.

Moreover, this is not a purely legal dynamic. Confronted with other civic cultures and with different habits and social links, citizens tend to see their own culture differently. The process of permanent comparison between national experiences – through benchmarking, or simply tourism – gradually transforms national identities. Once they enter the Union, and accept its principles of reconciliation and co-operation, nations are encouraged to rethink their own history. Because they are part of a broader community, and because of the peaceful confrontations this community generates – through intergovernmental meetings, in parliaments or before courts – citizens and nations become more reflective. Citizens remain very proud of their national identities – as is constantly shown by Eurobarometer polls. But this civic pride becomes more tolerant, less aggressive and less exclusive. By analogy with psychological theories of moral development, one could say that national identities in Europe are slowly moving from a conventional to a post-conventional (reflective) status, due to the effect of transnational contacts.[35] European citizenship is not merely a 'federal' set of rights to which national citizenship must conform; it is, rather, a principle which generates horizontal confrontation between diverse national visions of common basic norms.

This is not a unilateral movement. European citizenship is not the formal definition of the most liberal philosophy, imposed upon traditionalist national legacies by an enlightened federal elite. The confrontation between different versions of citizens' rights also challenges the European Union itself. Euroscepticism cannot be reduced to a reactionary answer to the modernism of the Brussels-based elites. The EU has no monopoly of 'civilisation' and Euroscepticism cannot be reduced to passionate or utilitarian reactions against a destabilising open market. True, these fears can sometimes feed xenophobic reactions. But they also offer cognitive and motivational resources for criticising the European Union and thereby counter-balance the abstractness and remoteness of the European project. When, for example, attachment to a national model of solidarity leads to rejection of the Union, this is not necessarily a reactionary attitude. The national consciousness, forged and strengthened by mechanisms of inter-personal solidarity, helps us understand the asymmetric 'political economy' of European citizenship and provides arguments to criticise it. In the same vein, criticism of the EU's democratic deficit, which is always based on implicit analogy with national civic processes, can be seen as a useful contribution to a critical understanding of the EU, which forces its actors to improve it. These 'national' oppositions to the EU are the root of reforms which tend to make the Union more respectful of 'diversity' and more modest. While a dynamic European citizenship forces national identities to think about their prejudice, it also constrains the actors of the EU to contemplate the limits of their own ideology.

This dynamic offers an original 'third way' between the two most radical conceptions of citizenship. The nationalist version, notably defended by Hegel, saw war as a necessity to preserve the vitality of national consciousness. The radical cosmopolitan view, illustrated by Anarchasis Cloots and leading figures of the French Revolution, on the contrary argued that national identities had to be banned, in order to build a purely universalistic citizenship.[36] Paradoxically, this abstract cosmopolitanism led to aggressive nationalism and imperialism. If it had not, it would probably have produced anomie and despair in an abstract community, by creating 'a moral void that opens the way for intolerance and other misguided moralisms'.[37]

European citizenship tries to avoid these two forms of corruption of collective identity. The ancients, and those, like Machiavelli, who followed them, argued that, to avoid corruption, a polity must organise a permanent confrontation with the roots of corruption. Since it was impossible to change human nature to make citizens virtuous, the system had to be built on the people's vices; it had to be conceived as an engine which turned individual vices into collective virtues. The polity would be stable if abuse by one of its elements was counterbalanced by its other elements.

In a sense, transnational citizenship applies this dynamic political reasoning to the question of identity. By creating a permanent confrontation between national identities and common principles, it erodes the parochialism of national polities, while strengthening their capacity of resistance against the most dangerous trends of modernity.[38] This might help break the vicious cycle which leads from local prejudice to abstract universalism and from abstract universalism to a rebirth of xenophobic reactions. If these two types of identity are permanent features of social groups – and since a perfect synthesis of the virtues of liberalism and communitarianism does not seem to be possible – their peaceful confrontation at least offers a 'negative substitute' of an ideal form of membership.

NOTES

1   We use here the now classic expressions of Eric Hobsbawm and Benedict Anderson. *Cf.* E. Hobsbawm and T. Ranger (eds), *The Invention of Traditions* (Cambridge, Cambridge University Press, 1983) and B. Anderson, *Imagined Communities: Reflections on the Origin and Spread of Nationalism* (London, Verso, 2nd ed. 1991).

2   Some sociologists go so far as to express the hypothesis of a causal link between the two movements: as states become more porous, human groups are encouraged to come closer across borders and contest state monopoly. *Cf.* Y. Soysal, *Limits of Citizenship: Migrants and Postnational Membership in Europe* (Chicago/London, University of Chicago Press, 1994).

3   J.S. Mill, *Considerations on Representative Government*, edited by J. Gray (Oxford, Oxford University Press, 1991).

4   W. Kymlicka, *Multicultural Citizenship: A Liberal Theory of Minority Rights* (Oxford, Clarendon Press, 1995), p. 182–3.

5   *Cf.* I.M. Young, *Democracy and Inclusion* (Oxford, Oxford University Press, 2000).

6   Kymlicka, *Multicultural Citizenship*, p. 178.

7   A. Gutmann, *Identity in Democracy* (Princeton, Princeton University Press, 2003), p. 8.

8   D. Schnapper, *La communauté des citoyens: Sur l'idée moderne de nation* (Paris, Gallimard, 1994), p. 99.

9   *Ibid.*, p. 100.

10 D. Miller, *On Nationality* (Oxford, Oxford University Press, 1995), p. 194.

11 *Ibid.*, p. 153.

12 These issues are far from being theoretical. In contemporary societies, marked by strong pluralism, these questions appear in eminently practical situations, placing public authorities in the face of insoluble dilemmas. Should wearing religious insignia be banned, and believers forced to relegate their convictions to the private sphere, if one wishes to maintain the cohesion of the civic body? Can some groups be allowed to have their own schools, to teach their children in a language or a religious and moral context that is not shared by other citizens without endangering the community as a whole? Can some religions be exempted from civil

obligations that are contrary to their beliefs without this undermining equality between citizens? Should religious practices that are contrary to the fundamental rights of the citizen, such as the circumcision of young girls, be prohibited?

13 A. de Tocqueville, *Democracy in America*, translated by Henry Reeve (London, Longman, Green, Longman and Roberts, 1862).

14 T.J. Lowi and B. Ginsberg, *American Government: Freedom and Power* (New York, Norton & Cq, 1996), p. 64.

15 This belief became all the more widely shared because German and Swiss experiments confirmed as early as the end of the nineteenth century that dual citizenship tended to go through a centralisation phenomenon.

16 *Cf.* for example, D. Held, *Democracy and the Global Order: From the Modern State to Cosmopolitan Governance* (Cambridge, Polity Press, 1995) and, in the case of the European Union, E. Meehan, *Citizenship and the European Community* (London, Sage, 1993).

17 This opinion is not confined to the French or Anglo-American space. It is also found in Germany and Italy and no doubt elsewhere.

18 R. Aron, 'Is multinational citizenship possible?', *Social Research* 1974, 41/1, pp. 638–56.

19 As Justine Lacroix very rightly notices, 'For a constitutional patriotism', *Political Studies* 2002, 50/5, pp. 944–58. I disagree with Lacroix, however, on the idea that this opinion is essentially 'communitarian'. It is found indeed in the writings of a number of liberal authors such as R. Dahl, 'Can international organizations be democratic? A skeptic's view', in I. Shapiro and C. Hacker-Cordon (eds), *Democracy's Edges* (Cambridge, Cambridge University Press, 1999).

20 Miller, *On Nationality*, p. 185.

21 *Ibid.*, p. 187.

22 M. Sandel, *Democracy's Discontent: America in Search of a Public Philosophy* (Cambridge, MA, The Belknap Press of Harvard University Press, 1996), p. 339.

23 We follow here in Jean Leca's footsteps. He defines four forming dimensions of citizenship: the genealogical dimension (where do we come from?), the teleological dimension (where do we go to?), the commercial dimension (with whom do I exchange?) and the polemical dimension (who is my enemy?). Jean Leca. 'Sur la citoyenneté européenne', in O. Beaud *et al.*, *L'Europe en voie de constitution* (Bruxelles, Bruylant, 2004).

24 Sandel, *Democracy's Discontent*, p. 321, 351.

25 *Cf.* J. Habermas, 'Citizenship and nationhood, some reflections on the future of Europe', *Praxis International* 1992, 12/1, p. 1–19.

26 J. Habermas, 'Why Europe needs a constitution', *New Left Review* 2001, 11, pp. 5–26, p. 15.

27 *Ibid.*, p. 16.

28 *Ibid.*, p. 18.

29 *Ibid.*, pp. 6, 21, 9 and 19.

30 Miller, *On Nationality*, p. 163.

31 Schnapper, *La communauté des citoyens*, p. 79.

32 J. Weiler, 'To be a European citizen – Eros and civilization', *Journal of European Public Policy* 1997, 4/4, pp 495–519, p. 341.

33 According to Kant, once a state entered a 'federation of free states', it must accept a new kind of law. Beside the *ius civitatis*, which defined the internal organisation of the state and

the relations between the state and its citizens, and beside the *ius gentium*, which codified relations between states, a third legal corpus must be forged, the *ius cosmopoliticum*. This third dimension of the public law ruled relations between citizens of a state and other states – a horizontal legal relation that had long been ignored in a legal tradition dominated by the concept of sovereignty, and the strict division between the sphere of the state and the international space.

34 *Cf.* P. Magnette, *La citoyenneté européenne, Droits, politiques, institutions* (Bruxelles, Editions de l'Université de Bruxelles, 1999).

35 *Cf.* J.-M. Ferry, *La question de l'Etat européen* (Paris, Gallimard, 2000). Ferry argues that constitutional patriotism is different both from 'historical patriotism', which is based on a non-critical national narrative, and from 'legal patriotism', which ignores history by focusing on rights. Constitutional patriotism is based on national historical resources but these are submitted to a critical self-examination in light of the common legal principles enshrined in the constitution.

36 This cosmopolitan viewpoint is defended nowadays by neo-stoic thinkers. See M. Nussbaum, *For Love of a Country: Debating the Limits of Patriotism* (Boston, Beacon Press, 1996).

37 M. Sandel, *Democracy's Discontent*, p. 323.

38 Paul Ricoeur, interpreting Karl Mannheim, suggests a virtuous democratic confrontation of ideologies and utopias, to strengthen the integrative virtue of ideology while attenuating its paralysing effect. See P. Ricoeur, *Lectures on Ideology and Utopia* (New York, Columbia University Press, 1986).

conclusion | the alternatives of citizenship

The concept of citizenship was charged with various connotations, according to the intellectual and political context it was immersed in: it was invested with the republican ethos in the small autonomous cities of Ancient Greece or of the Italian Renaissance; it evoked the freedoms of the patrician bourgeoisie in the constitutional monarchies of the nineteenth century.

Beyond these variations, two contrasts form the continuous basis, and permanent structure, of citizenship. First of all: exclusion. Every political society that has formed a concept of citizenship has expressed it through the fundamental operation which sorts individuals, designating who is a member of the political community and who is excluded from it. The former have their part in the city, access to its rights and privileges, having the advantage of its law, and sometimes taking part in its formation. They have a common status, the right of the city, from which their political identity flows. They form a civic body, a community of rights and will. And they are recognised, by contrast, in opposition to the others, the excluded, those who – whether they are called foreigners, barbarians or the proletariat – are not citizens. The concept plays the role of 'social closure',[1] which nourishes the attachment of citizens to their community and upholds the legitimacy of the power that incarnates it.

The second constant element of the concept of citizenship is legality. From Aristotle to our own day, citizenship has evoked the freedom which flows from the 'benefit' of the law. It is defined, once again, by contrast, that is, by opposition to all forms of domination, private and arbitrary, paternal, patrimonial, despotic or tyrannical. A power without laws is, as Montesquieu said a 'government where nobody is a citizen'.[2] The citizen is he who is only submissive to the law, and is freed by it from any personal dependency. The law is general, the same for all, whereas despotic orders are arbitrary; the law is the expression of collective rationality, whereas the *ukases* of princes are the voices of their passions. The antinomy between the rule of law and arbitrary rule once again has a function in the legitimisation of power. The theories of the social contract, which opposed civil society to the state of nature, and right to force, legitimised the action of the state in ensuring that the citizen was freer under the law than in its absence.

These two constants have, over time, taken different forms. Diverse motives have founded, and organised, exclusion. The rule of law has covered changing meanings, according to the nature of the power which decreed it. Each civilisation, even each political society or each author, gave its own version of these structures of citizenship. The forms are infinitely varied but behind them constants can be found.

NATURE AND ARTIFICE

In ancient languages, citizenship and nationality were designated by the same word – the Greek *politeia* and the Latin *civitas*. Most modern languages consider these two words as interchangeable – *citizenship* or *cittadinanza* can designate both belonging to the state and participation in the exercise of sovereignty.

Now, the modalities of exclusion have varied a great deal over time. Each political society has formulated its own criteria for access to citizenship, modulating gender, age, blood-right (*jus sanguinis*) and right of soil (*jus soli*, or being born in the state's territory regardless of bloodline), social rank and personal merits. In the humanities, two generic conceptions of access to the rights of the city are distinguished, inspired by the two classic versions of the nation.[3] The first one, which, according to Jean Leca, can be considered naturalist, 'evokes the idea of an organic nation of which the Nation-State must be a natural emanation, and denies to those who do not belong the possibility really to be citizens, this is translated in various codes of nationality by the provision linked to the *jus sanguinis*'. The second one, called artificialist, 'evokes the idea of an artificial city formed by a contract of adhesion whose respect brings about incorporation in the nation'.[4] These contrasting attitudes can be discerned from ancient times: the Greeks invested their *politeia* with an ethnic signification, and only opened it up exceptionally to individuals who merited it; whereas the Roman *civitas*, which was founded on adhesion to constitutional values, was likely to be extended limitlessly to all those who shared them. These contrasting attitudes are found in contemporary Europe, and it is classic to oppose the universalism of French citizenship, constructed on abstract values – natural rights – and in principle open to all those who acknowledge them,[5] to the German *Bürgerschaft*, reserved to individuals who possess the attributes of the German nation, which are inborn and not acquired. In the scientific literature, these two countries constitute archetypes, which other nations are reputed to partake of to varying degrees.

Like every analytical dichotomy, this one has exposed itself to criticism. It has been reasonably emphasised that the purely artificialist type has never existed, and that the universalism of French citizenship was an aspiration, much more than a rule – the succeeding codes of French nationality having also reserved a place of choice to *jus sanguinis*.[6] In the same way, by concentrating attention on the philosophical corpus, one may refuse to rank authors like Rousseau and Fichte in either of these two categories and call for scholars to 'overcome the opposition between the free-membership-nationality and the determination-nationality'.[7] These remarks do not invalidate the analytical opposition, however. On the contrary, emphasising that many historical realities borrow from one pole or the other pays tribute to the explanatory strength of the idea. The crucial point is not to take these distinctions for exclusive descriptions. W.R. Brubaker has remarkably demonstrated that, even if modern France and Germany are not perfect illustrations of these two types, the weight of these conceptions on collective mentalities can nevertheless be perceived in the history of the reforms of their codes of nationality.[8]

The major defect of this opposition is that, although it claims to have an analytical aim, it is strongly normative. In our multicultural societies, the affirmation of ethnic nationality seems reactionary, and the open conception seems the only one able to break with the ethnic exclusions, which we would like to believe are now a thing of the past. Placed in an historical perspective, these two versions of nationality divulge part of their ambiguity. To affirm the universalist character of French citizenship is to forget that it required the cultural standardisation of the nation and the eradication, or at least the dimming, of particular regional cultures; to insist on the ethnicism of the German conception is to occult the discursive process of formation undergone by the Germanic nation, which proceeded from the dialogue of its particular cultures.[9]

Today, these opposing conceptions continue to mark debates relative to nationality and to the citizenship to which nationality gives access. Choices between the *jus soli* and the *jus sanguini*, integration or assimilation, civic or cultural identity, determine the rhythm of parliamentary debates on the reforms of the right of nationality in numerous countries.[10] But their meanings deviate. The major part of the political class in Europe has taken note of the need to open nationality to descendents of immigrants who have been domiciled in the host country for a long time, therefore acknowledging a place for the 'right of soil'. The issue of cultural identity is no longer posed in the same terms: it is less and less understood as an objective criterion of exclusion but rather as a condition of political integration. The pertinent dichotomy today no longer opposes closed and open conceptions of nationality but two variants of the open version, which is slowly imposing itself. Cultural criteria, when they are still exacted, are no longer inborn but to be acquired.

EQUALITY AND HIERARCHY

The boundaries of citizenship have not always coincided with those of the state and nationality. It has been only a half-century, and sometimes less, since all adult nationals were made citizens in liberal democracies. All former political societies excluded certain categories of individuals – women and children, slaves and 'domestics' – from citizenship.[11] The main boundary separated the private and public spheres: modern societies kept until the middle of the twentieth century the Roman distinction between *domus* and *civitas*. The Roman Republic was only acquainted with the public domain and left to each citizen the care of managing his 'home'. Only the head of the family had a public existence, whereas all those who depended on him in the domestic sphere: his wife and children, his slaves and employees, were held to be minors, of whom he was the tutor. Pufendorf said it again in the middle of the seventeenth century: 'that the name "citizen" belongs to these (the heads of families) first of all, but only indirectly and through them to the women, boys and slaves of their establishment, whose wills were included in the will of the father of the family, in so far as they enjoy both the common protection of the state, and some rights by reason of that relation'.[12]

In these abstract terms, exclusion was a carbon copy of the limits of the state, which did not get involved in domestic life and was oblivious of those who remained bound in it. But it also dissimulated a patent mistrust of the elite concerning the 'reason' of the 'little people'. Women, children and domestics could not take part in public life for two overlapping reasons: firstly because they were 'dependants' of the head of the family, and thus they could not make an autonomous judgement; next because, being confined in the *domus*, they did not possess the level of understanding of public affairs needed to exercise active citizenship. And even if a few isolated voices, like Condorcet and John Stuart Mill, emphasised the perverted character of this reasoning – women couldn't acquire 'public spirit' as long as they were confined to the private sphere – it is only when women's participation in the economic and social areas was recognised, blurring the boundary between private and public, that the idea of extending them the right to vote won over.

Property ownership was, until the end of the nineteenth century, the 'objective' criterion for the exclusion of certain adult males in Europe. Only those who possessed goods, measured by the payment of a property tax, could participate in the life of the city. The argument was one of independence: the absence of property made members of the 'proletariat' submissive to their employers and prevented them from reasoning in an autonomous manner. It was also anchored in an instrumental conception of the state: for Locke, government having been instituted to protect property, those who had none to defend had no reason to be active citizens. The argument was extended to the nineteenth century's liberal theory of the state: the *raison d'être* of public power being to harmonise the interests of individuals, subjects with no interests – in the material sense of the term, and thus likely to be measured by their property – had no entitlement to civic participation either. Once again that distinction between property owners and the proletariat dissimulated the modern bourgeoisie's mistrust of the 'working classes': the bourgeoisie thought itself reasonable, serenely calculating its interest in political life as in its commercial activities, and feared that salaried workers might be, on the contrary, passionate and lacking the temperance and leisure judged necessary to involvement in public life. Ownership (the material criterion) designated those who had enough independence of mind and free time to form a political opinion (the intellectual criterion), and who, after all, were not inclined to overthrow the established order since the protection of their goods depended on that order (the social criterion). The liberal bourgeoisie could render these restrictions compatible with its universalist rhetoric, since every adult male – as long as the domestic criterion remained pertinent – could, in theory, by his work, accede to property and through it to citizenship. It is not by chance that the struggle for universal male suffrage and the social question were concomitant: only when the state was conceived as having other vocations than the protection of property, when it could legitimately interfere in the so-called 'private' sphere of economics, that everyone, owners and proletariat, could be considered as having an 'interest' in taking part in its direction.

At the very heart of the body of citizens, implicit forms of exclusion have at times been instituted. In the ancient republics, which did not acknowledge political representation and where every citizen could take part directly in voting on laws, diverse institutions worked together to minimise the 'people': elaboration of proposals of laws by the Senate, counting of votes by orders, material constraints imposed on civic participation; all allowed, under the Roman Republic, limitation of the influence of the masses on political life, all the while proclaiming their participation. Laws were the work of the *populus*, abstract people, but the plebs, concrete people, small people, remained on the sidelines. The moderns have made political representation explicit. Since the Renaissance, the opinion according to which 'a wise man must never apprehend the judgement of the people on specific facts like the attribution of rank and position, the only thing on which the people never err'[13] has spread. The active political capacity, that of governors, and the passive capacity, that of the governed, who can choose their governors but not govern themselves, have been distinguished. This justified the mechanism of representation: the election of the mandated was to operate a selection among the citizens and give the highest functions to the best ones among them. In the eyes of the nineteenth century, the republic was characterised by its representative character, which distinguished it from democracy, reserved to a people so virtuous that it was in the domain of utopia. The ruling classes' mistrust of the civic body was so strong that the representative guarantee long seemed insufficient: when the right to vote was largely extended, as it was under the French constitution of 1791, which relegated to the set of 'passive citizens' only one-third of male adults, a two-turn voting mechanism saw to it that, among the 'active citizens', certain ones had only the right to elect and not to be elected.

These prejudices were hardy. They weakened but did not disappear. The fear still prevalent among vast segments of the political class regarding the mechanisms of direct participation of citizens bears their mark. The referendum is often pejoratively perceived as a plebiscitary institution, an 'irrational' form of expression of popular sovereignty. The spectre of Bonapartism, an alliance between a despot and the little people, continues to play strongly in the imagination of the French ruling classes. Both with the moderns and with the ancients, there is ceaseless fear of the corruption of democracy into demagogy. Moreover, the limits which subsist in the access to 'public offices' bear the stamp of past prejudices. The weak presence of women among governors, and the rejection of positive discrimination in the name of equality, are symptoms of this. The elitism which continues, particularly in centralised states like France and Great Britain, to mark access to high public office, hides behind its meritocratic pretensions a persistent prejudice in regard to capability.

Theoretical political equality is, by definition, limited: it allows social hierarchies to subsist, which socialist critics have virulently denounced; but it also leaves actual political inequalities unscathed. For the former are nourished by the latter: every empirical study has confirmed the intuition that social inequalities and differences in instruction favour the domination of superior classes over electoral mechanisms.[14] Equality between citizens is equality of rights, which only refers to political equality as an ambition.

OBEDIENCE AND PARTICIPATION

The distinction between active and passive citizens, which the French constitution of 1791 cast in judicial terms, reflects a permanent tension at the heart of the concept of citizenship. Aristotle acknowledged that certain citizens, who could exercise the powers of judge and magistrate, were 'more' citizens than others. As we would say in contemporary language, those were active because they took part in the formation of the law, whereas passive citizens only have the right to profit from it. By inscribing two antagonistic conceptions of freedom, of the ancients and the moderns, Benjamin Constant reformulated this theme. Contemporary political philosophy has reintegrated this dichotomy in discussions about citizenship: 'We have, then, two different understandings of what it means to be a citizen. The first describes citizenship as an office, a responsibility, a burden proudly assumed; the second describes citizenship as a status, an entitlement, a right or set of rights passively enjoyed'.[15] And Walger establishes, on the basis of that distinction presented as analytical, intellectual relationships, the first running from Aristotle to Rousseau passing by Machiavelli and Harrington, the second developing from St Paul to Constant, crossing through Bodin and Montesquieu.

One must avoid defining these categories in exclusive terms, classifying authors as belonging to one or another line. Firstly, because there is an historic rupture in the history of the concept. Up to the middle of the seventeenth century, citizenship was reduced to the enjoyment of the law, and the idea that it referred to popular sovereignty was unknown to Hobbes and his contemporaries, citizen and subject were synonymous, and active citizenship existed only in an historical exception – ancient Athens, whose extraordinary character was used to emphasise the impossibility of its rebirth. From the end of the eighteenth century, on the contrary, citizenship separated from the idea of civic participation appears as an anomaly. Kant, who strained his ingenuity to justify the political exclusion of non-owners, confessed it, when he conceded, as Aristotle had done in his time, that 'the concept of a passive citizen seems to contradict the concept of a citizen as such'.[16] It was only during the one hundred and fifty years that separate these two milestones (1650–1800) that the active and passive conceptions coexisted.[17]

This distinction admits, also and above all, the inconvenience of presenting as an antagonism what in fact makes the modern concept of citizenship coherent. The first modern authors who defined citizenship as a civic activity all considered it as the indispensable guarantee of individual liberties, and understood these liberties in return as an indispensable condition for the exercise of citizenship. The operation of the social contract translated, in its abstract language, the idea of intimate solidarity between the 'active and passive dimensions' of citizenship: the savage must make himself a citizen, submit himself to the law which he himself has set forth, to protect his natural rights, say, in substance, Locke, Rousseau and Kant. The Declaration of the Rights of Man and of the Citizen of 1789 emphasised the same complementarity of the two aspects of citizenship: 'The aim of all political association is the conservation of the natural and inalienable rights of man' says its Article 2, clearly consecrating individual liberties. But its Article 6 also stated that 'all citizens have the right to participate personally or by their representatives in its formation', instituting active citizenship. The contractualist idea is underlying: the only way to ensure that natural rights would be respected by the law was to entrust its formation to those who have every interest in guaranteeing those rights: the citizens themselves. Active and passive citizenship are not antinomical but complementary, even indissociable.[18] Since the democratic revolutions, citizenship is not itself unless it admits these dimensions.

The alternative remains pertinent if it is not seen as a strict dichotomy: it permits the distinction between authors who value civic participation in itself, such as Rousseau or John Stuart Mill, and those who primarily give it instrumental value, as a means of protecting private liberties, like Bentham or Constant. Tocqueville embodies an intermediate position. Society ruled by the state, says he, tends to weaken; and the members of an apathetic society, in turn, become passive citizens. In the other way, the vitality of a society that the state leaves free to govern itself favours civic activity, which in turn diffuses its 'anxious activity' in the social body and keeps it vigorous. Privatism and public spirit do not exclude one another, they complete each other.

This alternative also draws attention to the variations that affect over time the balance of these two components, active and passive, of citizenship. Contemporary representative democracies suppose simultaneously a certain dose of activity and privatism on citizens' part: too much civic involvement leads citizens to contest the monopoly of power held by elected leaders; too much private interest undermines the legitimacy of representatives.[19] Today, according to general opinion, liberal democracies suffer from a deficit of civic involvement: as Tocqueville had feared, and as contemporary political scientists, from the left or the right, have underlined, the development of state competencies in ever-growing fields favoured a passive attitude of citizens towards the state, an 'interest in the achievements of the administrative system in the areas of regulation and social security, with a weak participation in the process of legitimisation'.[20] But contrarily to what Tocqueville hoped, the valorisation of 'civil society' – evident in the 1980s, at the time when the state was withdrawing and when the private field was growing independent from public custody – far from encouraging the rebirth of civic identity, contributed to weaken the little collective interest for the public sphere, seen as an obstacle to the development of the market and of private life.

TRANSPARENCY AND REPRESENTATION

Modern citizenship is innately representative. When the 'democratic revolutions' of the eighteenth century overturned the principles of power, stating that authority did not stem from God but from the people, they also instantly and firmly stated that the people could not govern itself. At the end of the eighteenth century, all thought like Rousseau that 'In the strict sense of the term, there has never been a real democracy and there never will be'.[21] The people being unable to govern itself, it must accept a role limited to choosing those who will govern in its name.[22] Two main arguments were put forward in favour of representation. The first, of a pragmatic nature, had been formulated by Montesquieu and was ceaselessly repeated: in a big modern state it was *materially impossible* for the people to assemble and deliberate. The second was a bit more complex and had a few variants; but beyond the nuances, the arguments of the American and French revolutionaries, and then of their followers, all admitted that representation had the tremendous advantage of ensuring a *social selection* that allowed the representatives of the people to deliberate more serenely than the whole of the people could have done. It was necessary to, as the Founding Fathers of the American Constitution said, 'refine and enlarge the public views, by passing them through the medium of a chosen body of citizens, whose wisdom may best discern the true interest of their country, and whose patriotism and love of justice will be least likely to sacrifice it to temporary or partial considerations'.[23] Representatives have cognitive qualities – they can *discern* the general interest – and moral qualities – they can *respect* the general interest – superior to those of the mass. The men of the eighteenth century called this system republican, because they acknowledged that it was a far cry from the ideal of democracy; and it is only because of a progressive shift in meaning that we call it democracy today.[24]

Here lies the cardinal difference between the citizenship of the ancients and that of the moderns: in Athenian democracy, the citizen 'took part in the power of judge and magistrate' according to the formula of Aristotle; in the Roman republic, the citizenry was renowned to be the author of the laws. In modern liberal democracies, citizens elect their representatives, who make and apply the laws in the citizens' name. This delegation, which reduces citizenship to the power of giving a mandate, was severely criticised by proponents of a transparent, direct and immediate citizenship. Historically, it was first the idea of conditioning the mandate to do away with the separation it entails. The idea of an imperative mandate, supported by Robespierre and his followers, changed the meaning of representation: it must not create a difference, but a similarity, between the citizen and the elected representative. Only the first motive of the election, the material need to deliberate amongst a limited number, remained valid, while the second was denied

– they refused to admit that the representative could be more intelligent and more virtuous than those he represents. Citizenship was no longer only giving power but was also a constant attention, vigilance towards the acts of the representatives, which could lead to their dismissal. The chaos this brought about long discredited this institution – whose spirit remains only in the attitude of members of parliament towards their ministers: giving power, controlling and sanctioning.

In the modern age, the representative mechanism seems so deeply lodged in the heart of the concept of citizenship that the denial of representation was also, most often, a denial of citizenship. In its original purity, liberalism conceived a transparent society, which abrogated the mediation of electoral citizenship. It imagined the ideal civil society as a natural harmony, ruled by the complementary character of interests. Modern individuals are above all workers and tradesmen, whose needs complete each other spontaneously, with no need for exterior regulations, for public power. Man no longer needs to tear away from himself, to leave his particular interests aside to contemplate the general interest; he no longer needs to make himself citizen to reach happiness. The condition of the individual, in the liberal anarchy, is civilness, direct relations of citizens amongst themselves. This conception was rarely found in its pure expression in contemporary theories. The nineteenth-century liberals at least acknowledged a correcting role for the state, because society was not totally harmonious. And from here stems the fact that, like Constant, they gave an instrumental value to citizenship as a necessary mediation to correct the faults of the transparent society. But the condition of man was still essentially seen as civilness. Liberal criticism of citizenship still plays this role of reducing the public sphere and the state, by valuing private identity and activity.

Socialist criticism of citizenship, as radicalised by Marx, pursued the same objective of transparency. It thought that the political emancipation of citizenship was a sham, because it allowed social alienation to survive. Socialists called for the borders between state and civil society, and between politics and economics, to be wiped out, and for all collective issues to be submitted to the direct deliberation of the assembled citizens. The modern idea of citizenship was rejected because it was mediated and because it was geographically limited. Communism thought of the condition of man along different lines, as a *sociability*, an autonomous development of all his faculties in a society expunged of all hierarchy and all obstacle to communication between men. This criticism did not eradicate modern citizenship. It nourished all forms of direct assemblies of workers in mutualism, co-operatives and trade unions acting directly, which are as many partial and imperfect realisations of the ideal of sociability. It also explains why, when they had to resign themselves to agree to the game of political representation, socialist movements tried to set up mechanisms to control their representatives in order to abolish the distance between representatives and represented, in case they were tempted by a corporatist rather than a political mode of representation. They shifted their criticism: since representation was unavoidable from the moment one chose liberal democracy, the representative had to *politically* represent his voters, by passing on their aspirations but also *socially* by being like them.[25] The representation of society as class antagonism reversed the meaning of representation: representatives were no longer seen as a moral and intellectual elite, in charge of finding the general interest and translating it into law; opposing fractions, political parties, had the mission of aggregating a compromise between conflicting class interests.

MONISM AND PLURALISM

If citizenship is universally conceived as representative, there are different ways of understanding the meaning of representation. In its Anglo-Saxon version, representation is understood as the reproduction of social differences, and representatives believe themselves to have a mission of aggregating their particular interests in a general compromise. Historically, the British Parliament was first the spokesmen of the orders, corporations and counties, before being that of abstract and isolated citizens. The legislative work consisted in making the demands of different social groups compatible. Representation meant administrating social pluralism. The Americans understood representation in the same way, and thought that the multitude of factions and minorities were a guarantee against the tyranny of the majority.

In its French version, representation had another kind of logic. It aimed to go beyond social differences, which were supposed to disappear in the unity of the nation. The National Assembly was not the offspring of the General Estates, which had represented the social orders, but its negative. When the Third Estate proclaimed itself the nation, it claimed to represent the abstract people, not its differences and hierarchies. Natural-law theory marked their minds and representatives long thought of themselves as the interpreters of a natural law that only needed to be unearthed. They did not claim to reconcile individual wills in a will of all, in a logic of compromise, but to go beyond individual wills to find the general will they hid. The mistrust towards the imperative mandate, and all kinds of intermediate bodies, shows the Rousseauian fear of seeing the unitary will of the people contaminated by particular interests. The strength of these conceptions explains the fact that, in France, parties were always thought of as enemies of democracy. The sociological conception of society, seen as a class antagonism, only legitimised parties at the end of the nineteenth century. If the nation was not fundamentally united, but conflictual, representation must not hide but rather bring to light these divisions. Workers' movements hoped, through the partisan representation of workers' interests, to bring the conflict of classes to the parliamentary arena; to break with the hypocrisy of representation-sublimation, which, by denying antagonisms, protected the interests of the bourgeoisie. But the aspiration to national unity and the disdain for corporatism survived and is still today the cause of French exceptionalism.[26]

All the liberal democracies, even when they were inspired by French monism, came to recognise the undeniable fact of social pluralism. The advent of universal suffrage made the formation of political parties a material necessity. Citizenship could be materialised in a direct relation between the representative and his voter, when taxation and capacity reduced the size of the civic body. When representatives were no longer able to know their voters personally, they had to rely on electoral machines. From the beginning, political parties were both praised and criticised. Their socialising value was acknowledged when they contributed to the animation and structuring of the political debate; when they were the 'schools of citizenship' that Tocqueville deemed indispensable to modern democracies. But their oligarchic tendencies were criticised when they reproduced in their structures the distance between the voter and the representative, the contraction of power at the summit they were supposed to battle.[27] In any case, there is a consensus that parties structure political space, by reproducing social differences in the political sphere. And in the time of mass-parties, citizenship is expressed by membership in a party, whose ideology filters the vision of the world and determines attitudes. The citizen is no longer an abstract being, orienting his electoral choice by reasoning in the silence of his passions, but a 'situated' man who intends to have his particular interest taken into account in the elaboration of compromises.[28]

This 'second age' of representative democracy is, according to some, coming to a close.[29] Social identities are losing their strength, competing with other forms of recognition, such as cultural, regional, ethical and ethnic; party membership and voting are more volatile; strong ideologies are dulled; the media are no longer strongly partisan; in short, pluralism is spreading. Thus reappears, in a new form, the ancient dilemma of citizenship: how to prevent the liberty of the individual causing the destruction of the freedom of the citizen.

NOTES

1   This Weberian expression is used by W.R. Brubaker in *Citizenship and Nationhood in France and Germany* (Harvard, Harvard University Press, 1992).

2   Montesquieu, *The Spirit of the Laws*, edited and translated by A.M. Cohler, B.C. Miller and H.S. Stone (Cambridge, Cambridge University Press, 1989), V, XXIII, p. 193.

3   On the durability of this duality in the theories of the nation *cf.*, in particular, D. Schnapper, *La communauté des citoyens, Sur l'idée moderne de nation* (Paris, Gallimard, 1994).

4   J. Leca, 'La citoyenneté entre la nation et la société civile', in D. Colas, C. Emeri and J. Zylberberg (eds.), *Citoyenneté et nationalité* (Paris, PUF, 1991), pp. 479–505.

5   On structural durability, from the Roman Republic to contemporary France, *cf.* C. Nicolet, 'Citoyenneté française et citoyenneté romaine: essai de mise en perspective', in *Da Roma a la Terza Roma, Documenti e studie II* (Roma, Edizione Scientifiche Italiane, 1985), pp. 145–73.

6   *Cf.* D. Schnapper, *La France de l'intégration, Sociologie de la nation en 1990* (Paris, Gallimard, 1991) and the classical study of French law of nationality, M. Vanel, *Histoire de la nationalité française d'origine* (Paris, Ancienne Imprimerie de la Cour d'appel, 1945).

7 A. Renaut, 'Logiques de la nation', in P.-A. Taguieff (ed.), *Les théories du nationalisme* (Paris, Kimé, 1994), pp. 29–46, p. 36.

8 *Cf.* W.R. Brubaker, *Citizenship and Nationhood* (Cambridge MA, Harvard University Press, 1992).

9 *Cf.* J.-M. Ferry, *Les puissances de l'expérience, vol. II, Les ordres de la reconnaissance* (Paris, Le Cerf, 1991), pp. 194–203.

10 *Cf.* in particular, *Pour un modèle français d'intégration, Rapport du Haut Conseil à l'intégration présidé par M. Long au Premier Ministre* (Paris, La Documentation française, 1991); G. Zincone, 'Due vie alla cittadinanza: il modello societario e il modello statalista', *Rivista italiana di scienza politica* 1989, XIX/2, pp. 223–65.

11 Until the beginning of the nineteenth century, 'domestic' meant all those who depended on others for their livelihood, that is, employees as opposed to owners.

12 S. von Pufendorf, *De Jure Naturae et Gentium, Libri octo*, edited by J.B. Scott, 2 vols. (Cambridge, Cambridge University Press, 1934), vol. 2, VII, II, 20, p. 995.

13 N. Machiavelli, *The Discourses*, I, XLVII, see also I, XX. edited by B. Crick (Harmondsworth, Penguin, 1970).

14 *Cf.*, particularly, S. Verba, N.H. Nie and J.-O. Kim, *Participation and Political Equality, A Seven-Nation Comparison* (Cambridge, Cambridge University Press, 1978); D. Gaxie, *Le cens caché* (Paris, Seuil, 1978).

15 M. Walzer, 'Citizenship', in T. Ball, J. Farr and R.L. Hanson (eds.), *Political Innovation and Conceptual Change* (Cambridge, Cambridge University Press, 1988), pp. 211–19, p. 216.

16 I. Kant, *TheMetaphysics of Morals,* introduced, translated and annotated by Mary Gregor (Cambridge, Cambridge University Press, 1991) §66.

17 It seems to me that it is misleading to call the first conception 'liberal citizenship' and the other 'republican citizenship'. Liberal thinkers of the eighteenth and nineteenth century neglect the concept of citizenship, loaded with republican 'ethos', precisely because they favour individual liberties. 'Liberal citizenship' is an anachronism, it is better to keep making this distinction under the concept of liberty, which was valued as much by liberals as by republicans. *Cf.* P. Magnette, 'La citoyenneté dans la pensée politique européenne. Eléments pour une histoire doctrinale du concept', *Res Publica* 1995, XXXVIII/3–4, pp. 657–78.

18 *Cf.* J. Habermas, *Between Facts and Norms: Contributions to a Discourse Theory of Law and Democracy*, translated by W. Rehg (Cambridge, Polity Press, 1996); R. Bellamy, 'Citizenship and rights' in *Theories and Concepts of Politics* (Manchester, Manchester University Press, 1993), pp. 43–76. Q. Skinner, also, underlines the virtuous relation between liberal and republican conceptions of liberty, asserting the superiority of the latter, which, according to him, postulates positive freedom as a value and as a means to defend negative freedom. *Cf.* Q. Skinner, 'The paradoxes of political liberty', in S.M. McMurrin (ed.), *Tanner Lectures on Human Values*, VII (Salt Lake City, University of Utah Press 1986), pp. 227–50.

19 This is one of the central themes of G.A. Almond and S. Verba, *The Civic Culture, Political Attitudes and Democracy in Five Nations* (Princeton, Princeton University Press, 1963).

20 J. Habermas, *Legitimation Crisis,* translated by T. McCarthy (London, Heinemann, 1976) p. 107. For a similar analysis from a liberal viewpoint, *cf.* R. Aron, 'La corruption des démocraties' (1952), in *Introduction à la philosophie politique, Démocratie et révolution* (Paris,

Editions de Fallois, 1997), pp. 99–117.

21 J.-J. Rousseau, *The Social Contract*, III, 4, edited and translated by V. Gourevitch (Cambridge, Cambridge University Press, 1997), p. 91.

22 The Rousseauian exception, interpreted at length, remains ambiguous. His statement of the inalienable character of sovereignty and his strong criticism of representation have been put forward. But it has been less often noted that: 1. He thought a distinction between the legislative and the executive power was necessary (*SC*, III, I); 2. He confined the role of the legislative power to the promulgation of a few general laws (*SC*, II, VI); 3. He considered elective aristocracy to be the best form for the executive power in a medium-size state (*SC*, III, IV); 4. He acknowledged this executive a vast discretionary power: 'This does not mean that the commands of the rulers cannot pass for general wills, so long as the Sovereign, being free to oppose them, offers no opposition. In such a case, universal silence is taken to imply the consent of the people' (*SC*, II, I). Taken together, these concessions lead to a regime close to contemporary liberal democracy, which is, in the words of the Enlightenment an 'elective aristocracy'.

23 *The Federalist*, X (Madison), in A. Hamilton, J. Jay and G. Madison, *The Federalist Papers* (New York, Bantam Books, 1982).

24 *Cf.*, on this semantic shift from 'republic' to democracy, J. Dunn, 'Democratic Theory', in *Western Political Thought in the Face of the Future* (Cambridge, Cambridge University Press, 1993), pp. 1–28; P. Rosanvallon, 'L'histoire du mot démocratie à l'époque moderne', *La pensée politique* 1993, 1, *Situations de la démocratie*, pp. 11–29.

25 *Cf.* P. Rosanvallon, *Le peuple introuvable, Histoire de la représentation démocratique en France* (Paris, Gallimard, 1998), pp. 191–217.

26 *Ibid.*, pp. 303–20.

27 For a synthetic approach to the analysis of political parties in the twentieth century, *cf.* B. Manin, *Principes du gouvernement représentatif* (Paris, Calmann-Lévy, 1995, republished by Flammarion, 1996), pp. 264–78.

28 G. Burdeau, *La démocratie* (Neuchâtel, Editions de la Baconnière, 1956, republished by Seuil, 1975).

29 *Cf.*, particularly, Manin, *Principes du gouvernement représentatif*, pp. 279–308; J. Habermas, *The Structural Transformation of the Public Sphere: An Inquiry into a Category of Bourgeois Society*, translated by T. Burger with F. Lawrence (Cambridge MA, MIT Press, 1989), particularly the preface of 1990.

| index

A

absolutism 81
Achean-Mycenian civilization 10
alienation 156, 157, 159
Althusser, Louis 165n.19
America *see* United States of America
anarchy 74, 75, 129, 132
ancien régime 124, 131, 141, 150
Ancient Greece
  citizenship in 7, 8–19, 37, 175,
    183, 187
  politics, origins of 7
  see also Athens
Anderson, Benedict 179n.1
Aquinas, Thomas 39, 40
  Aristotle and 40
  citizenship, concept of 40
Areopagos 11–12
Arezzo 43
Argians 10
aristocracy 79, 95, 142, 145
  abolition of privileges 140, 147
  see also monarchy; royal power;
    sovereignty
aristocratic age 142, 150
Aristotelianism 39–41, 52, 58
  anti-Aristotelians 64
  political nature of man 48
Aristotle 2, 15, 17–19, 41, 141, 182
  city and 29n.32
    definition of citizen 17–18, 19,
      41, 55, 67, 187, 189

politeia and 18, 29n.35, 39
Politics, The 39
republic, idea of 64–5
Aron, R. 193n.20
Athens 10–19, 28n.13
  citizenship in 8, 11–19, 29n.23
    deprivation of (*atimia*) 15
  democracy in 8, 10–14, 25, 189
  politeia in 48
  slavery in 11, 13, 14
Augustine of Ancona 58n.6
Augustine, St. 31, 32–6, 58n. 2, 58n.3
  City of God 32–4
Augustus 26, 27
autonomy 84, 92
  collective 159
  ethnic and religious minorities and
    169–70, 179n.12
  Kant and 122, 123
  liberal theory of society and 151
  republican idea of freedom as 127
  see also freedom
Azo 38–9, 40, 44, 46, 49

B

Babeuf, Françoise Noel 155
Bagehot, Walter 153
Baldus of Ubaldis 37, 45–7, 49,
  60n. 35, 60n.40
  definition of citizenship 47
Barbalet, J. M. 6n.5
Barbarossa, Frederick 36

Barber, Benjamin 136n.19
Barbeyrac 87
Bartolus of Sassoferrato 37, 44–5, 46, 49
Basques 169
Benhabib, Seyla 136n.19
Bentham, Jeremy 86, 110, 128–30, 151, 188
    critique of natural law 129
Bernstein, Eduard 162
Bescond, L. 29n.31
Bismark, Otto Edward Leopold von 161
Bodin, Jean 2, 63–9, 75, 78, 86, 94, 99n.3, 132, 141, 187
    doctrine of sovereignty 63, 64, 65–7, 68, 115
    redefinition of citizenship 67–9
Boeotia 16
Bonald, Vicomte de 125
Bonaparte, Napoleon 131
Bordes, Jacqueline 14–15, 29n.21, 29n.22
bourgeoisie 68, 92, 113, 140, 185–6
    bourgeois age 142
    Marx and 159
    new post-revolution 141, 145
    see also aristocracy
Bowsky, W. M. 44
Bracton 38
British Bill of Rights 126
Brubaker, W. R. 184, 192n.1, 192n. 8
Bruni, Leonardo 49-50
Brunner, O. 6n.8
bureaucracy 135
Burke, Edmund 86, 125-7, 129
    French Revolution and 125-6
    Reflections on the Revolution in France 126

C
Caere 20
Caesar 26, 27, 32
Cahiers de Doléances 112
Canning, J.P. 60n.40

capitalism 140–1, 154
    marxist critique of 161
    see also Marx, Karl
    social mobility and 145
caritas 33
Catholic Church 34
census 24–5
Chalier, J. 122
Charon, Pierre 69
Christianity
    medieval organicism of 34–5
    natural law and 31, 32, 71
    social theory of 31–6
Cicero 8, 21, 33, 41, 49, 106
    citizenship and 21, 23–6, 42, 55
    De Legibus 21, 23, 26
    De Republica 23–6
    use of civitas 23, 58
citizen, the
    as subject 74–5, 80, 86, 100n.28, 112, 132
    'good'/virtuous 51, 52
    man and 86, 98, 116–17, 158
        rule of law as reconciliation 118–19
citizenship
    active and passive 50–1, 114, 119–21, 123, 137n.50, 140, 186, 187–8
    civil law and 45, 86, 132, 163
    exclusion and 8–9, 140, 143, 149, 171, 182, 183–7
        class 140, 145, 149, 170
        foreigners 3, 67, 68, 122, 140, 182, 184
        women 22, 41, 54, 77, 86, 122, 140, 167, 170, 184
        see also identity, political; suffrage; women; working class
    global 3
    'industrial' 1, 2, 142–3
    moral and sociological bases of 151, 175, 178
    political freedom and 47, 86, 92,

96, 122–4, 150, 164
  see also freedom; natural rights
  revolutionary 104
  rule of law and 118-19, 140, 183
  social law and 163
  see also identity, political; nationality; suffrage
citizenship, concept of
  constant elements of 182–7
    exclusion 182, 183–4
    legality 182
  origins and definitions 1, 3–4, 5n.1, 14-16, 73, 150, 183, 187–188
    incorporation of social rights 162-4, 165n.11
    liberalism and redefinition 151, 152
    semantic changes 167
  political multiplicity and 170, 172–3
    federalism and 172–3
    multinational/transnational citizenship 176–9
    multiple citizenship 171, 174
    see also cosmopolitanism; European Union, citizenship in
  'social closure' and 182
  traditional, linked to nation-state 167–8, 170, 171, 176–7
    critique of 168, 170, 175–6
    Habermas and 176–7
    multiculturalism and 168–70
    separatist movements, use of 169
  see also nationality; sovereignty, popular; under names of individual theories/theorists;
city, the 5n.1, 7, 9, 40–1, 48, 182
  Aristotle's definition of 17–18
  Augustine's two cities 31, 32–6
  freedom of citizens and 43, 51
  medieval 36–7
  rights to 183
  Rome and 19

  see also civis/civitas
civic culture 15, 51, 177
civic humanism 5n.1, 49–55, 96, 105
  see also Florence
civic identity *see* identity, civic
civic virtue 51, 52, 57, 91, 105, 178
  working class and 144
civil freedom, doctrine of 49
civil rights *see* rights, civil
civil society 97, 98, 104, 148, 188–9, 190
  Marx and 157, 158–9
  separation of state from 162, 164
  social law and 163
civilitas 42, 43, 44, 47, 48, 49, 57, 183
civis/civitas 8, 19-28, 29n.36, 43, 45, 48, 58, 183
  Augustine and 31, 32–6
  citizenship and 49, 68
  romana 22, 27, 28, 31, 44, 57, 175
class 140–1, 142, 170
  citizenship and 140, 145, 149, 191
  Marx and class struggle 159, 191
  see also working class
Claudius 27
Cloots, Anarchasis 178
collective will 87, 88–9
  see also general will
common sense 129–30
common law 38, 86, 132
communism 159–60, 190
communitarianism, concept of citizenship and 2, 5n.4, 6n.5, 136n.21, 179
community, meaning of 4
Condorcet, Marquis de 112, 118, 136n.26, 146, 152, 185
  'social guarantee', idea of 149
  principle of 'legal state' 118
conscience
  freedom of 88, 90, 146
  philosophy of 87
consent 62
Constant, Benjamin 2, 4, 118, 143–6, 158
  citizenship and 146, 148, 187, 188,

190
critique of revolutionaries 143, 144, 146
public authority, role of 144–5
'constitutional patriotism' 176–7
constitutionalism 143
contractualism *see* social contract theory
Conze, W. 6n.8
corporatist conception of politics 132, 135
corruption, republican argument of 148
Corsica 91, 169
cosmopolitanism 174, 178, 181n.36
republican criticism of 174
Costa, Pietro 5n.1, 6n.8

D
Dahl, Robert 136n.19, 180n.19
Dante Alighieri 36
Declaration of the Rights of Man in Society 93
Declaration of the Rights of Man and of the Citizen 116–19, 124–5, 126, 128, 155, 188
democracy 189–91
Athens 8, 10–14
concept of citizenship and 2, 80, 140
deliberative conception of 136n.21
gender issues and 2
ideal of 189
Plato and 16–17
representative 103, 189–91
'second age' of 192
transfer of rights in (Spinoza) 80–1
virtue and 95, 96
utilitarianism and 130
see also liberal democracy
democratic socialism 161, 162
see also socialism and socialist theory
demokratia 13
Demosthenes 18, 29n.22
Descartes, René 69
despotism 95, 96

Dewey, John 111
Diderot, Denis 93, 112
discrimination 170
divine will 71, 85
Duguit, Leon 120
Dunn, J. 194n.24

E
education 125
citizenship and 152, 153–4, 163
egalitarianism 95
elite 113
Encyclopédia 87, 93, 101n.45, 112
England *see* Great Britain
Englebert of Admont 36
Enlightenment 125
Epicureans 70
equality, concept of 168
French Revolution and 125
Kant and 122–4
political 147, 164, 184–7
social 146, 147, 164
Etruscans 7
Eurobarometer polls 177
European Court 177
European Union
citizenship in
concept of common 172–3, 174, 175, 176–9
constitutional patriotism (Habermas) 176–7, 181n.35
'political economy' of 178
transnational citizenship (Habermas) 177
vertical and horizontal dimensions of 177
Constitution of 176
principle of free movement 177
principle of non-discrimination 177
democratic deficit in 178
Euroscepticism 178

F

Fabians 161
federalism 111, 150, 170
    USA and 172-4
Federalist Papers 105–109
Ferry, J.-M. 181n.35
feudalism 36, 132, 141
Feuerbach, Ludwig Andreas 156
Fichte, Johann Gottlieb 156, 183
fidelis/fidelitas 31, 32-6
Filmer, Robert 81
    Patriarcha 81
Finley, Moses 7
Flanders 169
Florence 42, 43-4, 49-58, 61n.56
    civic humanism and 49-55
    influence of Roman republic 57-8
    radical populism in 51-3
    use of the term citizenship in 50-1, 57
foreigners, citizenship and 3, 67, 68, 122, 140
    see also nationality
France 124-5, 191
    citizenship in 183
    French exceptionalism 191
    French monism 192
    Napoleonic Empire 141, 186
    post-Revolution 141, 155
    see also French Revolution
freedom 144
    Burke's definition 127
    civil, doctrine of 49
    collective security and individual 88-9
    Constant and individual 144-5
    Hegel's state and 135
    Hobbes and 79, 80, 83, 86, 100n.23
    individuality and 84
    Kant and 122-4
    liberal thought and 143, 146
    Locke and 83, 84
    Marx and emancipation 158

    natural pre-civil 85-6
    natural right, as (Rousseau) 88-9, 91
    'negative' 86, 150
    of the press 118
    'positive' 150
    republican idea of 127
    Spinoza and 79, 80, 86
    see also autonomy; natural law; natural rights
French Revolution 5n.1, 103, 114–16, 122, 124-5, 126, 128, 131, 140
    citizenship, concept of 107, 112-22
        active and passive 114, 119-21, 137n.50, 141, 186, 187
        rule of law and 118-19
        suffrage in 121, 137n.56
    Constitution (1791) 118, 186, 187
    Declaration of the Rights of Man and of the Citizen 116-19, 124-5, 126, 128, 188
    effects of 140, 141, 162
    judiciary and 107
    'Nation', concept of 113-15, 119, 120, 121
    National Assembly 115-16, 117-18, 119, 120, 191
    Republic, birth of 111, 115
    popular sovereignty 110, 112, 121, 124, 131

G

'general will' 90, 91, 92, 93, 103, 113, 117, 119
    Bentham and 130
    Hegel's legislative function and 134-5
    Kant and 123
    suffrage and 121, 164
Genoa 43
Germany 176
    Bürgerschaft 183
    Constitution 132, 133
Giles of Rome 39

Godechot, Jacques 124
Gonfaloniere 52, 54
government
  Hegel's tasks of 134–5
  Locke's theory of 82–4
  see also sovereignty; state
Gratian 37–8
Great Britain 126–31
  aristocracy in 141
  British Bill of Rights (1688) 126
  effects of French Revolution in 141
  English Declaration of Rights 126
  Parliament 191
  Poor Laws 161
  Revolution of 1688 75–6, 126
  suffrage in 130–1, 153
  utilitarianism in 130–1
Greece, Ancient *see* Ancient Greece; Athens
Grotius, Hugo 69–73, 74, 75, 76, 79, 83, 84, 85, 87, 96, 156
  concept of rights and 70, 71–3
Guicciardini, Francesco 53–5, 57, 58, 95, 149
  citizenship and popular government 54–5, 60n.48, 61n.64
  freedom and 53–4, 61n.63
guilds 36, 37, 38

H

Habermas, Jürgen 5n.4, 175–7
  'constitutional patriotism' 176–7
  'transnational citizenship' 177
Hagias 9–10
Halévy, E. 139n.83
Hamilton, Alexander 105, 108
Hansen, M. H. 29n.33
Harrington, J. 187
Hazard, Paul 84
Hegel G.W.H. 106, 131–5, 156
  Elements of the Philosophy of Right 133, 134
  German Constitution 133

state and citizenship 132–3, 151, 178
Herder, Johann Gottfried 125, 126
Herodotus 9–10
history 143
  liberalism and 168
  philosophy of 125, 168
Hobbes, Thomas 2, 73–75, 76, 77, 78, 79, 80, 83, 85, 87, 141, 142, 156
  citizen as subject 74–5, 86, 100n.23, 112, 132, 187
  Leviathan, The 74–5, 81
  social contract 74–5, 88, 124
  sovereignty, concept of 74–5, 79, 85, 154
Hobsbawm, Eric 179n.1
human nature 127
  see also natural law
human rights *see* natural rights; rights
humanism 158
Hume, David 96, 127–8, 129

I

identity, political
  civic 171, 176–7, 184, 188–9
  corruption of 178
  national 2–3, 169–70, 171, 174, 178
  transnational citizenship and 179
  see also nationality
imperialism 131, 178
individualism 62, 116
  Locke and 84
industrial revolution 140, 141, 155
inequality
  of opportunity 170
  social and economic 154, 162
  see also socialism and socialist theory; working class movements
interests
  citizenship and 114, 130
  conflict of 107
  'general' 149
  liberal thought and 142
  natural (Smith) 97, 106, 130
  principle of 106

public 129
intuitionism 125
irrationalism 125
Isocrates 15, 17, 18, 29n.22
isonomia 13, 15
Italy
city-republics 53, 54
Renaissance 47, 51–2, 54–8, 147, 167
see also civic humanism; Florence; Rome

J
Janowitz, M. 6n.5
Jaurès, Jean 161
Jennings, W.I. 153
John of Salisbury 34–5
John of Viterbe 36, 43, 59n.26
judicial power 107–9

K
Kant, Immanuel 122–4, 138n.65, 146, 156
autonomy and citizenship 92, 122–4, 149, 187, 188
Metaphysics of Morals 123
Perpetual Peace 124
'right of hospitality' 177, 180n.33
Kleisthenes 12, 14
Koselleck, R. 6n.8
Kymlicka, Will 169–70

L
Lacedaemonians 9, 27
Lacroix, Justine 180n.19
Lanjuinais, Jean-Denis Conte de 121–2
law, common 86, 127
law, positive 126, 129
law, public
synthesis of order and freedom (Kant) 122, 123–4
see also rights
Leca, Jean 180n.23, 183
Lewis, Ewart 36

Levellers 75–6
Lévy, E. 29n.32
liberal democracy
American 103, 104, 136n.18
civic involvement, deficit of 188
as individual development (JS Mill) 152
European 103–4
modern 189–91
nationalist movements, challenge from 169
liberalism 92, 93–4, 96, 97–8, 141–51, 154
concept of citizenship and 2, 4, 5n.4, 98, 141, 143, 146, 153, 168–9, 179, 185–6, 190, 193n.17
language of 151
redefinition of citizenship 151, 152
Tocqueville's civic identity 149, 188
conception of political life and society 127, 142, 151, 190
Constant's axioms of 143–6
economic 96, 97–8, 154
English 'liberal' movement 128, 130–1, 142, 143, 151, 153
etymology of 142–3
French political 142, 143
history, importance of 94, 127
natural law theory and 93–4, 128
state, theory of 94, 97–8, 134, 142, 143, 144, 153–4
libertas 22–6, 27, 42, 175
liberty 2, 127, 168, 193n.18
Constant and civil 144, 145–6
Tocqueville, democracy and 147
Lipsius, Justus 69
Locke, John 79, 81–4, 85, 86, 87, 141, 143, 154
citizenship and 149, 188
concept of law 84
individualism of 84
theory of government 82–4, 85, 86, 185

Two Treatises of Government 81–4, 104
London 47

M
Machiavelli, Niccoló 2, 4, 55–8, 61n.59, 61n.63, 63, 64, 69, 75, 84, 94, 105, 142, 146
    Christianity and 55
    citizenship and 57, 89, 187
    civic virtue and 57
    corruption and 178
    popular participation and 56–7, 148
    principle of force 79
    theory of the state 141
Magnus, Albertus 39
Maistre, Joseph-Marie, Comte de 125
majority, tyranny of 106, 190
Mandeville, B. 97
Manin, B. 194n.27
Mannheim, Karl 3, 181n.38
Mantua 43
Marat, Jean Paul 155
Marathon 13
Marcuse, Herbert 177
markets and the state 1, 97, 98, 142
Markus, R.A. 58n.2
Marshall, Thomas H. 1, 161, 162–3
Marsilius of Padua 40–2, 49, 55
    definition of citizenship 41–2
Marx, Karl 4, 86, 154–61
    citizenship and 157–8, 160–1, 190
    civil society and 157, 158–9
    communism, idea of 159–60, 190
    critique of contractualism 155–6
    critique of state 156–7, 158–9, 160
    emancipation, idea of 158
    Paris Commune 160
marxism, citizenship and 6n.5
materialist psychology 144
Melampous 10
Mill, James 151
Mill, John Stuart 2, 4, 130, 151–4,

168–9, 188
    citizenship as individual development 152–3, 165n.11
    equality and 146, 165n.12, 185
minorities 168
    contemporary citizenship, challenge to 169, 170, 171
    rights of representation and 170
Mirabeau, Honoré Gabriel Riqueti, Comte de 93, 117
Monarchomacs 64
monarchy
    absolute 115, 134
    authority of 63, 64
    Bodin and 66–7
    constitutional 134
    Hegel's state and 133–4
    medieval 36
    Montesquieu and 95
    neutral force, as a 145
    Spinoza and 79, 80
    see also royal power; sovereignty
    monism 191–2
Montaigne, Michel Eyquem de 69
Montesquieu, Charles-Louis de Secondat 2, 90, 93–7, 102n.40, 105, 106, 141, 143, 189
    balance of powers, theory of 95–6, 107, 141, 143, 144, 149
    citizenship and 94–5, 96, 112, 113, 182, 187
    critique of Hobbes 94
    The Spirit of Laws 94–6
More, Thomas 63, 64
multiculturalism 174
    concept of national citizenship and 168, 169–70
    republican view of citizenship and 171
    state structure and representation 170

N
nation

concepts of 174, 175, 192n.3
  naturalist and artificialist 183–4
myth of 140, 155, 168
see also French Revolution, 'Nation'
nationalist movements 169, 178
nationality 174, 183–4
  assimilation 184
  citizenship and 3, 5n.1, 7, 10, 14, 67, 167, 171, 175, 183
    civic nationalism 176
    multicultural challenge and 168, 184
  civitas and 20, 48
  integration 184
  see also identity, political
natural law 38, 40, 45, 62, 69, 76–7, 78, 84, 85, 87, 93, 103, 125, 127, 131, 154, 191
  citizenship, concept of and 143, 150
  civil law and 72–3
  Grotius, principles of modern 70–3
  Herder's critique of 125
  Hobbes and 74, 79
  Hume's critique of 128
  language of 93, 103, 104
  liberalism and 93–4
  Locke and 81-2, 83, 154
  revolutions of 18th century and 103, 116
  Rousseau and 87–8, 91, 92, 93, 191
  theoretical basis of 94
  utilitarian critique of 129
natural rights 62, 71, 84, 85, 86, 116, 119, 125, 150, 154
  Bentham's critique of 129
  citizenship and 150, 188
  civil rights and 116, 119
  common law and 86
  Marx's critique of 158
  positive law and 126
  see also rights
nature, state of 71, 76, 85, 116, 150
  Hobbes and 73–5

Locke and 81–2
Rousseau and 87–8
Spinoza's 'continuation of' 79–80
see also society
Nero 27
Nicolet, Claude 26, 192n.5
Nussbaum, M. 181n.36

O
obedience 2
obligation 62
oligarchy 135
  citizenship and 55
Opizo of Piacenza 43
Orvieto 43

P
pact 62
  social 74
Padua 43
partecipazione 87
Paine, Thomas 104, 110
participation, political 186–9
  freedom of the law and 96
  popular sovereignty 140
  see also representation; sovereignty, popular; suffrage
patriotism 91
Paul, St. 31, 32, 125, 187
Peisistratos 11–12
Pennington, K. 59n.15
Peripatetics 70
Persians 13
Pericles 10, 14
Peter of Auvergne 39
Plato 16-17, 63, 64
  equality and 25
  Republic 17, 19
pluralism 107, 191–2
Plutarch 34
Pocock, J.G.A. 50–1, 57, 60n.48
Podestá 54
Poland 91
polis 9, 11, 12–13, 14, 15, 16, 19, 40

politeia 8, 9, 11, 14, 15–16, 20,
29n.36, 48, 183
  Aristotle and 17–18, 19, 29n.35
  Plato's view of 16–17
  sovereignty (arche) 15
  William of Moerbeke's translation
  of 39
polites 9, 19
political philosophy 143
  conscience and 87
  fundamental method of (Grotius) 71
  natural law theorists and 94
political science 4, 84–5, 106, 143,
150, 155, 168
  Bodin's system of primary definitions 64–5, 85
  Cartesian method and 85
  empiricism 126, 153
  liberalism and 94, 97, 127, 143–6, 154
    intellectual break of 143–4
  medieval intellectual system and 84–5
  method of knowledge and 69
  organic ideas and 65, 127
  political sociology 153–4
  reason and rationalism in 79, 85,
  88, 90, 97
  subjective rights and 69, 127
  traditionalist 127
  see also names of individual theo-
  ries/theorists e.g., social contract
  theories
Polybius 25, 58
popular sovereignty see sovereignty,
popular
positive discrimination 186
potestas 24
power, state see state power
Privernates 57
progress, idea of 125
proletariat 141, 182, 185
  see also socialism and socialist
  theory; working class
property 131, 132
  citizenship and 83, 86–7, 134, 145,
185
  right to 154, 161
Proudhon, Pierre Joseph 161
Pseudo-Xenophon 10
public opinion 146
public sphere 11, 62, 184
  distinction between domestic and 65
Pufendorf, Samuel von 76–8, 79, 83,
85, 87
  definition of citizenship 77–8, 86,
  100n.28, 185
Putnam, Robert 136n.19
Pythia 9
Pyrrhonism 69

R
racial discrimination 167, 170
Ramée, Pierre de la 64, 67
rationalism 62, 127
  Enlightenment 125
  Spinoza and 79
  theory of the state and 62
religion
  authority of (Grotius) 71
  Marx's critique of 156, 157
  primacy of 32
  see also Christianity
Renaissance see Italy, Renaissance
representation 8, 42, 62, 106–7, 114,
186, 189–91
  legitimacy of 188
  liberal thought and 143
  Marsilius of Padua and 42
  modern state and 189–91
  Renaisannce and 58
  popular moods and 106–7
  sovereignty, connection with 114
republic, the 39, 64–6, 71, 107, 140,
148, 186
  Aristotle and 64–5
  Bodin's definition 64–5, 67
  civic identity and 149
  conflict of interests and passions in
  106–7

consent and 86
difference with democracy 106, 140, 194n.24
freedom in 144
Grotius and 71–2
Hobbes' sovereign 74–5, 79
ideal 63–4
Kant and 124
Marx's critique of 161
revolutions, 18th century and 103, 125, 140
Rousseau and collective reason and 89–90
social contract theory and 96
socialism and 162
Spinoza's rationality and 79
utopian 91
see also Plato; Rome, Republic, The
republicanism
American political thought and 105–11, 135
concept of citizenship and 2, 4, 5n.1, 5n.4, 24, 73, 96, 110, 113, 161, 175
concept of society 142
democracy and 189
Habermas' critique of 176
Jaurès and 162
Marx's critique of 156, 157, 158, 160–1
multiculturalism and 171
nationality, importance of 174–5
res publica 20, 24, 30n.36
revolutions, 18th century 103, 124–5, 140, 150, 189
see also French Revolution; United States of America, Revolution
Ricoeur, Paul 181n.38
rights 62
British Bill of Rights 126
Burke's 'real' 126
civil 2, 68, 100n.24, 110, 133, 162
concept of citizenship and 2, 73, 76, 80, 83, 84, 85–6, 103, 129, 143, 176
Declaration of the Rights of Man in Society 93
Declaration of the Rights of Man and of the Citizen 116–19, 124–5, 188
Constant and 146
critique of 126, 128, 129, 155
socialist critique of 155–6
development of the language of 62, 70, 73
inalienable 146
laws of nature and 70–1, 72
modern concept of freedom and 85–6
of property 71, 83, 86
philosophy of 169
political 119, 120–1, 164
social law and 163–4
subjective 127
to life 71, 86, 100n.23
to vote 119–20
see also natural rights
Robespierre, Maximilien 119, 121, 131, 146, 155, 161, 189
Rokkan, Stein 3
Romanticism 125
Rome
census 24–5
civic law (*civitas romana*) 7–8, 19–28, 31, 37, 170, 184–5, 186
equality and 21, 23, 24–6, 183
medieval/Renaissance rediscovery of 37–9, 57–8, 59n.15
Republic, The 22–6, 32, 48, 58, 184–5, 189
fall of 26–8
slaves in 22, 185
women in 22, 185
Romulus 27
Rosanvallon, Pierre 163
Rousseau, Jean-Jacques 2, 79, 81, 87–93, 96, 101n.45, 105, 117, 124, 142, 154, 158, 183, 189, 194n.22
'Body politic' 89

citizen, concept of 89, 90, 91–2, 103, 112, 116, 122, 149, 187, 188
Discourse on Inequality 87, 88
Émile 92
freedom of conscience and 88
'general will' 90, 91, 92, 194n.22
La Nouvelle Héloïse 93
republic, conception of 89–90, 92, 144
Social Contract 88–90, 91, 92, 93
royal power 38, 63, 64, 75–6
England, Revolution of 1688 75–6
see also monarchy
rule of law 164
concept of 118–9
state and 134

S

Salamis 13
Salutati, Coluccio 49
Savonarola 51–3, 60n.52, 61n.59
Sceptics 71, 73
Schnapper, Dominique 5n.4, 171, 192n.3
Scotland 169
Seyssel, Claude 63, 64
Sienna 43
Sieyès, Abbé 78, 113–15, 119
concept of 'Nation' and 113–14
Siger of Brabant 39
Sinclair, R. K. 28n.13
Skinner, Quentin 4, 57, 193n.18
slaves 11, 13, 14
citizenship and 67, 68, 184
Rome and 22
US abolition of slavery 173–4
Smith, Adam 96, 97–8, 105, 128, 130, 144, 157
role of state 142
Wealth of Nations 97–8
social contract theories 66–7, 68, 73, 85, 96, 116, 130, 150, 154, 156
Hobbes and 74–5, 88, 124
Hume's critique of 127–8

liberal critique of 94, 96, 128
Kant and 124
Locke's theory of government and 82–4
Marx's critique of 155–6
Pufendorf and 77
Rousseau's reformulation of 87, 88–90, 124
Spinoza's limited contract and 79–80
see also natural law; nature, state of
social equality 146, 164
Tocqueville and 147
social law 162, 163
social security 161, 162, 163, 164, 167
socialism and socialist theory 96, 125, 131, 141, 154, 161–2
citizenship and social rights 161–4, 187, 190-1
democratic 162
Jaurès and 161–2
liberalism and 162
Tocqueville's condemnation of 148
see also Marx, Karl; working class, movements
society 143, 144, 191
liberal and republican conception of 142
science of 150
Solon 10-11, 14, 94
sovereignty 2, 8, 15, 62, 65, 79
Bartolus of Sassoferrato and 44–5
Bodin's doctrine of 63, 64, 65–7, 68
Christian social theory and 31
citizenship and 45, 48, 78, 80–1, 83, 86, 121
division of 108–9
expression of law and 79
Italian Renaissance 54
Marsilius of Padua and 41
national, doctrine of 120
popular 39, 44–5, 76, 78, 84, 86,

133, 140, 186
  American political thought and
    105, 106, 108–9, 110
  citizenship as 140, 149
  European liberal democracy 104
  France's 'Nation' 110, 121
  rational collective will and 87
  Rousseau's 'Body politic' and 89,
    90–1
  social contract theories and 85, 88–9
  see also monarchy; natural law;
    royal power
Sparta 14, 16
Spinoza, Baruch of 78-81, 154
  citizenship and sovereignty 80–1,
    83, 86, 149
  democracy and 80–1, 86
  The Political Treaty 80–1
  politics of reason and 79
state, the 32, 76, 141, 142, 150–1, 161,
  163, 167–8, 189
  abolition of 162
  Bodin's theory of 67
  concept of 46, 60n.36
  Hegel's model of 131–2, 133–5,
    156, 157
  Hobbes' Leviathan 74-5
  interests and 142
  'legal', principle of 118
  liberal political economy and
    97–8, 144, 158
  Locke's theory of government
    82–4, 185
  Marx's critique of 156–7, 158–9,
    160, 162
  republican tradition and 98
  social law and 162, 163
  see also government; social con-
    tract theories; sovereignty
state of nature *see* nature, state of
state power 141, 144-5, 149–50, 153
  balance of 149, 153
  executive 133, 145
  federalism/decentralisation and

150, 153
  Hegel's organisation of 134
  individual freedom and 93, 94–5
  legislative 133, 134, 145
  liberalism and 94, 143, 144, 149
  minorities, challenge of 169, 179n.2
  see also monarchy; sovereignty
Stoics 69, 70
suffrage 121, 140, 184-6
  education and 152
  Great Britain and 152–3
  J.S.Mill and 152–3, 185
  universal 120, 145, 153, 160, 186,
    192
  utilitarianism and 130–1

T
Tacitus 27
Taylor, Charles 5n.4
Thebes 16
Thermidorians 120
Thompson, Dennis 6n.5
Thucydides 10
Tisamenus 9–10
Tocqueville, Alexander de 2, 4, 103–4,
  146–50, 192
  citizenship and 148–50, 152, 188
  civic identity 149, 172–3
  Democracy in America 107, 109,
    110–11, 147–8, 149–50, 154, 172–3
  equality and 146–7, 149
trade unions 162, 190
  see also working class, movements
transparency 189–91
Trajan 34

U
Ullman, Walter 35, 40
United States of America
  abolition of slavery 173–4
  Bill of Rights 108, 116, 174
  citizenship, nature of 107, 108,
    109–11, 136n.19, 148, 149–50, 170
    dual citizenship 172–4, 180n.15

Civil War 173
Constitution 96, 105–9, 149, 172, 173–4
  Fourteenth Amendment 173–4
  'judicial power' 107–8
Declaration of Independence (1776) 104–5
democracy in 103–111, 147–8, 149–50
federalism of 111, 172–4
popular sovereignty in 105, 106, 108–9, 110–1
republicanism in 105–6, 136n.19
Supreme Court
  Dred Scott v. Sandford (1857) 110
Revolution 103, 140, 189
universitas 38, 39, 41, 44
utilitarianism 129–31
  concept of citizenship 129, 130–1
utility principle 129
Utopia 90

V
Veca, S. 5n.4
Venice 43, 52
Vernant, Jean-Pierre 12
virtue, public 90, 96
  democracy and 95
Visconti, Duke 49
Voltaire, François-Marie A. 101n.45

W
Walzer, Michael 5n.4
Weber, Max 4, 47-8
Weil, Eric 122
Weiler, J. 177
welfare state 163, 164, 167, 175
Whigs, the 125
William of Moerbeke 39
William of Orange 76
women
  citizenship 41, 77, 86, 122, 140, 152, 167, 184, 185
    Italian Renaissance and 54

  Rome 22, 185
  democracy and 16
French Republic 120, 136n.26
working class
  liberals and 154
  movements 161, 162, 163, 190, 191
  political participation and 145, 170, 185

X
Xenophon 17

www.ingramcontent.com/pod-product-compliance
Lightning Source LLC
Chambersburg PA
CBHW050437280326
41932CB00013BA/2147